THE BALANCE BETWEEN INDUSTRY AND AGRICULTURE IN ECONOMIC DEVELOPMENT
Volume 1: BASIC ISSUES

This volume is IEA conference volume no. 86

THE BALANCE BETWEEN INDUSTRY AND AGRICULTURE IN ECONOMIC DEVELOPMENT

Volume 1 BASIC ISSUES
Kenneth J. Arrow (*editor*)

Volume 2 SECTOR PROPORTIONS
Jeffrey G. Williamson and Vadiraj R. Panchamukhi (*editors*)

Volume 3 MANPOWER AND TRANSFERS
Sukhamoy Chakravarty (*editor*)

Volume 4 SOCIAL EFFECTS
Irma Adelman and Sylvia Lane (*editors*)

Volume 5 FACTORS INFLUENCING CHANGE
Nurul Islam (*editor*)

These volume are, respectively, nos. 86–90 in the IEA/Macmillan series

IEA conference volume series

Series Standing Order

If you would like to receive future titles in this series as they are published, you can make use of our standing order facility. To place a standing order please contact your bookseller or, in case of difficulty, write to us at the address below with your name and address and the name of the series. Please state with which title you wish to begin your standing order. (If you live outside the United Kingdom we may not have the rights for your area, in which case we will forward your order to the publisher concerned.)

Customer Services Department, Macmillan Distribution Ltd, Houndmills, Basingstoke, Hampshire, RG21 2XS, England.

The Balance between Industry and Agriculture in Economic Development

Proceedings of the Eighth World Congress of the
International Economic Association, Delhi, India

Volume 1
BASIC ISSUES

Edited by
Kenneth J. Arrow

MACMILLAN
PRESS

in association with the
INTERNATIONAL ECONOMIC
ASSOCIATION

First published 1988

Published by
THE MACMILLAN PRESS LTD
Houndmills, Basingstoke, Hampshire RG21 2XS
and London
Companies and representatives
throughout the world

Printed in Hong Kong

British Library Cataloguing in Publication Data
International Economic Association, *World Congress*: 8th : *Delhi, India*
The balance between industry and agriculture
in economic development: proceedings of the
Eighth World congress of the International
Economic Association, Delhi, India.—
(Macmillan/International Economic Association).
Vol. 1 : Basic issues
1. Economic development
I. Title II. Arrow, Kenneth J. (Kenneth Joseph),
1921– III. International Economic Association
330.9
ISBN 0–333–46713–2

HD
73
˙I57
1986
V. 1

Contents

Preface

The Eighth World Congress of the International Economic Association was held in Delhi from 1 to 5 December 1986, presided over by Professor Kenneth J. Arrow, President of the IEA from 1983 to 1986. The subject of the Congress was 'The Balance between Industry and Agriculture in Economic Development.' It was organised by the Indian Economic Association.

Participation in the Congress was broadly based in terms both of geography and of the types of economy from which participants came; market-orientated and centrally-planned; developed and developing; mainly agricultural and predomantly industrial.

The Congress included a number of plenary sessions, but much of the work of the Congress was undertaken in eighteen specialised meetings. The volume of papers was too large for them all to be published, but the five volumes in this group, together with a volume on the Indian economy being published separately in India, represent the major viewpoints expressed. The volumes generally contain reports on the discussions which took place during the specialised sessions.

The volumes are:

1. *Basic Issues*, edited by Kenneth J. Arrow
2. *Sector Proportions*, edited by Jeffrey G. Williamson and Vadiraj R. Panchamukhi
3. *Manpower and Transfers*, edited by Sukhamoy Chakravarty
4. *Social Effects*, edited by Irma Adelman and Sylvia Lane
5. *Factors Influencing Change*, edited by Nurul Islam

The Indian volume is edited by Dr P. R. Brahmananda and Dr S. Chakravarty under the title *The Indian Economy: Balance between Industry and Agriculture* and will be published by Macmillan India.

This volume contains papers from the Plenary Session and selected papers from Session 16 on Agriculture, Industry and Economic Development in a Historical Perspective organised by Professor Paolo Sylos-Labini.

The International Economic Association

A non-profit organisation with purely scientific aims, the International Economic Association (IEA) was founded in 1950. It is in fact a federation of national economic associations and presently includes fifty eight such professional organisations from all parts of the world. Its basic purpose is the development of economics as an intellectual discipline. Its approach recognises a diversity of problems, systems and values in the world and also takes note of methodological diversities.

The IEA has, since its creation, tried to fulfil that purpose by promoting mutual understanding of economists from the West and the East as well as from the North and the South through the organisation of scientific meetings and common research programmes and by means of publications on problems of current importance. During its thirty-seven years of existence, it has organised seventy-nine round-table conferences for specialists on topics ranging from fundamental theories to methods and tools of analysis and major problems of the present-day world. Eight triennal World Congresses have also been held, and these have regularly attracted the participation of a great many economists from all over the world. The proceedings of all these meetings are published by Macmillan.

The Association is governed by a Council, composed of representatives of all member associations, and by a fifteen-member Executive Committee which is elected by the Council. The present Executive Committee (1986–9) is composed as follows:

President: Professor Amartya Sen, India
Vice-President: Professor Béla Csikós-Nagy, Hungary
Treasurer: Professor Luis Angel Rojo, Spain
Past-President: Professor Kenneth J. Arrow, USA
Other members: Professor Edmar Lisboa Bacha, Brazil
Professor Ragnar Bentzel, Sweden
Professor Oleg T. Bogomolov, USSR
Professor Silvio Borner, Switzerland
Professor P. R. Brahmananda, India

	Professor Phyllis Deane, United Kingdom
	Professor Luo Yuanzheng, China
	Professor Edmond Malinvaud, France
	Professor Luigi Pasinetti, Italy
	Professor Don Patinkin, Israel
	Professor Takashi Shiraishi, Japan
Adviser:	Professor Tigran S. Khachaturov, USSR
Secretary-General:	Professor Jean-Paul Fitoussi, France
General Editor:	Mr Michael Kaser, United Kingdom
Adviser to General Editor:	Professor Sir Austin Robinson, United Kingdom
Conference Editor:	Dr Patricia M. Hillebrandt, United Kingdom

The Association has also been fortunate in having secured the following outstanding economists to serve as President:

Gottfried Haberler (1950–3), Howard S. Ellis (1953–6), Erik Lindahl (1956–9), E. A. G. Robinson (1959–62), G. Ugo Papi (1962–5), Paul A. Samuelson (1965–8), Erik Lundberg (1968–71), Fritz Machlup (1971–4), Edmond Malinvaud (1974–7), Shigeto Tsuru (1977–80), Victor L. Urquidi (1980–3), Kenneth J. Arrow (1983–6).

The activities of the Association are mainly funded from the subscriptions of members and grants from a number of organisations, including continuing support from UNESCO.

Acknowledgements

The host for the Eighth World Congress of the International Economic Association was the Indian Economic Association and all Congress participants are in its debt for the organisation of the Congress itself and for the welcome given to economists from all over the world. The preparation for such a gathering, culminating in a week of lectures, discussions and social activities, is an enormous undertaking. The International Economic Association wishes to express its appreciation on behalf of all participants.

Both the Indian and the International Economic Associations are grateful to the large number of institutions and organisations, including many states, banks, business firms, research and trade organisations which provided funds for the Congress. They particularly wish to thank the following Indian Government Departments and other official agencies:

Ministry of Finance
Ministry of External Affairs
The Reserve Bank of India
The State Bank of India
The Industrial Development Bank of India
The Indian Council of Social Science Research
The Industrial Credit and Investment Corporation of India
The Industrial Finance Corporation of India
The National Bank for Agriculture and Rural Development
The Industrial Reconstruction Bank of India
The Punjab National Bank
The Canara Bank
Tata Group of Industries
The Government of Uttar Pradesh
The Government of Karnataka
The Government of Kerala
The Government of Madhya Pradesh

Valuable support was given by the Ford Foundation and the International Development Research Centre. The Research and Information System for Non-aligned and Other Developing Countries and the Institute of Applied Manpower Research provided valuable assistance in staffing and in the infrastructure of the Congress.

The social events of the Congress provided a useful opportunity for informal discussion as well as being a source of great enjoyment. The hospitality of the Indian Economic Association, the Export Import Bank of India, the Federation of Indian Chambers of Commerce and Industry, the Punjab Haryana and Delhi (PHD) Chambers of Commerce and Industry and DCM Ltd created memorable occasions. Thanks go to the Indian Council for Cultural Relations, which organised a cultural evening. In addition there were many small social gatherings which stressed the international flavour of the Congress.

Lastly, and vitally important, was the contribution of the members of the IEA Organising Committee and the Indian Steering Committee listed overleaf; in particular, Dr Manmohan Singh, Chairman of the Steering Committee, Professor S. Chakravarty, President of the Indian Economic Association, and then Vice-President of the International Economic Association, and Dr V. R. Panchamukhi, Convenor of the Steering Committee; the authors; the discussants; the rapporteurs and the ever-helpful students. The International Economic Association wishes to thank them all for the success of the Congress in Delhi in 1986.

Thanks are expressed to the International Social Science Council under whose auspices the publications programme is carried out, and to UNESCO for its financial support.*

* Under the auspices of the International Social Science Council and with a grant from UNESCO (1986–87/DG/7.6.2/SUB.16 (SHS)).

The IEA Programme Committee

Indian Steering Committee

Dr Manmohan Singh (*Chairman*)
Professor S. Chakravarty (*President, Indian Economic Association, then Vice President of the International Economic Association*)
Dr V. R. Panchamukhi (*Convenor*)

Dr Malcolm S. Adiseshaiah
Dr M. S. Ahluwalia
Dr D. S. Awasthi
Dr Mahesh Bhatt
Professor P. R. Brahmananda
Shri M. Dubey
Professor Alak Ghosh
Professor P. D. Hajela
Dr Bimal Jalan
Professor A. M. Khusro
Professor D. T. Lakdawala
Dr M. Madaiah
Professor Gautam Mathur
Professor M. V. Mathur
Professor Iqbal Narain
Professor D. L. Narayana
Dr D. D. Narula
Professor Kamta Prasad
Dr C. Rangarajan
Dr N. K. Sengupta
Professor Shanmugasundaram
Dr R. K. Sinha

List of the Contributors

Professor Kenneth J. Arrow, Economics Department, Stanford University, USA

Professor Krishna Bharadwaj, Centre for Economic Studies and Planning, Jawaharlal Nehru University, India

Academician Oleg T. Bogomolov, Institute for the Socialist World Economic System of the Academy of Sciences of the USSR, Moscow, USSR

Mr Walter Eltis, National Economic Development Office and Exeter College, Oxford, UK

Professor Giorgio Fuà, Department of Economics, University of Ancona, Italy

Professor Shigeru Ishikawa, School of International Politics, Economics and Business, Aoyama Gakuin University, Tokyo, Japan

Professor D. T. Lakdawala, Centre for Monitoring Indian Economy, Bombay, India

Professor V. K. R. V. Rao, Institute of Social and Economic Change, Bangalore, India

Professor Alessandro Roncaglia, Università degli Studi di Roma, Italy

Professor Ignacy Sachs, Ecole des Hautes Etudes en Sciences Sociales, Paris, France and the United Nations University

Professor Theodore W. Schultz, University of Chicago, USA

Professor Amartya K. Sen, Littauer Center, Economics Department, Harvard University, USA

Dr Manmohan Singh, Planning Commission of India, Delhi

Professor Paolo Sylos-Labini, Instituto di Economia, Università degli Studi di Roma

Professor Antonio Vásquez-Barquero, Universidad Autonoma de Madrid and Instituto del Territorio y Urbanismo, MOPU, Madrid, Spain

RAPPORTEURS FOR PART II

Professor P. Jegadish Gandhi, Department of Economics, Voorhees College, Vellore, India

Dr Jayatí Ghosh, 78 Munirka Enclave, New Delhi, India

Abbreviations and Acronyms

ARTEP	Asian Regional Team of Employment Promotion
BE	Budget estimates
CMIE	Centre for Monitoring Indian Economy
CPSU	Communist Party of the Soviet Union
ECU	European Currency Unit
GDP	Gross Domestic Product
GNP	Gross National Product
IDA	International Development Association
ILO	International Labour Organisation
ITUR	Instituto de Territorio y Urbanismo
MOPU	Ministerio de Obras Públicas y Urbanismo
NABARD	National Bank for Agriculture and Rural Development (India)
NDP	Net Domestic Product
NEC	North-East and Centre (of Italy)
NREP	National Rural Employment Programme (India)
NSS	National Sample Survey
PL 480	Public Law 480 (USA)
RE	Revised estimates
RLEGP	Rural Landless Employment Guarantee Programme (India)
UNIDO	United Nations Industrial Development Organisation
WIDER	World Institute of Development Economics Research (Helsinki)

Introduction

Kenneth J. Arrow

This volume introduces the series in which the proceedings of the Eighth World Congress of the International Economic Association will be published. Not only is it the first in order but its contents set forth in broad outline the leading themes pursued in greater detail in the later volumes.

The Congress was held on 1 to 5 December 1986 in New Delhi, and the Association is grateful to the Indian Economic Association, the Indian government, and many others in the Indian public and private sectors for essential support. The theme of the Congress was 'The Balance between Industry and Agriculture in Economic Development'. This volume contains the invited addresses to the plenary sessions, and the proceedings of the session on the treatment of that topic in the history of economic thought. We see here the workings out of that balance in the practical experience of developing countries in the past and the present, reflections which seek to find generalisations drawn from experience, treatments of the theme in early economic thought in Europe, when the role of agriculture was at least partly analogous to that in many developing countries today, and, perhaps most surprising, studies of the emerging role of the countryside in modern economies.

The use of agriculture and industry as opposed categories stems from the view, widespread from at least the seventeenth century to the present, that an increase in industry is an essential component of economic growth. This observation has frequently been held to imply a policy of deliberate encouragement of industrial development. The Duc de Sully, the famous finance minister of Henry IV of France, Alexander Hamilton at the beginning of United States history, and many of the newly independent developing countries all took or at least urged strong steps in pursuit of this policy: protection, subsidies, low interest rates, and so forth. The concern over 'deindustrialisation' in the United States and Great Britain shows how widespread is the concern about a special role for industry in economic progress.

The following pages show well enough that there is a consensus on the proposition that the preference for industry may well have been taken too far. Bogomolov's address has stressed the problems of imbalance in socialist agriculture, and Singh has given us a nuanced account of Indian experience in intersectoral balancing. Agriculture and especially the growing of food crops is of the greatest importance in the early stages of development, and there is great need for investment and productivity improvements in those areas, if only to permit the supplying of necessities to workers in manufacturing. Further, as Lakdawala shows, industry does not absorb as many workers as was believed; industrial development does not insure full utilisation of resources. The disequilibrium relationships induced by shifts in agricultural methods and sectoral proportions have been well demonstrated by Schultz.

It is as important for both scientific and practical purposes to ask whether the appropriate questions have been asked as to answer them, perhaps more so. Let me present a few reflections and questions that have been raised in my mind by reading and pondering the interesting and insightful addresses and essays which follow.

In particular, I want to ask if the distinction between agriculture and industry is in fact interesting from an analytic point of view. Is there any significant information gained for either theoretical or practical purposes by classifying an activity in one or the other category? Rao's address casts grave doubts on the existence of systematic relations betweens sectoral proportions and economic development.

Related to this is a second classificatory issue. Every one recognises and has recognised at least since the pioneering work of A.G.B. Fisher and Colin Clark in the 1930s that agriculture and industry do not exhaust the varieties of economic activity. The service or tertiary sector is now recognised to be of major importance and apparently always was. Its significance, at least in terms of employment opportunities, was reaffirmed many times during the course of the Congress. This sector seems to be more sharply differentiated from agriculture and industry than either is from each other, in that the product is not embodied in a physically defined object. Yet it may also be asked whether from a fundamental economic point of view services are systematically separate from activities producing physical goods. To suggest the relativity and flimsiness of the distinction, we need only consider the familiar contrast between home cooking and restaurants. Production of food for home use is in the primary and secondary spheres, restaurants are services, but both yield the same outcome.

One defence of the distinctions is that implicit in the terminology of primary, secondary and tertiary goods. We are led to think of a one-way sequence on inter-industry flows with primary goods being used by the secondary and tertiary sectors and secondary (industrial) goods being used by the tertiary sector. This picture does not imply a unique value interpretation. As discussed in Eltis's paper, the Physiocrats inferred the supreme importance of agriculture as the only source of wealth, with industry and services merely ways of transforming the primary goods created by nature (or, perhaps better for the eighteenth century, Nature). To Adam Smith and to Karl Marx, the dividing line was the physical or material nature of the product; services were 'unproductive', primary and secondary sectors 'productive'. To the neoclassical economists, and indeed to many of the classicists, any activity for which individuals are willing to pay adds to the creation of economic value.

But regardless of the value interpretation, the facts do not conform to the unilineal ordering of production, which the Austrian School starting with Carl Menger made so much of. As Marshall clearly saw and as has been emphasised in the empirical work of Wassily Leontief, inter-industry flows are circular. Certainly modern agriculture is heavily dependent on the products of industry, and from 1000 BC or even earlier, at least the implements of agriculture were products of specialised metalworkers, the industrialists of their day. Similarly, trade, certainly one of the services, and transportation are and always have been inputs into industry; the Greek bronze-makers of the classical period used tin from Britain through Phoenician and Gallic intermediaries. Certainly, in the modern sophisticated world, the input–output table is a maze of interrelations which permit no rearrangement into a triangular (unilinear) form, certainly not along the traditional tripartite division.

Similarly, as the example of reataurants and home-cooked meals suggests, the distinction between services and material goods is of problematic economic significance. Fundamentally, all goods are ways of producing services. Housing protects us from the elements, clothing serves the functions of warmth and display, food keeps us from hunger and gives us pleasure. The distinction nevertheless points to some real issues in economic analysis but at a very different level than has been suggested. What is true is that the *organisation* of

economic activity creates different boundaries than the *technology* of
those activities. This is true even in inter-industry flows. A firm may
do its own repair work or purchase the service from another firm.
(This choice exists under socialism as well as under capitalism.) If, as
is usual, our unit of statistical inquiry is the firm, then the proportion
of the service sector in the total economy will appear to depend on
the vagaries of the organisation. I am not suggesting that the boundaries of economic organisations are irrelevant, but surely they are of
lesser importance than the activities which are in fact carried out
within whatever organisations exist.

The location of economic activities within one industry or another
is primarily a statistical problem. However, a more fundamental
division is the location of activities as between the household and
firms in general, as the paper of I. Sachs brings out so clearly. The
pressures of economic criteria are lessened, economies of scale are
greatly reduced, the interrelations between social values and economic performance made much greater. The importance of the role of
households is made more evident when one reflects on the close
relation between farms and households. Agricultural production in
developing and developed countries alike is to a very considerable
extent organised along family lines with all that that implies about
motivation, division of labour, other aspects of economic efficiency,
and the social structure of the family.

A very different criterion for distinguishing industry from other
economic activities is the general perception that industry is capable
of more rapid technological advance. This in turn can take two forms,
one that it so happens that technological advance based on science is
more directed to process and product innovations in manufacturing
and one that industry is more likely to exhibit increasing returns to
scale (including, as a dynamic version, learning by doing). The first
argument, that increases in factor productivity are empirically more
concentrated in industry than in agriculture seems to have no basis
whatever as a generalisation. Not only the Green Revolution but the
whole history of agricultural productivity since 1800 or so has been
one of constant increases thoroughly comparable and perhaps ex-
ceeding those of industry as a whole.

The second argument, that industry exhibits more increasing returns than agriculture, has somewhat more merit. In the past it has
been especially emphasised by Allyn Young and by Nicholas Kaldor.
Static economies of scale in agriculture undoubtedly exist, especially
in the presence of agricultural machinery, but they are exhausted at

levels very small compared with the economy. Further, the much greater role of the individual farmer in achieving adaptation to changing conditions means that the diseconomies of large-scale organisation are very pronounced. Gigantism in agriculture has been a failure where tried, as in collective farming. Undoubtedly there is learning by doing, but at the level of the individual farm it does not create significant economies of scale at the national level. There are many problems of agricultural policy in developing and developed countries, but the achievement of perfect competition, where desired, is not one of them.

On the other hand, in many but by no means all industries economies of scale are by no means trivial. Even in such a large market as the United States, some industries may have no more than two or three viable firms and in many industries have no more than ten or twenty. The propensity towards economies of scale is concentrated in continuous-process industries, such as chemicals, steel, or electric power generation and is much less apparent elsewhere. This suggests that a more fruitful classification would not lump all industry together but distinguish according to the degree of economies of scale.

A similar contrast has frequently been drawn, for example by Kaldor, between industry and services. While the category of services is so heterogeneous that generalisations are difficult, there are at least some, such as professional services, where economies of scale are weak. But even retail trade has exhibited great opportunities for technological progress and great receptivity to economies of scale. Deprecation of trade as a source of economic progress has not proved fruitful.

We may draw, however, a different distinction in which some of the most modern economic trends echo aspects of the beginning of European development, the distinction between *rural* and *urban*. It is noteworthy, as Roncaglia shows, that Sir William Petty, writing at the end of the seventeenth century, did not distinguish sharply between agriculture and industry, for the good reason that they were so much intertwined. Now Fuá and Vázquez-Barquero tell us of the strength of industrial development in the rural areas of Italy and Spain. Rural economies are characteristically different from those based in cities; they have the advantages and disadvantages of low population density. The economies of agglomeration are strong, but the diseconomies of urban congestion are equally so. An American (and especially an inhabitant of Santa Clara Valley, better known throughout the world as Silicon Valley) may be forgiven for wondering whether rural industrialisation is merely a transient state leading to all the consequences of full urbanisation.

There is still another special sense in which agriculture differs from other economic activities. It is especially subject to the forces of nature, to the rhythms of the seasons, and, at least in most places, to the irregularities and unpredictabilities of weather and climate, whether the monsoons of southern Asia, the blizzards and hailstorms of Midwestern United States, or the periodic droughts of East and West Africa. These have real consequences for economic organisation and above all for the social structure within which economic forces are embedded, as Ishikawa's address brings out. Agricultural organisation and, in particular, village organisation differ sharply under the pressure of different needs for collective action, whether for water management or for risk-sharing. In some areas, the value of large-scale irrigation, as in parts of China and in Egypt, forms the foundation for large and powerful states.

To sum up, the three-way classification may be of very limited value. It does not reflect anything about economic value (contribution to surplus in the language frequently used in studying the classical political economists, as in the paper of Bharadwaj). It does not bear any significant relation to the direction of input–output flows, especially under modern agricultural conditions.

The discussion does bring out some categories which are useful:

(1) Agriculture (*not* primary production, a category which includes mining) is a useful category because its relation to the household and to social structure is so much different from and greater than that of most other economic activities. Even this role is but a special case of the importance of social structure in the economy, some aspects of which are brought out in Sen's address.

(2) Economies of scale differ very much from one economic activity to another, and a categorisation along these lines may be very useful.

(3) The rural–urban difference is of significance for the possibilities of certain kinds of economic growth, even of an advanced kind, and for the special economic and social problems of urbanisation.

Part I

Plenary Papers

1 Inaugural Address

V.K.R.V. Rao

INSTITUTE OF SOCIAL AND ECONOMIC CHANGE,
BANGALORE

Mr President of the International Economic Association, Professor Kenneth Arrow, former President of the Association, Professor Sir Austin Robinson, Chairman of its Steering Committee, Dr Manmohan Singh, President of the Indian Economic Association, Professor Sukhamoy Chakravarty, Vice-President of the Indian Economic Association, Dr Alak Ghosh, distinguished economists and delegates to the Congress, ladies and gentlemen:

I must begin by thanking the organisers of the Eighth World Economic Congress, the Chairman of its steering Committee, Dr Manmohan Singh, and President of the Indian Economic Association, Professor Sukhamoy Chakravarty for the honour they have done me in inviting me to deliver the inaugural address to the Congress. This honour, which was unsought by me and has been given to an undeserving person, makes me feel very humble in your presence. I hope you will bear with me if my address does not come up to what you legitimately expect from an inaugural address.

Historically and traditionally, development has been identified with economic growth. The most frequently used indicator of economic growth is the change that takes place in a country's per capita GDP [gross domestic product]. And the economist, who has used the best and largest quantitative data extending over many years and many countries is Professor Simon Kuznets. I am deeply indebted to his writings for a great deal of what I am going to say in the inaugural address. For later years than those covered in his classic work on the *Economic Growth of Nations*, I have used the latest data from the *World Bank Reports on Development*.

Professor Kuznets had shown conclusively that there is a positive relationship between the growth of GDP and in terms of shares, that of the industrial sector, while it is negative in the case of the agricultural sector, and somewhat mixed, though positive, in the case of the agricultural sector and somewhat mixed, though positive, in the case of the tertiary sector. The quickest way of demonstrating the truth of

3

Table 1.1 Shares of production sectors in GDP
(Groups of countries in increasing order of 1958 per capita GDP)

Group	I	II	III	IV	V	VI	VII	VIII
No. of countries	6	6	6	15	6	6	6	6
1. GDP per capita (US$)	52	83	138	221	360	540	864	1382
2. Share of agriculture	53.6	44.6	37.9	32.3	22.5	17.4	11.8	9.2
3. Share of industry	18.5	22.4	24.6	29.4	35.2	39.5	52.9	50.2
3A. Share of industry (excluding transport and communication)	13.3	16.5	18.8	23.5	28.7	32.5	43.6	42.4
4. Share of services	27.9	33.0	37.5	38.3	42.3	43.1	35.3	40.6
4A. Share of services (including transport and communication)	33.1	38.9	43.3	44.2	48.8	50.1	44.6	48.4

Source: S. Kuznets, *Economic Growth of Nations: Total Output and Production Structure* (Cambridge, Mass.: The Belknap Press of Harvard University Press, 1971, Table 12).

---

the formulation was by a cross-section analysis of GDP at factor cost for as many developed and developing countries as possible and a look at the shares of the three sectors in one particular year linked with a Census year with its availability of occupational distribution of the labour force engaged in the production of the GDP. Accordingly, he selected 1958 (or about 1958) for some 57 countries which he grouped in increasing order of per capita product in 1958 converted to US dollars by relevant exchange rates. He also grouped them together into eight groups of six countries each (except for one group which included 15 countries), using their average per capita GDP, and the percentage of sectoral shares in increasing order of their 1958 GDP (see Table 1.1 for relevant extracts from this table).

Kuznets' table shows a strong positive relationship between the growth of the per capita GDP and the sectoral share of industry and, conversely, a declining sectoral share of agriculture, the difference in percentage points between the highest group coverage of per capita GDP of 1382 dollars and the lowest of 52 dollars being *plus* 31.7 points in the case of the industrial sector and *minus* 44.4 points in the case of the agricultural sector. Agriculture has lost its percentage not only to industry, but also to services, though by a smaller measure. Kuznets has included in the industrial sectors the subsector, transport and communication, which is mainly a producer of services and should, therefore, in my view, be excluded from the share of the industrial sector and added to that of the services sector. I have, therefore, included in Table 1.1 items 3A and 4A to indicate the resulting revised shares of the two sectors. According to these revised figures, while the share of industry still shows the same strong positive connection with the growth of the GDP, the magnitude is less, the difference between its share in the highest and lowest group average per capita GDP coming down to 29.1 percentage points as compared to 31.7 points in Kuznets' table. My revised version of Kuznets' table gives a share of 13.3 per cent to industry in the lowest per capita GDP group which is more realistic. The intriguing thing in the table, both in the original and as revised, is in regard to the behaviour of the share of services. Kuznets' table shows a fall in the share of services sector from 43.1 per cent in group VI of 540 dollars average per capita GDP to 35.3 per cent in the next higher group of 864 dollars of per capita GDP and then a rise to 40.6 per cent in the highest per capita group of 1382 dollars; while the figures as revised show a fall from group VI of 540 dollars of 50.1 per cent to 44.6 per cent in group VII of 864 dollars and then a rise to 48.4 per cent in the highest group of 1382 dollars per capita GDP. It appears that the services sector does not show a consistently steady increase in its share of the GDP growth as contrasted with the industries sector. Moreover, the share of the industries sector in the per capita GDP shows a much higher rate of growth from 13.3 per cent in the lowest category to 42.4 per cent in the highest category, or by 29.1 percentage points, while that of the services shows an increase of only 15.3 percentage points from 33.1 per cent to 48.4 per cent. But in recent years the position has changed, with the industries sector showing a decline and the services sector claiming a dominant share in the growth of the higher income group countries. This is illustrated by the anatomy of employment change for five industrialised countries between the years 1975 and 1980 from an issue of *Industry and Development* (UNIDO, 1985, Table 1b). Thus while there was an increase in employment of 13.5 million in the USA, services accounted for 9.4 million or 70 per cent of the total increase, while the industrial sector showed an increase of only 2.5 million. In the case of the FRG, the total increase was 504 000. While the services sector increased by 819 000, the industrial sector declined by 32 000. In the case of France, the corresponding figures were, total increase of 413 000, with the services sector increasing by 1.1 millions and the industry sector declining by 335 000. In the case of Japan, the total increase was over 1.2 millions, the services sector increased by more than that at approaching 1.5 millions and the industry sector declined by 310 000. In the case of the United Kingdom, the total increase was 161 000, with services increasing by 888 000, and industry declining by 647 000. This rapidly ascending order of the services sector is a new feature of the technological revolution now taking place in the industrially developed countries. There is a great deal of quality difference in the share of the service sector in the economic growth that is taking place in the industrially developed countries and in the industrially developing countries. In fact, the role of the services sector in economic development has always intrigued me and I wish some younger economist could take up the subject for a detailed study.

To revert to the role of industry in economic growth, there is no doubt that in the case of developed countries, industry has played the most important role in the earlier years, with the service sector taking its place in recent years and the share of agriculture continuing to decline till it reached in some countries the ridiculously low level of 2 per cent of GDP. The newly-industrialising countries have also shown a similar trend of increase in the sectoral share of industry and decline in the share of the agricultural sector and some increase in the services sector. This is seen in Appendix Table A1.1 which shows GDP in 1984, and the share of industry, agriculture and services for 22 countries, both developed and developing. But the intriguing fact that emerges from this table is that some of the middle income countries like Poland, Yugoslavia, South Korea, Mexico, and Argentina, with a per capita GDP ranging around 2000 dollars, show a high share of about 40 per cent of the GDP for the industrial sector, while even low income countries like Indonesia with a per capita GDP of 540 dollars shows an industrial sector share of 40 per cent, while a very low income country like India shows an industry sector share of 27 per cent.

The table does not reveal any consistent and continuous link between the GDP and the share of the industry sector or even the service sector, the only consistent and continuous trend shown being that of the declining share of agriculture with increasing amount of the GDP. There can be no doubt that the nature of industry is not the same between the developed and the developing countries, the former representing the use of advanced technology and the latter using backward technology, including historically inherited traditional technologies. Thus economic growth involves not only an increased role in sectoral shares for the industrial sector but also the use of modern or advanced technology in its operation. In fact, technology is an all-embracing factor in economic growth and covers not only industry but also agriculture and services. And it seems that advance in the technology used, rather than a mere percentage increase in the sectoral share of the industrial sector, is the key to rapid economic growth. In fact, in recent years, the use of better technology and higher investment in agriculture in some of the developing countries is becoming a notable feature of their economic growth as in the case of India. To quote from the *World Bank Report of 1986*:

> The past several decades of development have demonstrated that growth in agricultural production and productivity in developing countries can match or surpass the growth in industrial countries. The record has shown that agriculture can be a dynamic sector in developing countries and contribute greatly to growth in real incomes, employment, and foreign exchange earnings and to the alleviation of poverty.

Thus agriculture is still a dynamic sector in economic growth, but this does not mean that it can take the place of industry in maximising the growth of the GDP. In fact, it is the role of better technology and supporting investment for its use that has made the difference to the agricultural sector and the same would be even more true for the industry and services sectors. In other words, the emphasis in planning for rapid economic growth must now shift from sectoral attention to that of the methods used in production, supporting investments, and appropriate but modern technology.

So far I have been dealing with economic growth, identifying it with development and using the GDP as the measure of development, and sectoral growths as the means for maximising GDP. But development means much more than mere economic growth or an increase of GDP. Development deals with human beings and economic growth has to be linked with productive employment. Development should also take into account not only the positive aspects of economic growth in terms of maximising incomes and employment, but also its negative effects on the stock and continuity of natural resources, and the quality of the environment. In the last analysis, development implies a continuing improvement in the quality of life and the extension of this improvement in quality to the lives of all the people in the country concerned. Indeed, with the growing interdependence of the countries of the world, not only in economic terms but also in social, cultural and ethical terms, what we should mean by development is *sustainable* development for the continuing improvement of the quality of life to global dimensions and covering the entire human race. But I will not go into all that in the remaining part of my address, as that would take me too far from the main theme before this Congress.

The alarming feature of economic growth in the developing countries is not the change in their sectoral shares in GDP which is following the classical pattern of a rising share for industry and a falling share for agriculture, but the employment linkage with the changing sectoral shares and the level of productivity per worker accompanying the change. I have given in Appendix Tables A1.2, A1.3 and A1.4 comparative figures of the percentage sectoral shares of GDP and the percentage share of the labour force in the years 1960 and 1980 or 1981. Table A1.2 gives the relevant figures for industry, Table A1.3 for agriculture and Table 4 for services. The figures have been compiled from the *World Bank's Development Reports* for 1979, 1983 and 1986. I have taken as the initial year 1960, not only because of the availability of comparative data, but also because it corresponds with the Census year which contains the figures of occupational distribution of the labour force; and I have stopped with 1980 (or 1981 for GDP) as it is the latest year (also a Census year) for which occupational data is available.

Appendix Table A1.2, which gives the figures in the descending order of the percentage of the labour force engaged in industry, includes their corresponding shares in the GDP and the figures of the GDP to which they relate. The change in the link between the sectoral share of industry in GDP and the labour force has also to take into account the changes which have taken place in the share of the services sector over this period of 20 years, and to which I shall turn later.

For six industrially developed countries, namely, USA, Federal Republic of Germany, France, Canada, The Netherlands and the United Kingdom, whose per capita GDP ranged between 9110 dollars and 13 450 dollars in 1981, we find that their industry sectoral share ranged between 32 and 46 per cent in 1981, while their industry share in the labour force ranged from 29 to 44 per cent in the census year 1980. But all of them showed a decline of varying dimensions ranging from 2 percentage points to 13 percentage points in their sectoral industry shares of the GDP and a decline of varying dimensions ranging from 4 to 10 per cent of their share in the labour force. But in all cases, there was a positive link between the decline in this sectoral GDP and its sectoral labour force share. The only exceptions were Japan, which showed a decrease in its industry sectoral shares in GDP but an increase in the labour force, the former from 45 to 43 per cent and the latter from 30 to 34 per cent and Denmark where the sector share of GDP increased but the labour force decreased. It is also remarkable that the percentage figures for the sectoral share of industry in both the per capita GDP and the labour force are round about an equal figure.

When we come to the developing countries, we find in varying dimensions a rise in the share of the labour force in industry accompanying the rise in its share of the GDP. Among the countries with a per capita GDP between 2250 dollars (Mexico) and 1700 dollars (South Korea), we find a rise in the industry share of the labour force ranging from 9 to 27 per cent in the case of South Korea, from 12 to 19 per cent in the case of Malaysia, the corresponding share in per capita GDP being from 20 to 39 and 18 to 36 per cent. Argentina has retained its industry sectoral share in per capita GDP at 38 per cent, while there is a decline from 36 to 34 per cent in the share of the labour force. Yugoslavia, while showing a slight decline from 45 to 43 per cent in the industry share of its GDP, its industry labour force has shown a significant rise in its percentage from 18 to 33. On the other hand, Pakistan with a per capita GDP on only 350 dollars in 1981 records an increase of ten percentage points in its industrial GDP share as against a fall in its labour force share from 18 to 16 per cent. Even among the low income countries with per capita GDP ranging from 870 dollars (Nigeria) to 140 dollars (Bangladesh), there is immense variation. All of them show a percentage rise in their industry share of both the GDP and the labour force; the comparative rise in industry labour force is low in the case of India, Nigeria, Zaire, Indonesia, Kenya, Tanzania and Bangladesh; while the comparative growth in their industry's GDP share shows startling variations, with Indonesia showing a rise to 42 per cent from 25 per cent and Nigeria from 11 to 37 per cent. In the case of India, acclaimed for its industrial progress among the developing countries, the rise is only from 20 to 26 per cent. It is clear from the table that the type of technology used has a great deal to do with the growth of the industrial sector in the developing countries in respect of changes both in the shares in the GDP and the labour force.

The 22 countries in Appendix Table A1.3, listed therein in descending order of the share of agriculture in their labour force, begin with Tanzania with 86 per cent going down to only 3 per cent for the United Kingdom. While all of them show a decline in the share of agriculture in their GDP during the period, the magnitude of the decline shows a great deal of variation and so does the decline of the share in the labour force. Of the 13 countries which had an agricultural share of more than 50 per cent of their labour force in 1960, only five showed a marked decline to below 50 per cent in this share in 1980; South Korea from 66 to 36 per cent, Yugoslavia from 64 to 32 per cent, Malaysia from 63 to 42 per cent, Mexico from 55 to 37 per cent, and Brazil from 52 to 31 per cent. India's agricultural sector share in the labour force has only come down from 74 to 70 per cent in the labour force, though its GDP share has come down from 50 to 37 per cent or by 13 percentage points as compared to a fall of only 4 percentage points in its GDP share.

I have already strained your patience and endurance by the statistics I have been retailing. I shall only refer you to Appendix Table A1.4 which lists 22 countries in a descending order of the share of their service sectors in their labour force in 1960 together with their share of GDP, and also the corresponding figures for 1980. This table clearly bears out the thesis I have been emphasising, namely, the increase that has taken place between these two years in both shares in the GDP and in the labour force of the services sector. This has taken place particularly in the industrially developed countries, among which the United States had reached the high figure of 66 per cent for the Service sector in the labour force and 63 per cent share in the GDP. The less developed countries have also recorded a rise, though in absolute terms their service sector is much smaller; the lowest share in its rise is in the case of India, from 15 to 17 per cent in the labour force and from 30 to 37 per cent in the GDP.

The three tables seem to show that economic growth is taking place in most of the developing countries along the lines of the early experience of the developed countries, though with much smaller GDPs and a slower growth of the industrial sector. But this similarity should give no cause for complacency. The major problem confronting the most populated developing countries, including mine, is that of the large lag between the fall in the share of the labour force and that of the GDP of the agricultural sector. This leads to a variety of undesirable consequences, such as fall in the productivity of the labour force engaged in agriculture in spite of the fairly wide application of modern technology, underemployment and unemployment in the rural areas, exodus of the rural poor to urban settlements with increasing incidence of slums and urban deterioration, and an increasing dichotomy between the rural and the urban areas in their access to the basic elements that underlie the quality of life. Even in the case of the less populous countries, in some of which the share of industry is reaching high proportion, productivity as reflected by per capita GDP is low, there is increasing dependence even for food and other agricultural products, and an increasing gap in the quality of life between rural and urban areas. The growth of the industry sector share does not by itself either bring about a significant increase in economic growth nor does the fall in the GDP share of the agricultural sector reflect a surplus of food or other agricultural products. The increase in the services sector is also not a matter for satisfaction in so far as it does not mean a corresponding increase in educational, cultural and health facilities which are so important in constituting the quality of life. Employment – and productive employment at that – remains the keynote of both economic growth and human development, and there does not appear to be much of a rational nexus between changes in sectoral employment with the historically accepted sectoral pattern for economic development.

As regards the link between the trade and development, I do not think that a solution lies in the export-oriented production of food and agricultural raw materials. Apart from the fact that, in the food area, developed countries like the United States, Canada and Australia dominate the world market, it should not be forgotten that developing countries do not have genuine food surpluses which they can export (I include India in this category), nor are they in a position to offer their food exports to developed countries at competitive prices. Incidentally, I am not one of those who decry the policy of developed countries to protect their domestic agriculture, as I can appreciate the necessity to do so in their aesthetic, social and ecological interests. What the developing countries should do is to increase their food supplies primarily for the purpose of providing for their own population a balanced and adequate nutritional diet. I must also refer to the increasing difficulties which developing countries have in exporting raw materials, because of the advance of technology, leading to the emergence of synthetic substitutes for industrial raw materials, a concrete example being the substitution of cotton by synthetic fibres. Export–oriented agricultural development in foods and raw materials is no solution nor export-oriented industrial development with backward technology and semi-skilled or unskilled labour. Agricultural exports may help if they are in new avenues such as vegetables, flowers and processed foods; and similarly, industrial production for exports may help if they cater to the changing tastes of the paying markets and are based on competitive technology and skilled labour. Both these ways of export-oriented growth have their own limitations for most of the developing countries. In any case, these constraints cannot be overcome without massive humane-oriented international action on the part of the industrially developed countries.

I must now say a word about the demographic associations of agriculture and industry. The recent population explosion in the developing countries is only a corollary of the development that is taking place, which includes improvement in health services and their effect in promoting a decline in mortality. It was the same in the earlier stages of the development of the now industrially developed countries, which have now managed by their development to achieve a balance between their economic growth and their population. The same thing will happen in the case of the developing countries as well, provided they are able to have an accelerated rate of economic growth. This is dependent not only on their resources and economic policies but also on what the developed countries do to help them by implementing the new international economic order. Meanwhile the transitional problems of demography and development are creating great difficulties in the developing countries by both excessive dependence on agriculture and a massive exodus of the rural poor to urban areas, adding to their slums and unemployment. India is a conspicuous illustration of this transitional crisis of rural underemployment and unemployment and slum-laden urbanisation and unemployment. At the same time, I certainly agree that the governments of developing countries should follow a more positive population policy by expanding access to population control techniques, and providing motivation for population restriction by better health care, education, particularly of women, reduction in infant mortality, and economic incentives for adopting the small family norm.

There can also be no denying the fact that land and natural resources are limited in volume even when they are renewable; and there is certainly a specific limit to the area of cultivable land that a country has. The increase in direct employment that agriculture can give is limited, and one cannot deny the need for shifting a part of the labour force away from agriculture. How this is to be done in terms of an industrialisation that is both capital intensive and energy intensive and does not have the required employment magnitude, as in the case of India, is a question to which an answer has still to be found.

On the top of all this is the negative effect that modern economic growth and industrialisation is having on environment and the ecological balances. Quite apart from a nuclear war, or even preparations to wage it, making nonsense out of all our discussion on development, there is now increasing knowledge of the effect of modern industrialisation on the sustainability of development, including even the ecological imbalance created by the attempts at modernising our agriculture. Deforestation, denudations, desertification, recurring floods, loss of top soils, degeneration of land, noise and air pollutions, disposal of wastes and effluents damaging the quality of our water resources and marine wealth – all these and other environmental damage, both domestic and imported, are a growing constraint on the developing countries which have to cross the barrier of poverty, and enter on a course of economic growth, abolition of underemployment and unemployment, increase in the production of goods and service that determine the quality of life, and the creation of equality of access and equitable distribution of the dividends of development. We in India have just enacted legislation for the protection of the environment which is bound to increase the costs of industrialisation; but it cannot be helped, as life and health are more important than an industrialisation that seeks to bring about an appropriate balance between agriculture and industry in our development or even the modernisation of our agricultural growth that brings about ecological imbalance and threatens the very foundation of an enduring and productive agricultural existence. And yet, thanks to the advance in transport, communication, and audiovisual media, the world can no longer live in isolated compartments. National curtains, whether iron or bamboo or other varieties, have become out of date; and both Soviet Russia and Communist China are going in for an encouragement of tourist traffic with its promise of foreign exchange earnings and disregard for its adverse demonstration effects on consumer behaviour among the domestic population. Elitism and consumerism, with increasing wants and new and newer wants, are growing in the developing countries, and the industrialisation that is promoted tends to concentrate on this profitable market, to the neglect of the wage goods and mass consumption sector, which is justified in economic terms by their lack of purchasing power and effective demand.

For countries with small populations, there may be a possibility of elitism trickling downwards both in terms of demand and of production, though I am not sure how this would promote the quality of life or generate an egalitarian social order. But for large population countries like India or China, consumerism of an élitist character can only accentuate, as in the case of India, or create as in the case of China, social tensions and class conflicts that can end up in civil war and destruction of national integrities. This danger is greater for a country like India, which has a parliamentary democracy, adult franchise, periodic elections and multi-parties competing for vote banks through the use of populist rhetoric. We cannot isolate ourselves from the developed world which has built its economy on the basis of unlimited wants aided, if not also generated, by purposive advertisement which have acquired a significant role in their business economics. Nor can we escape the onward march of science and technology that is being increasingly geared either to profit making in the private sector or the politics of power and aggrandisement on the part of national governments. Nor can we escape the lure of modern consumer gadgets even if we can make them available only for a tiny section of our population.

We need capital from abroad even for a healthy development of our economy; and our domestic savings are not adequate for the purpose. We also need to import technology from abroad, partly because of our failing to exploit the scientific and technological potential that exists in our country. Our previous revenue surpluses have now turned into bulging deficits, partly resulting from the consequences of inflation and partly from the fall-out on our defence requirements of the superpower conflicts that are now entering so rapidly into our neighbouring regions and oceans. There has been a lot of rhetoric about the new international economic order, but it has not gone beyond talking, holding conferences and passing resolutions in UN bodies. Import of capital has to be paid for, and, mostly at market rates: and our long standing record of credit–rating and avoidance of the debt trap may soon come to an end with our planned efforts to speed up development. Imported technology carries with it, its own unwelcome conditions and gives no chance for its indigenisation and subsequent domestic development. Our balance of payments is getting out of gear. Export-induced investments and operations may themselves induce more inputs, creating a vicious circle of imports chasing exports, even assuming that our export drive, shorn of incentives at the expense of public revenues and domestic requirements, will take off the ground and not fall a victim to the lure of a profitable élitist domestic market.

In the midst of all these problems, I wonder what special importance can be attached to the question of balance between agriculture and industry in development. I am not denying the linkages, forward and backward, between industry and agriculture in economic development. Agriculture in its producer aspect meets the needs of industry in respect of both food for its workers and raw materials for its products. Agriculture, as producer-consumer, provides a market for the industrial production of agricultural inputs like fertilisers, tractors and tillers, and steel and cement for building dams, reservoirs, and canals, also for lining the canals, with the plastic industry now stepping in as a substitute, and also for the new system of sprinkler irrigation. Agriculture as consumer needs the basic mass and, hopefully, also the conventional consumption goods required by its population that are produced by industry. The vast numbers of our agricultural population constitute an immense potential market undisturbed by quotas and tariffs; but to realise this potential into an actual mass market, agricultural incomes will have to increase, not only those of small cultivators, and medium and big farmers, but also of the labourers they hire for cultivation; and this means higher prices for agricultural produce and higher wages for agricultural workers. It also means high investment, both public and private, not only to make land more productive but also for post-harvest operations such as storage, inland transport, and marketing. Increase of the purchasing power of the rural masses must also include the marginal cultivators who are underemployed, and the rural non-agricultural workers who have lost their markets to the products of modern urban industrialisation and now swell the ranks of the rural unemployed.

All this means increased resource mobilisation on the one hand and higher cost of living for the urban population and non-agricultural workers in the rural region on the other. Unless industrial employment is taken into the rural areas and there is decentralisation in the industrial development process, there can be no substantial decline in the percentage of the labour force now employed in agriculture and other traditional rural occupations; and if this is not done, there can be no reduction in the existing disparity between the per capita income in the rural sector and that in the urban sector or in the per capita product of rural and urban economic activity. The balance one needs between industry and agriculture in development must necessarily involve both a dispersal of industrial activity and its decentralisation, along with markets additional to, or even exclusive of local markets and dependence on local materials.

Also, a third variable has to be brought into the development process besides industry and agriculture namely, the environment. For sustained and sustainable development, one needs a balance not only between agriculture and industry in terms of mutual exchange and markets but also in terms of the economic processes involved in both agriculture and industry not adversely affecting the environment and disturbing, if not actually destroying, the ecological balance. And this balance, between agriculture, industry and environment need not, indeed, should not, be confined within national boundaries but must cross them, increase international trade, and permit the harnessing of comparative advantages in costs and supply of natural resources. Natural resources are not evenly distributed by national boundaries; nor is the environment and the help it can give, and the harm it can do, confined within national frontiers. The environment is both local and world wide; and only a global attitude and its implementation in policies and programmes can protect the environment and ensure human harmony with nature to the mutual advantage of both in terms of sustenance and further development. The balance between agriculture and industry has to be global and equitable in its operations, not only across national boundaries but also within them. The balance between economic growth, which includes all the three sectors of the GDP, and the environment which covers them all, has not only to be implemented across national frontiers but also within them. Development cannot be left without a qualifying adjective which will take it out of the short period and from purely personal or group selfish interests into the broader field of the long period and a harmonisation of the personal and the social interest; and it must deal with the quality of life rather than merely with material goods and needs. Science must be combined with spirituality.

I had no hand in the choice of the theme for this Eighth World Economic Congress. If I had my choice, I would have broadened and deepened the theme and called it BALANCE BETWEEN AGRICULTURE, INDUSTRY, ENVIRONMENT AND THE QUALITY OF LIFE IN SUSTAINABLE DEVELOPMENT.

It is a long and clumsy title to give to the theme of such an august body as the World Economic Congress. But it is in line with the reputation I justly have for long–windedness, besides indicating my preference for comprehensiveness over conciseness. The classic Indian tradition is to prefer the whole to the part; and one cannot see the parts in clear perspective except in the context of the whole. I have only been applying my ancient national tradition in straying so far from the field strongly bounded by the announced title of the theme.

I now conclude my inaugural address with the hope that in the discussions that follow on the theme set for the Congress, at least some of you will step beyond its boundary and bring in the completeness indicated by my references to the quality of life, ecological balances, global implications, the new international economic order and sustained and sustainable development.

I thank you for your patience.

Note

I am indebted to Sri R. P. Tyagi of the Institute of Economic Growth for statistical assistance.

Reference

UNIDO (1985) 'Industrialisation and Employment Generation in the Services Sector of Developing Countries: An Appraisal', *Industry and Development* No 15 September pp. 55–108

Appendix Table A1.1   GNP per capita and share of sectors in GDP–1984

Country	Per capita GNP (US$)	Percentage share in GDP of:		
		Industry	Agriculture	Services
1. USA	15 390	32	2	66
2. Canada	13 280	24	3	72
3. Denmark	11 170	25	5	70
4. Federal Republic of Germany	11 130	46	2	52
5. Japan	10 630	41	3	56
6. France	9 760	34	4	62
7. Netherlands	9 520	32	4	64
8. UK	8 570	36	2	62
9. New Zealand	7 730	32	9	60
10. Argentina	2 230	39	12	50
11. Yugoslavia	2 120	46	15	40
12. South Korea	2 110	40	14	47
13. Poland	2 100	52	15	33
14. Mexico	2 040	40	9	52
15. Malaysia	1 980	35	21	44
16. Brazil	1 720	35	13	52
17. Nigeria	730	30	27	43
18. Indonesia	540	40	26	34
19. Pakistan	380	29	24	47
20. Kenya	310	21	31	48
21. India	260	27	35	38
22. Bangladesh	130	12	48	39

Source: *World Bank Development Report 1986* (New York: Oxford University Press for the World Bank, 1986) Tables 1 and 3.

Appendix Table A1.2 Importance of industry in GDP and labour force
related to per capita GNP (in order of 1960 labour force share)

Country	% Share of labour force in industry		% Share of industry in GDP		Per capita GNP (in US$)
	1960	1980	1960	1981	1981
1. Federal Republic of Germany	48	44	53	46	13 450
2. UK	48	38	43	33	9 110
3. Netherlands	42	32	46	33	11 790
4. France	39	35	39	35	12 190
5. Denmark	37	35	31	32	13 120
6. USA	36	31	38	34	12 820
7. Argentina	36	34	38	38	2 560
8. Canada	34	29	34	32	11 400
9. Japan	30	34	45	43	10 080
10. Yugoslavia	18	33	45	43	2 790
11. Mexico	20	29	29	37	2 250
12. Pakistan	18	16	16	26	350
13. Brazil	15	27	35	34[1]	2 220
14. Malaysia	12	19	18	36	1 840
15. India	11	13	20	26	260
16. Nigeria	10	12	11	37	870
17. Zaire	9	13	27	24	210
18. South Korea	9	27	20	39	1 700
19. Indonesia	8	13	25	42	530
20. Kenya	5	7	18	21	420
21. Tanzania	4	5	11	15	280
22. Bangladesh	3	6	7	14	140

Note:
1. 1980 figure
Source World Bank Development Reports (New York: Oxford University
Press for the World Bank).
1983 volume, Table 21, for labour force 1960.
1986 volume, Table 30, for labour force 1980.
1983 volume, Table 3, for GDP 1960 and 1981.
1983 volume, Table 1, for per capita GNP in 1981.

Appendix Table A1.3 Importance of agriculture in GDP and labour force related to per capita income (in order of 1960 labour force share)

Country	% Share of labour force in agriculture		% Share of agriculture in GDP		Per capita GNP (in US$)
	1960	1980	1960	1981	1981
1. Tanzania	89	86	57	52	280
2. Bangladesh	87	75	58	54	140
3. Kenya	86	81	38	32	420
4. Zaire	83	72	30	32	210
5. Indonesia	75	57	50	24	530
6. India	74	70	50	37	260
7. Nigeria	71	68	63	23	870
8. South Korea	66	36	37	17	1 700
9. Yugoslavia	64	32	24	12	2 790
10. Malaysia	63	42	36	23	1 840
11. Pakistan	61	55	46	30	350
12. Mexico	55	37	16	8	2 250
13. Brazil	52	31	16	13[1]	2 220
14. Japan	33	11	13	4	10 080
15. France	22	9	10	4	12 190
16. Argentina	20	13	16	9	2 560
17. Denmark	18	7	11	4	13 120
18. Federal Republic of Germany	14	6	6	2	13 450
19. Canada	13	5	5	4	11 400
20. Netherlands	11	6	9	4	11 790
21. Australia	10	7	12	5	11 080
22. USA	7	4	4	3	12 820
23. UK	4	3	3	2	9 110

Note:
1. 1980 figure.
Source: As Appendix Table A1.2.

Appendix Table A1.4 Importance of services in GDP and labour force related to per capita GNP (in order of 1960 labour force share)

Country	% Share of labour force in services		% Share of services in in GDP		Per capita GNP (in US$)
	1960	1980	1960	1981	1981
1. USA	57	66	58	63	12 820
2. Canada	52	66	61	64	11 400
3. UK	48	59	54	65	9 110
4. Netherlands	47	63	45	63	11 790
5. Denmark	45	58	58	64	13 120
6. Argentina	44	53	46	53	2 560
7. France	39	56	51	61	12 190
8. Federal Republic Germany	38	50	41	49	13 450
9. Japan	37	55	42	53	10 080
10. Brazil	33	42	49	53[1]	2 220
11. Mexico	25	34	55	55	2 250
12. Malaysia	25	39	46	41	1 840
13. South Korea	25	37	43	44	1 700
14. Pakistan	21	30	38	44	350
15. Nigeria	19	20	26	40	870
16. Indonesia	17	30	25	34	530
17. India	15	17	30	37	260
18. Yugoslavia	19	34	31	45	2 790
19. Bangladesh	10	19	35	32	140
20. Kenya	9	12	44	47	420
21. Zaire	8	16	43	44	210
22. Tanzania	7	10	32	33	280

Note:
1. 1980 figure.
Source: As Appendix Table A1.2.

2 Presidential Address: General Economic Theory and the Emergence of Theories of Economic Development

Kenneth J. Arrow
STANFORD UNIVERSITY

I welcome the delegates of the Eighth World Congress of the International Economic Association. We come from countries containing the bulk of the world's population and represent economies with widely varying modes of economic organisation and income levels. The International Economic Association was founded thirty-three years ago as a federation of national economic associations from as wide a variety of nations as possible. Among us today are two of the early leaders of the Association, Sir Austin Robinson and Academician Tigran Khachaturov. Throughout its history the Association has continued to maintain and strengthen the ties of intellectual interaction among economists, regardless of changes in the political climate. We have contributed, I am proud to say, to the common elements of mankind in seeking better understanding and contributing to the universal aspiration for a better material life. We have had, and will have, many and strong differences of opinion. It is only by frank expression that we understand and learn from each other. The serious and unpolemical nature of the papers at this Congress shows the underlying universality of respect for evidence and logical argument.

Words are inadequate to express the gratitude of the Association and the participants in this Congress for the work and contributions of the Indian Economic Association and the Indian Government. Both the financial contribution and the hard and unremitting labour of the Steering Committee for more than a year have produced a superbly organised Congress. The delegates may find it hard to realise the vast number of major decisions and seemingly minor details which must be handled to produce a deceivingly smoothly-running meeting. I hesitate to mention particular names for fear of neglecting others, but I must express the Association's thanks to our Vice-President, Professor Sukhamoy Chakravarty, to the Convener of the Steering Committee, Dr V. R. Panchamukhi, and to Professor P. R. Brahmananda and Dr Manmohan Singh. They have disrupted their normal busy and important schedules to make this Eighth World Congress the success that it is.

I am not, as you all know, a specialist in economic development, and doubtless most of you here have more knowledge of the problems of developing countries than I do. I intend here a modest aim. It is to review selectively some of the early formulations of the theory of economic development during the period 1945–60, approximately, and show how they related to developments in general economic theory at that and somewhat earlier periods. I am referring particularly to developments in neoclassical economics as it evolved under the pressure of the problems of developed countries. I also refer to that offspring of neoclassical theory which threatened to eat its father, Keynesian theory, also a response to the conditions of the advanced world. These had a strong and inevitable influence on thinking about economic development.

Let me briefly characterise neoclassical economics as I understand it. It is rather a general viewpoint than a highly specific theory. It is constantly evolving. Neoclassical economics is an approach or mode of thinking which assumes optimising behaviour by individuals, together with an all over coherence of the economy in the form of balancing supply and demand. From the viewpoint of application, what is relevant is a general tendency to balance rather than a moment-by-moment clearing of the market.

The charge is sometimes made that neoclassical economics is completely static and, therefore, unsuitable for analysing change and growth. This charge cannot be maintained. Sir John Hicks, Gerard Debreu, and I, among many others, have shown how the future, and even uncertainty, can be brought into general equilibrium analysis, with suitable understanding and sophistication (Hicks, 1948; Arrow, 1953; Arrow and Debreu, 1954, pp. 266, 268; Debreu, 1959, p. 29). Recent research has even extended the analysis to the role of information in the economic system, but this topic takes us beyond the period to be discussed.

Another recurrent theme is that neoclassical economics tends to the study of small-scale resource allocation problems rather than the grand themes which classical political economy is supposed to have displayed. Personally, I believe that classical economics has the same fundamental world viewpoint as neoclassical, but is much less developed analytically. For example, technological unemployment in the long run is certainly a fallacy, but Ricardo's struggles with the problem in his chapter on machinery can only be described as confused. Consider also the meaning of gains from trade. Though Ricardo, of course, believed in and emphasised them, he had no way of explaining them, since in his system foreign trade represented an equal exchange of 'values'. He had to make some vague allusions to something different from value, which he called, 'riches'; this is simply, 'utility', in later language.[1]

I want to relate some of the 'grander' themes of development theory in its formative period to neoclassical paradigms, including the failures of some paradigms to apply. I note that there are fewer and fewer of these grand theories and more and more highly specific applications. The neoclassical insight lends itself to this kind of analysis of specific situations, for example, the effects of a change in tariffs or agricultural subsidies. Indeed, the tendency to the specific is one of the advantages of the neoclassical approach. Grand visions do not lend themselves to useful policy. Following Ricardo or Marx leads one either to urge free markets everywhere or to say that there is no solution short of revolution.

It is useful to recall the state of economics and the preoccupations of economists in the period before and after the Second World War and during the great era in which the developing countries achieved independence. It was at this time that the modern economics of development took its form. To oversimplify, the main concerns of economists were (1) the ways in which the economy deviated from competitive behaviour and competitive efficiency, and (2) unemployment. Let me make these in reverse order.

Unemployment in the 1930s was too palpable and prolonged a phenomenon to be conveniently ignored by economists. In many ways, the presence of unemployment, of a failure to clear one of the most important of all markets, is a serious critique of neoclassical economics, with its emphasis on markets as a co-ordination of behaviour. Of course, Keynes's *General Theory* (1936) provided an intellectual representation which gave economists a tool for analysis.

From the viewpoint of development economics, Keynesian theory gave encouragement to models in which labour played no constraining role. In particular, dynamic Keynesian models emerged, associated with the names of Harrod, Domar, and later, Joan Robinson (1969). It was the unemployment problem of the developed countries that was under consideration, but these theories provided a major stimulus for development planning. They were convenient analytic tools, and there was a factual correspondence in that many of the development countries exhibited large-scale urban unemployment, and at least a perceived underutilisation of labour on the farms.

An intellectual problem remained: why is there unemployment in either developed or underdeveloped countries? The neoclassical (or, I would maintain, even classical) argument that competition should drive wages down to eliminate unemployment is not on the face of it ridiculous Policy-oriented economists and those whom they advised may at one time have regarded this kind of question as one for theorists to amuse themselves with. In the analysis of both developed and developing countries it was assumed that wages would remain constant as demand rose, at least until a period of full employment (in developed countries) or labour scarcity (in developing countries) was achieved. The passage of time and better observation have shown the fallacy of this assumption if taken literally. Wages do rise even when the reservoir is not empty. A deeper understanding of the nature of unemployment still eludes us. Some version of the efficiency wage theory, with different interpretations for developing and developed countries, is the currently most coherent explanation of unemployment, but it is so far not very useful.[2]

The presence of unemployment, of course, presents an opportunity for growth by providing a resource with zero shadow price, and indeed that was the assumption of even quite sophisticated planning models.

My second theme, you will recall, was that economic thought from about 1930 or so was much concerned with imperfections in competition and, related to that, the extent to which the actual market falls short of an optimum, however defined. It has long been traditional in neoclassical economics to study market failures and defend state intervention as a way of overcoming them. The topic is not absent from Walras (1874–3 pp. 256–7) and is given considerable prominence by Marshall (1890, Book V, Chapter XIII). It is, however, Marshall's student A. C. Pigou, who presented the most complete catalogue of market failures and externalities (Pigou, 1920), after his earlier efforts on faulty foundations were corrected by Allyn Young (1913) and Frank H. Knight (1924).

Market failure and indeed any departures from Pareto optimality share with unemployment one important characteristic: there is the apparent possibility of a large gain in welfare, an impossibility if resources are already optimally allocated.

It is very frequently asserted that in developing countries the market fails to achieve equality of wage rates in different sectors of the economy, the dual economy hypothesis. This doctrine seems to have been first expressed in a general form by Paul Rosenstein-Rodan (1943), while discussing the economic development of south-eastern Europe. When wage rates differ, marginal productivities differ, and there is room, perhaps considerable, for increases in welfare.

The simplest form of the idea is that farm wages or marginal productivities are lower than industrial or urban wage rates. At least three different causes are possible; all can be operating. (1) Since the members of a farm family share their receipts, the individual receives average productivity on the farm and only marginal productivity in the city. To induce mobility, urban wages would have to equal average farm productivity. Put another way, the ownership of capital on the farm is not transferred on a market but linked to family membership and participation in the farm work. (2) The transaction costs of migration and of information about the urban sector and the uncertainty of the move constitute a second gap between rural and urban wages. (3) A third gap could be the political and collective economic power of the urban workers.

Instead of the gap between agriculture and industry, the dualism is sometimes found between traditional and modern sectors, in recognition of the importance and difficulties of the modernisation of agriculture.

The explanatory power of this hypothesis is that it locates the cause of international differences in income levels in the failure of markets and limitations on mobility between them. The policy implications are ambiguous. The most direct implication would be to lower the institutional barriers and let the free play of the market improve resource allocation. But usually the imperfection is taken as given, and policy has been oriented toward offsetting the imperfection with measures to subsidise and protect the industrial or, more generally, the modern sector.

The extreme version of the dual-economy hypothesis has a zero shadow wage for labour and thus is another form of the unemployment hypothesis. A constant real wage is needed in the urban sector. There is a striking and not accidental parallel to early Keynesian economics, where wages would be constant until full employment is achieved, and, of course, the shadow wage is zero. In both spheres, those of developed and developing countries, more realistic analysis suggests that wages will rise as more workers are drawn into employment, in the Keynesian case, or into the modern sector, in the dual economy. The marginal productivity of farm labour is far from zero, as Theodore Schultz has shown.

No doubt many developing countries show dual economies. But the question remains, can a significant part of the international differences in income levels be attributed to dualism? Calculations of the production possibility curve for two-sector models, even with large distortions, suggest relatively small losses in industrial output for a given level of agricultural output. Further, the presence of large-scale urban unemployment or underemployment in a number of developing countries suggests that immobilities due to income-sharing by farm families are not a constraining factor in growth.

Dualism is one example of the application of welfare economics or the theory of market failure to help understand economic development. Another application of this point of view gave rise to the idea of balanced growth, strongly advocated by Ragnar Nurkse (1953) and given analytic expression by Tibor Scitovsky (1954). Industry A will not develop in the absence of assured demand from Industry B or from consumers. But Industry B or the consumer sector in turn will develop only with assured or expected demand which, in turn, will come from the development of Industry A.

Parenthetically, the form in which the argument has just been stated implies that the balanced growth is entirely domestic. It was presented at a time when there was pessimism about the prospects for exports by developing countries. Obviously, if the source of some demands is partly external to the country, the chicken-and-egg problem is not as acute. But I want to avoid the foreign trade aspects of development in this address, not because they are not important but because they would take me too far afield.

How are the externalities suggested by the balanced growth argument consistent with the usual theorems about the optimality of competitive equilibrium? Monopoly is not presupposed nor are there any technological externalities of the type of pollution in the argument. Technically, the market failure is the non-existence of forward markets for the products of each industry. If steel is needed for the production of automobiles, while no one will invest in automobile production in the absence of a domestic source of steel, all that is needed to get started are markets today for delivery of automobiles and steel tomorrow. The steel producers will invest today on the basis of simultaneous sale of their product for delivery in the future, while the automobile manufacturers will put up their plants with the security of steel deliveries when the plants are ready to produce.

In the absence of forward markets, expectations perform much the same role. Indeed, trial and error by individual producers will get the economy to a balanced resource allocation without intervention, if constant returns to scale prevail. If a steel producer starts producing on a small scale, risking little, automobile producers will enter on a small scale, encouraging further entry on both sides. There is a loss of welfare, of course, compared with a development fully co-ordinated by a complete set of intertemporal markets or by an ideal planner, but the welfare loss will not persist and cannot be an explanation for large long-run differentials in development.

As Hollis Chenery (1959) showed, the market will fail to co-ordinate if there are elements of increasing returns. More generally, the existence of increasing returns is recognised as one of the basic difficulties in both the viability of competitive equilibrium and the use of the price system to achieve a prescribed efficient allocation. The doctrines of imperfect competition developed by Joan Robinson and Edward Chamberlin in the 1930s were developed to show how an economy with many competing firms could exist in the presence of increasing returns.

From the perspective of development, the concept of increasing returns seems to offer an endogenous explanation for economic growth. Indeed, as we all know, Adam Smith emphasised that growth in productivity was due to division of labour, which is limited by the size of the market. This is a perfectly clear statement of the role of indivisibilities, which is virtually synonymous with increasing returns. The idea dropped out of his classical successors; it has no role in Ricardo or Marx, where increases in productivity are solely the result of capital accumulation. With the diminishing returns, and the consequent stationary state envisaged by Ricardo and John Stuart Mill, long run international differences in income levels arise only from differences in natural resources and in the socially determined minimum wage that governs reproduction. Marshall reintroduced increasing returns into economic theory, but had difficulties reconciling them with perfect competition (Marshall, 1890, Book V, Chapter XII and Appendix H). In his model, increasing returns were always an externality, but as Knight (1924, fn 9) later argued, this cannot be universally true. Every externality is someone's internality. Allyn Young, in his 1928 presidential address to the Royal Economic Society, stressed increasing returns as a major factor in economic growth (Young, 1928).

Though Smith and Young were seeking to explain the remarkable development of Europe and its overseas extensions, the doctrine might be equally capable of explaining the differences between developing and developed countries today. Any simple growth model of the type made familiar to us by Robert Solow (1956) shows that, under increasing returns, a country that came into the growth process will always remain ahead, other things being equal. Of course, this rigidly deterministic model does not reflect the fact that leadership does change as the decline of Great Britain and the rise of Japan attest. But it does give an explanation of persistent international differences due only to the timing of entry on to the path of development.

The presence of increasing returns has other explanatory values. It helps explain why there is so much trade among technologically similar countries. The comparative advantage which drives the trade is derived from scale economies in particular, quite narrowly-defined industries. The notion of increasing returns should, of course, in many cases, be given a dynamic interpretation, so-called learning by doing.

The proposition that increasing returns are the, or even a, key element in understanding economic growth has striking policy implications. Since increasing returns inhere in very specific industries, including agriculture and services, one implication is that development should *not* be broad-based or balanced but rather directed to narrow sectors, to achieve economies of scale in one sector before going on to another. Obviously, such a policy is going to be constrained by the demands and needs of final consumers, unless foreign trade can provide substitutes for the underdeveloped sectors.

The implications for planning are ambiguous. On the one hand, the optimal allocation under increasing returns will not be obtained under free markets. In fact, as I have already remarked, the competitive equilibrium is not even viable, and the outcome will be some kind of imperfect competition. But optimal allocation under increasing returns is difficult. For one thing, the optimisation requires the use of integer programming, a procedure intrinsically more complex than linear programming, and impossible to carry out for large systems even with the most powerful computers. Even more serious are the data demands. The information needed is widely dispersed among the industries and cannot be effectively communicated. It is for these reasons that decentralised decision-making with some element of monopoly is likely to be more efficient.

In conjunction with the theme of this Congress, it is worth noting that all of the points of view that I have discussed can be used to justify allocative biases for industry as against agriculture or services; unemployment presumably cannot be fully absorbed in agriculture. This argues for development of industry, but, as experience confirms, even more strongly for services, including construction. The dual economy hypothesis gives the clearest argument for protecting industry, especially in the broader version in which urban service workers, sometimes not easily distinguished from the unemployed, are considered part of the traditional sector. In the balanced growth model there is no need for special intervention to enable agriculture to meet demand; it is industry that needs encouragement to get started and therefore be a source of demand. It is usual to associate increasing returns with industry as the late Nicholas Kaldor always held, but from a broader point of view, the argument is not so clear. Increasing returns in a form needed to explain long-term economic development and international income differences must be understood to include induced innovation, that is, innovations not worthwhile developing until the scale of application becomes high enough. Here, agriculture has proved to be a powerful stimulus to innovation.

I have talked in a very general way, as befits the occasion, of the relation of some important early strands of economic development theory to developments in the economic theory of developed countries, especially neoclassical economics, but also Keynesian theory. To a great extent neoclassical economics has developed its own internal critiques, which have enriched our economic understanding and led to applications beyond the original intended scope. It is for others, who know the facts of economic development much better than I do, to assess the role of the theories just discussed in understanding and guiding economic development.

Notes

1. Don Patinkin has pointed out to me that Ricardo suggests that both countries in foreign trade might have more of both commodities (in a two-country, two-commodity model) as compared with autarky (see Sraffa, (ed.) (1951) *The Works and Correspondence of David Ricardo* vol. 1, p. 140. This statement is not true in general, and it is not clear that Ricardo meant it to be more than an example. In any case, the statement is not one that is expressible in terms of 'values'.
2. See, among other papers, Yellen (1984), Schapiro and Stiglitz (1984), and Bowles (1985).

References

Arrow, K. J. (1953) 'Le rôle des valeurs boursières pour la répartition la meilleure des risques', *Econometrie* (Paris: Centre National de la Recherche Scientifique), pp. 91–6; English version (1963–4) 'The role of securities in the optimal allocation of risk-bearing', *Review of Economic Studies*, vol. 31 (1963–4). pp. 91–6.

Arrow, K. J. and Debreu, G. (1954) 'Existence of Equilibrium for a Competitive Economy', *Econometrica*, vol. 22, pp. 265–90.

Bowles, S. (1985) 'The Production Process in a Competitive Economy: Walrasian, Neo-Hobbesian and Marxian models', *American Economic Review*, vol. 75, pp. 16–36

Chenery, H. B. (1959) 'The interdependence of investment decisions' in Abramovitz *et al., The Allocation of Economic Resources* (Stanford: Stanford University Press) pp. 82–120.

Debreu, G. (1959) *Theory of Value* (New Haven: Yale University Press) p. 29, Chapter VII.

Hicks, J. R. (1948) *Value and Capital* 2nd edn. (Oxford: Clarendon Press).

Keynes, J. M. (1936) *The General Theory of Employment, Interest and Money* (New York: Harcourt Brace).

Knight, F. H. (1924) 'Some Fallacies in the Interpretation of Social Cost', *Quarterly Journal of Economics*, vol. 38, pp. 582–606.

Marshall, A. (1890) *Principles of Economics* 8th edn. (1920) (London: Macmillan).

Nurkse, R. (1953) *Problems of Capital Formation in Underdeveloped Countries* (Oxford: Oxford University Press).

Pigou, A. C. (1920) *Economics of Welfare* 4th edn. (1932) (London: Macmillan).

Robinson, J. (1969) *The Accumulation of Capital* 3rd edn. (London: Macmillan).

Rosenstein-Rodan, P. N. (1943) 'Problems of Industrialisation of Eastern and Southeastern Europe', *Economic Journal*, vol. 53, pp. 202–11.

Schapiro, C. and Stiglitz, J. (1984) 'Equilibrium Unemployment as a Worker Discipline Device', *American Economic Review*, vol. 74, pp. 433–44.

Scitovsky, T. (1954) 'Two Concepts of External Economies', *Journal of Political Economy*, vol. 17, pp. 143–51.

Solow, R. M. (1956) 'A Contribution to the Theory of Economic Growth', *Quarterly Journal of Economics*, vol. 65, pp. 65–94.

Sraffa, P. (ed.) (1951) *The Works and Correspondence of David Ricardo* (Cambridge University Press) vol. 1.

Walras, L. (1874–7) *Elements of Pure Economics*, English translation by Jaffe, W. (1954) (Allen & Unwin).

Yellen, J. (1984) 'Efficiency Wage Models of Unemployment', *American Economic Review Papers and Proceedings*, vol. 74, May, pp. 200–5.

Young, A. A. (1913) 'Pigou's Wealth and Welfare', *Quarterly Journal of Economics*, vol. 27, pp. 672–86.

Young, A. A. (1928) 'Increasing Returns and Economic Progress', *Economic Journal*, vol. 38, pp. 527–42.

3 Dealing with Economic Imbalances between Industry and Agriculture

Theodore W. Schultz
UNIVERSITY OF CHICAGO

1 INTRODUCTION

Attaining and maintaining an economic balance between industry and agriculture is an important, unsettled policy issue. How to do it is not obvious. Seeing what governments do, it could be argued that they are adept at producing such imbalances. We know that many governments pursue policies that distort product and factor values by various means and thereby induce economic imbalances. In low income countries, governments tend to specialise in policies that keep agricultural production down; in high income countries governments do the exact opposite. Nevertheless, while governments are not blameless, it would be a serious error to attribute all imbalances between industry and agriculture to what governments do.

My subject would be alarmingly formidable if I were to pursue all of the various concepts of balance or imbalance. The idea of a social balance between industry and agriculture, however appealing it may be, will not be pursued. Nor will the idea of an institutional balance. When it comes to policy issues, the concept of a political balance may be useful. In the language of this Congress I am mainly concerned with economic conditions that result in economic imbalances. I take this to mean that an economic balance has the properties of an economic equilibrium, and that an imbalance means that an economic disequilibrium exists. I shall concentrate on modern economic growth in the spirit of the approach of Simon Kuznets (1966). The economic growth of the last 40 years, the period since the Second World War, will be foremost in my thinking. I shall eschew development economics by staying with the much less complex process of economic growth.

33

We often bemoan the lack of political theory and supporting evidence to explain the politics of economic growth. But the limitations of our economic growth theory are also grievous. There are all manner of economic imbalances, whether they are between industry and agriculture, or between labour and capital, between human and physical capital, between traded and nontraded goods (this list goes on and on), there is no room for these imbalances in steady growth theory.

We do have useful specialised economic studies that reach beyond the existence of a general equilibrium. For the purpose at hand there are studies specialising in international trade, in rates of economic productivity, in agricultural economics, in human capital and in various other specialties that provide elements of theory along with evidence pertaining to the sources of economic imbalances and, to a less extent, to what can be done in dealing with them.

My personal reason for choosing this subject is that I gave considerable thought to it in my *Agriculture in an Unstable Economy* (Schultz, 1945) and then with more depth in *The Economic Organization of Agriculture* (Schultz, 1953). There are qualifications I would want to make about these works; yet, despite all the changes in economic conditions since 1950, my principal results, so it seems to me, are not wrong. My approach was restricted to the economics of agriculture in a national economy, mainly to that of the United States. Within the theme laid down for this Congress, and linking it with my 1945 book, my subject might well be, 'Industry and Agriculture in an Unstable World Economy'.

My experience since 1945 and my efforts to understand the process of achieving increases in real income, supports John Hicks's remark in the preface to *Capital and Growth* (Hicks, 1965). On a theory of economic growth which is to be defended as the theory that is superior in every respect, Hicks states,

> I do not think that there is such a theory; I doubt if there can be. The phenomena that are presented by a developing (changing) economy are immensely complex; any theory about them is bound to simplify . . . There is no known approach which is not based upon omissions, omissions that can easily prove to be of critical importance.

In truth a developing (changing) economy is immensely complex. It has become quaint to think of it as a 'progressive state', or seeing it as Adam Smith saw it, 'the cheerful and hearty state'. We now call it economic growth and thus try to avert the hassle about progress. At issue in dealing with the immense complexities of economic growth is how to simplify in order to devise a manageable and useful theory. A theory based on the assumption of steady economic growth may be made tractable analytically. But the omission of various changing economic conditions and their effects on growth is of crucial importance. Moreover, actual national economic growth is not a steady process even during fairly short periods.

Consider the economic stress and strain on the balance between industry and agriculture during modernisation. Is there ever a period when the growth of a national economy is in a true equilibrium with respect to all economic margins that matter? Data reporting trends can be made smooth and be shown nicely smooth, but smoothing does not create an economic equilibrium.

We can rationalise any observable economic state as being in equilibrium and it is sophisticated to do so by artful uses of particular assumptions about information, transaction costs, risk and uncertainty.

I hold fast to the proposition that it is not possible to have economic growth with no economic disequilibria. Even under the most favourable changes in economic conditions that result in economic growth consisting of increases in real income, *economic disequilibria are inevitable*. They cannot be prevented by law or by public policy and surely not by rhetoric.

But prevention is not the key economic issue. Surely we do not want to prevent the increasing division of labour and specialisation that are an integral part of growth. Who among us is set on preventing the increasing returns to be had from specialised physical and human capital? Modern growth is increasing the value of human time and also the real per capita income in many nation-states. It brings about a decline in the share of national income that is accounted for by agricultural land rent. It has in large measure made possible the remarkable increase in life span in many low income countries since 1950. If the economic growth that makes these achievements possible entails disequilibria, are we to forego the growth in order to prevent the disequilibria? Prevention is the wrong issue. The real issue pertains to the incentives that induce economic agents to reallocate the resources in their domain and to the efficiency of these agents in establishing a new equilibrium.

The policy implications of my argument up to this point consist of two parts. Where government policies induce malallocations of resources, more economic growth could be had by eliminating such policies. Where modern economic growth creates disequilibria that cannot be averted, if growth is to be had, the focus of policy should be on economic organisation that has the best record at inducing economic agents, be they urban or farm people, to equilibrate the economic activities in their domains.

My arguments that follow appear under two topics. The first features mainly particular agricultural changes in economic conditions that contribute to growth and in doing so beget disequilibria. The second deals with the economic value of the equilibrating activities of economic agents.

2   GROWTH SPAWNS DISEQUILIBRIA

There are changes in economic conditions that create opportunities for growth. Such changes disturb the then prevailing equilibrium and call for a reallocation of resources. For these growth opportunities to be realised it is necessary that economic agents perceive that such an opportunity has occurred and that they may gain by reallocating the resources in their economic domain. This class of changes in economic conditions occur unevenly over time. They also occur unevenly by locations within and among national states. A classic case, which is well documented (Dalrymple, 1986), is the time and location differences in the distribution and utilisation of the new high-yielding wheat and rice varieties within and among countries that have occurred since the Second World War. To label this process a *Green Revolution* does not give us any insights into the nature of the disequilibria that have occurred, or on the equilibration that has taken place, or on the extent to which a world-wide equilibrium has been attained in the distribution and utilisation of high-yielding varieties of wheat and rice.

At this Congress, my cup of hemlock is labelled agriculture. I have a little list of agricultural events in addition to the 'economic dynamics' that is specific to the high-yielding food grains during which disequilibria show their ugly heads.

2.1   The Fate of Agricultural Land

Modern economic growth reduces the importance of agricultural land. Contrary to the imprint of Ricardo and Malthus on economic thought, agricultural land rent declines as a fraction of national income. The political influence of landlords also declines. As this transition in the political balance occurs, there are periods of political instability.

Ricardo's concept of land, 'the original and indestructible powers of the soil', is a burden in comprehending the increasing elasticity of the supply of agricultural land. The supply of such land is not fixed by nature; it is in large measure a man-made factor of production. It is augmented by investments of various types. Substitutes for land are well illustrated in the case of corn. Biological advances, in the form of hybrid corn, fertiliser-responsive and disease-resistant varieties, became substitutes for corn land. The harvested corn acreage in the United States in 1982 was 24 million acres less than it had been in 1932, whereas corn production was over three times as large, namely 8.2 billion bushels in 1982 compared to 2.6 billion in 1932.

As such changes in economic conditions occur, they spawn disequilibria. The pioneer work on the economics of hybrid corn was done by Zvi Griliches (1960, 1964) who noted that had he assumed equilibrium he would have begged some of the most important questions pertaining to hybrid corn as an innovation.

The fate of land is such that it loses its political value as a sinecure of an unprogressive landed aristocracy. What has now become a paradox is the rise in the political influence of progressive farmers in most high income countries. Their political clout has increased decidedly, not withstanding that they and their families have become a very small fraction of the population. The rise of the political influences of these farmers remains a puzzle that neither political nor economic analysts have solved. The land tenure of these farmers varies widely. The rent derived from the productivity of the land is very small relative to that derived from their own labour and equipment from inputs they purchase from industry.

Governments and international agencies tend to overrate the economic contributions of land and by their actions worsen the land specific disequilibria. Harrod's (1948) big jump in his *Dynamic Economics* to a *growth model* with no land is, however, a bit premature.

Despite the marked increases in the nominal price of agricultural land during periods of high rates of inflation, my 1951 paper, 'The Declining Economic Importance of Agricultural Land', continues, so it seems to me, to be valid.

2.2 Movements of People out of Agriculture

One of the major consequences of modern economic growth is that many people leave agriculture. These movements of people are responses by farm people who perceive that the value of time working in agriculture has declined relative to that in industry. Where the option of leaving agriculture is not foreclosed by policy, it is widely observed that many farm people choose not to stay down on the farm.

These movements of people out of agriculture are compelled by disequilibria between industry and agriculture in earnings from work. These movements seldom occur evenly over time or evenly by locations. Most are like small, turbulent rivers; some, however, are large, massive movements.

The 1986 *World Bank Development Report* classifies 36 countries as low income economies. As of 1980, 70 per cent of the labour force in these countries was in agriculture. As a statistic it stood at 987 million. China and India accounted for three-quarters of this enormous number of labourers, ages 15 to 64, in agriculture. Meanwhile, world-wide, over half of the 128 countries listed by the Bank had less than half of their labour force in agriculture; 37 countries had less than a quarter and 18 less than a tenth.

If the labour force in Chinese agriculture in 1980 had been down to half of the national total, there would have been 126 million fewer labourers in agriculture. If the modernisation of agriculture in China were to proceed during the next several decades as it has in recent years, the prospects would be that the labour requirements of agriculture in China could well be down to half of the total labour force of China. Ponder the immense reallocations of labour in China for her to arrive at a *new* economic equilibrium implied by such prospects. The cards have long been stacked against reallocation of labour by severe restrictions on the movement of people into cities in China. Disequilibria in earnings between city and non-city labour increased as a consequence. A recent development brings considerable flexibility that favours labour reallocation. The household responsibility system, an important new economic organisational approach to agricultural production, is reducing the labour requirements of agriculture a great deal as Justin Lin showed in 1986.

Although movements of labour out of agriculture within the United States pale in comparison to the prospective movements in

China or in India, I turn to them because the available data show how very uneven the out-movements have been. My brief comment is restricted to the period since 1930, which is my date of entry with a PhD in hand. These movements out of agriculture have not been blissful. They have not been neutral in their economic effects. They did not conform to any knowable expected rate. Economic agents, whether they were rural or urban, or policy-makers, or economists, could not have foreseen as of any given date, the full array of changes in economic conditions and the resulting disequilibria that called for reallocation of labour.

The Great Depression reversed this movement, and a net movement into agriculture occurred during 1932 and 1933. Although the increases resulting from net changes in births and deaths within the farm population were appreciable, the labour force in agriculture declined from over 10 million in 1930 to 3.2 million in 1985. The annual net movement of people out of agriculture ranged from a half to eight-tenths of a million during 1936–40. In 1943 it was well over 3 million. In 1946 the movement reversed once again. From 1948 to 1970 there were 9 scattered years when the net out-movement ranged between 1 and 2.2 million (US Department of Commerce, 1975). To summarise, in 1930 the farm population count was 30.5 million. The natural increase of births over deaths in the farm population was about 12 million during the period between 1930 and 1985. Had there been no out-movement and adding the natural increase and a bit of fancy arithmetic, the 1985 farm population would have been 42.5 million. The actual farm population in 1985 was down to 5.3 million, which implies a net out-movement of over 37 million.

As long as modern economic growth continues, the changes in economic conditions that are an integral part of such growth will give rise to disequilibria between industry and agriculture in the allocation of labour. Labour in both sectors becomes increasingly more skilled and more specialised, and the human capital component becomes larger. These changes are important parts of the dynamics of the increasing value of human time over the years (Schultz, 1980a).

2.3 Upsurge in Life Expectancy

Gains in the state of health that account for longer life spans increase the lifetime productivity of workers as a consequence of their longer participation in the labour force, their greater physical ability to do

Plenary Papers

work, and less loss of working time because of illness. In many low income economies, growth along with investments in health accounts in large measure for the recent remarkable increases in life span. I turn to the first-rate Indian data. The 1951 Census gives the life expectancy at birth of males at 32.4 years and for females at 31.7 years (Ram and Schultz, 1979). As of 1984 it was 56 and 55 years respectively – a 73 per cent increase in 33 years. People in Western Europe and North America never attained anywhere near so large an increase in life expectancy in so short a period.

Longer life expectations make it worthwhile to acquire more schooling and more on-the-job experience as investment in future earnings.

Improvements in the state of health occur very unevenly, especially so in the case of agriculture in low income countries. The effects of this unevenness in health on the productivity of agricultural labour have not gone unnoticed. My quote pertains to India.

Public health programs initiated during the first five-year plan (1951–56) and carried on through the second plan (1956–61) had a much larger favorable effect on health than did the programs undertaken later. The program to suppress malaria tells the story. Official data indicate that the incidence of malaria dropped from 73 million cases in 1952–53 to about 1.1 million in 1959–60. But the malaria program suffered a setbak after 1965 (Schultz, 1980b, p. 38).

Differences within India in the decline in mortality alone explain about 28 per cent of the interstate variations in agricultural productivity. The fall and rise of malaria among districts provides an additional test of the effects of health on productivity.

The economics of health in low income countries has received all too little attention. Health is a component of human capital. Having attained a (much) higher life expectancy, traditional family human capital no longer suffices. Additional and new forms of human capital are required to equilibrate the investment opportunities and in doing so establish a new and more productive equilibrium. Furthermore, as Usher (1978) has shown, the value of the additional utility that people derive from improvements in health, especially so in low income countries, implies that the real rate of economic growth is appreciably higher than that reported in the national statistics of these countries.

2.4 Industry becomes the Major Supplier of Agricultural Inputs

The modernisation of agriculture entails ever more inputs that are purchased from non-farm sectors. These inputs are major carriers of the elements that contribute to the technical advances in agriculture. Here, too, disequilibria abound. These inputs become profitable. Farmers respond, agricultural productivity increases, and given time a new equilibrium becomes evident.

Suffice it to mention some of these inputs: chemical fertiliser and pesticides; tractors, trucks and automobiles; other equipment and machinery; fuel and electricity; high yielding seeds; communication facilities and various services.

These purchased agricultural inputs are a part of the intriguing story of increasing productivity events, each of which for a brief period give rise to 'increasing returns', and there are periods when output per acre, per man-hour and per unit of 'capital' all increase.

Another part of this story is based on the fact that before new and better agricultural inputs can be had, specialised human capital is required to create them. Growth economists who deal with the changes in technology, usually fail to see that specialised human capital is a prerequisite, exemplified by what plant breeders do when they create a new high-yielding crop variety. Specialised human capital is one of the essential components for doing this research.

In the USA the private agricultural input industries in 1979 spent about $860 million on research and development as Vernon Ruttan has shown (Ruttan, 1982, p. 185).

Since the Second World War it is the public sector that has produced the big bang in agricultural research. It has been propelled throughout the world, very unevenly however. The perceived high rate of return, supported by many studies, provided strong incentives to expand. Large as public sector agricultural research has become, it is still far from having arrived at an equilibrium viewed as an investment.

Scientist man-years serves as a measure of the specialised human capital involved in agricultural research. I turn to the studies by Robert E. Evenson and his associates (Evenson and Kislev, 1975; Boyce and Evenson, 1975; Judd *et al.*, 1986). Scientists engaged in agricultural research in the public sector world wide increased over three-fold from 1959 to 1980 (from 47 000 to 148 000). Total expenditure in constant 1980 US dollars increased from $2 billion to $7.4

billion. I would put it at about $9 billion presently, also in 1980 dollars.

Much of what we have learned about human capital can be stated briefly as follows:[1] (1) The human capital that people in high income modern economies have accumulated consists predominantly of specialised human capital; (2) A Crusoe or a self-sufficient farm family, or a small population on a small island with no trade with people at any other location, has little or no incentive to acquire specialised human capital; (3) During economic modernisation the rate of increase in human capital is higher than that of reproducible physical capital; (4) Human capital enhances the productivity of both labour and physical capital; (5) People at each skill level are more productive in a high human capital environment than in one that is low in human capital; (6) Two-way international trade in similar products between similar countries occurs as a consequence of increasing returns to scale made possible by human capital specialisation; and (7) Adam Smith's famous proposition that the division of labour depends on the extent of the market, encompasses the advantages of specialisation including the gains from specialised human capital (Rosen, 1983).

It is part of the folklore of economics to believe that agriculture is immune to specialisation that requires specific human capital. In fact, however, today's farmer is no Crusoe; self-sufficient is not his economic state. The case of the specialised corn belt farmer is instructive. He no longer maintains a few chickens for eggs and broilers, a few cows for milk and butter, or a large garden for vegetables and fruit. Such food items are purchased. So is the electricity, gas for fuel and the telephone service. Water is not infrequently piped in from off-farm sources and paid for. He no longer produces his own seed corn. He buys hybrid seed appropriate to his area. His corn production expenses to a large extent consist of inputs produced by industry. In the production of pigs some farmers specialise in producing breeding stock, others in farrowing and maintaining the piglets through weaning, and others who finish the growth of the pigs into hogs to suit the market. Yet the myth persists that agriculture is immune to specialised physical and human capital.

3 ECONOMICS OF EQUILIBRATION

The core of my argument is that modern economic growth spawns disequilibria. Those that I have featured have agricultural connections. Somehow, somebody does something to bring his domain of the economy into equilibrium. It is widely observed that this occurs. As yet, however, determining precisely what people do who are not in equilibrium is not one of the notable achievements of economics. It is all too convenient to assume that their optimising behaviour is such that they regain equilibrium instantaneously. Why quibble about a few lags?

In truth we know very little about the economics of equilibration. We do not inquire about the efficiency of economic agents in dealing with disequilibria. What are the costs of equilibrating and what are the gains? Is the prevailing economic organisation conducive to efficiency in attaining a new and presumably a more productive equilibrium?

We do well to keep in mind that neither farmers nor any other private economic agents march to the beat of the equilibrium drummer, as we do analytically. The adoption by India of the high-yielding Mexican wheat gave rise to a major disequilibrium in producing wheat. Farmers who produce wheat were not lackadaisical in taking advantage of the much higher yields. Their purpose, however, was not to bring the Indian wheat economy into a new and much more productive equilibrium. It was the profitability of the higher yields that induced the rapid adoptions. We now call this event the Green Revolution.

Profits did the trick despite the then strong view held by many in India that profitability was the wrong game. The prevailing doctrine was that small, poor, private farmers are immune to profits. I protested against that view then and I continue to do so.

But under what conditions are profits efficient in dealing with economic disequilibria? Surely not in a regime in which ambiguities abound as a consequence of procurement quotas, marketing quotas, subsidised agricultural inputs, controlled prices and all manner of regulations.

There are economic organisation choices for dealing with disequilibria. As a subsector, agricultural research has evolved a fairly efficient type of organisation to take advantage of new research opportunities. Farms are too small to do it. In low income economies private industries that produce agricultural inputs account for a small part of the on-going agricultural research. Most of it, as a world-wide activity, is being done in the public sector. Economists are doing their homework on these issues and also on the prospective research opportunities. The record of the success in this activity since 1950 is strong and clear.

The economic organisation that prevails in most low income countries results in underinvestment in various dimensions of human capital. My concept of specialised human capital includes proficiency in a language. My reasons for attributing a great deal of economic importance to primary schooling are as follows: (1) The acquired abilities to *read* efficiently and to *write* with competence are essential in achieving modern economic growth, and they are in general necessary prerequisites to investing in additional specialised human capital. For a refreshingly useful historical perspective on literacy in this context, we now have Jeffery Brooks's (1985) *When Russia Learned to Read*.[2] (2) The real costs of learning to read and write are at their lowest during the early years of primary schooling; these costs increase as the value of time of the maturing student rises. (3) The abilities to read and write are critical components of the quality of the human capital of any population.

All this is well known, but the investment disequilibria pertaining to primary schooling are chronic in many low income countries. Parents cannot come up with the required funds. Nor can these governments acquire funds by borrowing capital in international markets for this purpose, despite strong evidence that the rates of return to investment in primary schooling are, in general, higher than in secondary schooling or in higher education and that they also tend to exceed the normal rates of return to investments in physical capital.

Banks, however, are not in the business of providing funds for primary schooling. For banks human capital is a fancy idea that is harmless when it is confined to the ivory tower. On this score the World Bank is no exception; human capital is deemed to be all too intangible to qualify, no matter how high the prospective rates of return.

The World Bank, however, is not restricted to making hard loans. It has the IDA, which is a large window for doing soft financial business. The 'credits' provided by the IDA are so soft that for all practical purposes they are 'free funds', provided that the country receiving IDA funds does not reckon the political costs of getting them.

IDA credits beginning in 1961 and through 1982 (the last year for which I have figures), totalled $26.7 billion, which amounted to $43 billion in 1982 dollars. Less than 6 per cent of these credits were allocated to education. As far as I can tell, very little indeed was used to increase the stock of human capital that primary schooling creates.

In the case of physical capital the legal and institutional foundation of private property has evolved over centuries of experience. Specialised human capital which is private has no comparable foundation. Plant breeders, chemists and other scientists are not protected from time clocks, from mandatory retirement regardless of productivity, and from being organised as if their work were routine. To patent the fruit from specialised human capital is a fragile part of the required foundation.

'No matter what part of a modern economy is being investigated, we observe that many people are consciously reallocating their resources in response to changes in economic conditions'. Thus I began my 1975 paper, 'The Value of the Ability to Deal with Disequilibria'. The part that is acquired can be measured, and it is an important component in a modernising economy.

4 CONCLUSIONS

My conclusions pertain to economic imbalances between industry and agriculture that occur as a consequence of modern economic growth. I have not dealt with what governments do, although many governments exasperate these imbalances, some pursue policies that reduce the gains to be had from growth, but few, if any, concentrate on improvements in economic organisation to enhance the ability and efficiency of private economic agents in their endeavours to cope with disequilibria.

It is not that I consider governments blameless, for it is all too obvious that nation-states here and now pursue policies that distort world trade and reduce the gains to be had from trade. Nation-states in this and in other ways reduce specialisations, reduce productivity and reduce economic growth.

For me, what is important on this occasion is the state of economics. Economists are not blameless by virtue of the fact that the disequilibria spawned by growth receive all too little analytical attention and virtually no thought is given to possible improvements in economic organisation to deal with the various disequilibria that occur.

Economic organisation can be improved to take prompt and full advantage of the decline in the economic importance of agricultural land made possible by modern growth. Vast improvements in economic organisation are called for in the reallocation of labour as less and less labour is required in agriculture. Additional investments in schooling and health would improve this reallocation process. The success in the distribution and utilisation of the new high-yielding wheat and rice varieties is well known. But we do not know the nature and significance of the disequilibria that have occurred, or the equilibration that has taken place, or the extent to which a worldwide new equilibrium has been attained in the production of wheat and rice.

Prevention of the disequilibria that occur during modern growth is the wrong issue. The issue that matters pertains to incentives that are efficient at inducing private economic agents to reallocate the resource within their domain, and in doing so establish a new and more productive equilibrium.

The capital markets, including banks, are not organised to provide funds for investing in human capital. The World Bank is no exception. IDA credits distributed by the Bank are for all practical purposes 'free', i.e., costless. A very small fraction of these billions of dollars have been invested in human capital.

There are now indications that specialisation, human capital and growth are on the research agenda of a considerable number of economists. Our myopic view of specialisation is being corrected by appropriate lenses. Investigations are now under way to ascertain the extent to which *Specialised Human Capital*, *Increasing Returns* and *Growth* go hand-in-hand.

Notes

1. Based on part of my 1986 paper 'Investing in People: Schooling in Low Income Countries'.
2. Brooks, 1985, see especially Chapter 1 on 'Uses of Literacy' and Chapter 2 on 'Primary Schooling'.

References

Boyce, J. K. and Evenson, R. E. (1975) *National and International Agricultural Research and Extension Programs* (New York: Agricultural Development Council).

Brooks, J. (1985) *When Russia Learned to Read: Literacy and Popular Literature: 1861–1917* (Princeton, NJ: Princeton University Press).

Dalrymple, D. G. (1986) *Development and Spread of High-Yielding Wheat Varieties in Developing Countries* (Washington, DC: Bureau of Science and Technology, Agency for International Development).

Evenson, R. E. and Kislev, Y. (1975) 'Investment in Agricultural Research and Extension: A Survey of International Data', *Economic Development and Cultural Change*, vol. 23 (April), pp. 507–21.

Griliches, Z. (1960) 'Hybrid Corn and the Economics of Innovation', *Science*, vol. 132, no. 3422, (29 July), pp. 275–80.

Griliches, Z. (1964) 'Research Expenditures, Education, and the Aggregate Agricultural Production Functions', *American Economic Review*, vol. 54 (December), pp. 961–74.

Harrod, R. F. (1948) *Towards a Dynamic Economics* (London: Macmillan).

Hicks, J. (1965) *Capital and Growth* (Oxford: Oxford University Press).

Judd, M. A., Boyce, J. K. and Evenson, R. E. (1986) 'Investing in Agriculture Supply', *Economic Development and Cultural Change*, vol. 35, October, pp. 77–113.

Kuznets, S. (1966) *Modern Economic Growth* (New Haven: Yale University Press)

Lin, J. (1986) 'The Household Responsibility System in China's Agricultural Reform: A Study of the Causes and Effects of an Institutional Change', PhD dissertation, University of Chicago (April).

Ram, R. and Schultz, T. W. (1979) 'Life Span, Health, Savings and Productivity', *Economic Development and Cultural Change*, vol. 27 (April), pp. 399–421.

Rosen, S. (1983) 'Specialization and Human Capital', *Journal of Labor Economics*, vol. 1, pp. 43–9.

Ruttan, V. W. (1982) *Agricultural Research Policy* (Minneapolis: University of Minnesota Press) ch. 8, table 8.1.

Schultz, T. W. (1945) *Agriculture in an Unstable Economy* (New York: McGraw-Hill).

Schultz, T. W. (1951) 'The Declining Economic Importance of Agricultural Land' *Economic Journal*, vol. 61 (December), pp. 725–40.

Schultz, T. W. (1953) *The Economic Organization of Agriculture* (New York: McGraw-Hill).

Schultz, T. W. (1975) 'The Value of the Ability to Deal with Disequilibria', *The Journal of Economic Literature*, vol. XIII, no. 3, September, pp. 827–46.

Schultz, T. W. (1980a) 'The Economics of the Value of Human Time', *Investing in People* (Berkeley: University of California Press) ch. 4, pp. 59–84.

Schultz, T. W. (1980b) 'Investment in Population Quality', *Investing in People* (Berkeley: University of California Press) ch. 2.

Schultz, T. W. (1986) 'Investing in People: Schooling in Low Income Countries', presented at World Bank's Education Staff Retreat (10 January).

US Department of Commerce, Bureau of the Census (1975) *Historical Statistics of the United States*, part I, table series C76–80, 'Estimated Annual Movement of the Farm Population: 1920–1970' (Washington, DC) p. 96.

Usher, D. (1978) 'An Imputation to the Measure of Economic Growth for Changes in Life Expectancy' in Moss, M. (ed.) *The Measurement of Economic and Social Performances* (New York: National Bureau of Economic Research) pp. 193–226.

World Bank (1986) *World Development Report 1986* (New York: Oxford University Press for the World Bank).

4 The Balance between Industry and Agriculture in Economic Development: The Indian Experience[1]

D. T. Lakdawala
CENTRE FOR MONITORING INDIAN ECONOMY

I am highly obliged to the World Economic Congress for giving me this opportunity to discuss the Indian experience of the balance between industry and agriculture in economic development with this distinguished audience.

With economic development and the growth in per capita income the two important commodity sectors of the ecomony, agriculture and industry also grow. Because of the lower per capita income elasticity of demand for food and other agricultural products, and the relatively higher income elasticity for industrial products, the demand for agricultural products grows less rapidly than that of industrial products. If foreign trade can be ignored, the domestic supplies must grow similarly if they are to be kept in balance. Foreign trade may complicate the demand-supply balance relationship, but this has generally not been a factor of great importance in India. Relying on this relationship, the Indian planners have in all their exercises provided for higher industrial growth targets than the agricultural growth ones and strived to achieve them. The realisations have broadly borne out these expectations. The debate on balance has sometimes been carried out as if no third sector existed or its existence was of no consequence. This is a grave mistake. In India the services sector is now the most important, and has increased the fastest. The target agricultural growth rate in the Sixth Plan was just fulfilled, the industrial growth rate had fallen woefully behind. If the Sixth Plan still succeeded, it was because the services sector expanded rapidly (Table 4.1). In terms of constituents of income in the

Table 4.1   Targeted and anticipated growth rates in the Sixth Plan:
1980–85
(value added)
(per cent per annum)

	Sixth Plan targets	Anticipated achievements
Agriculture	3.8	4.3
Mining and manufacturing	6.9	3.7
Other sectors	5.5	6.6
Total	5.2	5.2

Source: CMIE, *Seventh Five Year Plan: 1985–90, A Comparative Picture*
(Bombay) November 1985.

pre-Independence era, agriculture was the most important, tertiary
second and industry the last. During the Sixth Plan, the roles of
agriculture and services were reversed. The contributions of the
primary, secondary and tertiary sectors changed from 59, 14, and 26
per cent in 1950–51, to 38, 22, and 40 per cent in 1984–5 respectively
(Table 4.2). Because of its dynamism, the industry sector may in due
course come to occupy the second position, but it will take long.

While the progressive industrialisation of the Indian economy and
growth on other commercial fronts had an impact on urbanisation,
there seem to be hardly any significant changes in the occupational
classification of workers, which showed no parallel shift. According
to the Decennial Census, the percentage of workers occupied in
agriculture and allied activities declined from 72.1 per cent in 1951 to
68.8 per cent in 1981 – a change of 3.3 percentage points only. This
was partly due to the definitional changes from Census to Census, but
even more refined analysis did not yield more clear-cut results. The
percentage of organised workers, i.e. workers in the public sector
and in non-agricultural establishments employing 10 or more workers, remained near 10 per cent. This meant a great increase in the
distance between agriculture and non-agriculture and between organised and non-organised non-agriculture (Table 4.3). In 1971 the
unorganised non-agricultural worker was earning 1.8 times the agricultural worker and the organised non-agricultural worker 4.2 times.
In 1981, the multiples had increased to 2.3 and 5.7 respectively.

We have spoken of the higher income elastic demand for industrial
products. This factor is likely to lead to a downward movement in the
terms of trade of agriculture. Increase in population will immediately

Table 4.2 Structural changes in the composition of India's gross domestic product (GDP) at factor cost: 1950–51 to 1984–85 (since the beginning of the planning era, by decades)

Sector/industry of origin	Percentage share in total GDP 1984–85				
	1950–51 (Pre-Plan year)	1960–61	1970–71	1980–81 (p)	Terminal year of the Sixth Plan – also latest available (q)
1. *Primary*	*59.14*	55.14	48.46	41.62	*38.08*
of which: Agricultural and allied activities	58.86	54.20	47.43	40.50	36.75
of which: agriculture	57.05	52.46	45.67	39.23	35.63
2. *Secondary*	*14.47*	17.28	20.67	21.57	*21.60*
of which: (a) Manufacturing	9.98	12.28	14.22	15.21	15.55
of which: registered	5.45	7.28	9.27	9.85	10.51
3. *Tertiary* (a + b + c)	*25.92*	27.58	30.87	36.81	*40.32*
(a) Transport, communication and trade	11.89	13.80	16.09	18.83	19.73
(b) Finance and real estate	5.24	5.06	5.76	6.62	7.05
(c) Community and personal services	8.79	8.72	9.02	11.36	13.54
4. Total: GDP at factor cost (1+2+3)	100.00	100.00	100.00	100.00	100.00
5. Net factor income from abroad	− 0.38	− 0.43	− 0.77	+ 0.17	− 0.44
6. Total: GNP at factor cost (+5)	99.62	99.57	99.23	100.17	99.56

Note:

(p) = provisional (and subject to revision).

(q) = 'quick' estimates (and subject to revision more than once).

Sources: 1. *National Accounts Statistics, 1970–71 to 1976–77* (January, 1979) Appendix A. 1.2, pp. 140–43 (for the years: 1950–51 and 1960–61) by the Central Statistical Organisation, Department of Statistics, Ministry of Planning, Government of India.

2. *Press Note: No. P.12015/3/85 NAD-9* entitled 'Quick Estimates of National Income, Consumption Expediture, Saving and Capital Formation, 1984–85', dt. 28 January 1986 (for the years: 1970–71, 1980–81 and 1984–85).

Table 4.3 Growing disparity between agriculture and non-agriculture

Sector	Per capita NDP		As multiple of agriculture	
	1971	1981	1970–71	1980–81
Agriculture	426	860	1.0	1.0
Non-agriculture:				
unorganised	765	1937	1.8	2.3
organised	1777	4931	4.2	5.7

Source: Dandekar, 'Agriculture, Employment and Poverty', *Economic and Political Weekly* (Bombay) 20–27 September 1986, p. A-94.

increase demand. The supply side acts quite the reverse. Though supply flexibilities of individual agricultural products are now recognised as widely prevalent, the supplies of agricultural production as a whole are much more price inelastic. In an old, heavily populated country like India, the scope for extensive land cultivation is very limited; the known techniques of land cultivation have been fairly explored; and unless new techniques of greatly improved productivities are introduced on a large scale, agricultural supplies cannot appreciably increase. Industrial supplies can be more easily expanded. A relative price change will be the result of these counteracting forces, relative demand leading to a price fall of agricultural products, and increase in population and relative supply genarally leading to the reverse. The large fluctuations in agricultural production not backed by imports or appropriate stocking policies can be a big price upsetting factor.

The demand for agricultural products is not only less income elastic, it is also price inelastic. The consequences of supply of agricultural products lagging behind demand can, therefore, be severe in price terms and in case of items like foodgrains, pulses, edible oils, etc., may affect the course of ecomomic development itself. The foodgrains production had to be supplemented by imports, mostly wheat imports (Table 4.4). Though a small proportion of production, they played a crucial role in the public distribution system. Till the 1970s in many years they were higher than internal procurement. A large part of these in earlier years was under PL (Public Law) 480, so that they did not raise the question of foreign exchange availability. Later on high priority was given to needed foodgrain imports. The only major problem in this connection was that the foodgrain to which a majority of the Indian people were accustomed, namely rice, was not available in the required quantities abroad. This was even more true of other cereals and pulses, where price change remained the only effective method of adjustment.

The most testing years were 1966 and 1967 when foodgrains production fell by more than 10 per cent and the rupee was devalued. To keep the prices in check and balance the budget, the Government of India resorted to the easy option of reducing public expenditure, especially plan investment. The concept of the medium-term plan was given up, the three annual plans followed. Even when the concept of the medium-term plan was reintroduced with the 1969–74 Plan, public investment was kept at a low level. In real terms, public investment reached the 1965–66 level only in 1972–73, and as a percentage of GNP in 1975–76 (Table 4.5). Since public investment stimulated demand for private industrial goods, this had the effect of stagnating demand. Industrial growth rate therefore slackened. A similar price rise in 1973–75 was met with rigid price controls including factor price regulations. Public investment was not checked.

In response to this situation, apart from increased imports which were regarded as a temporary expedient and which PL 480 greatly facilitated, a new agricultural strategy was evolved, concentrating on irrigated areas and providing them with ample improved high-yielding seeds, fertilisers, credit, extension services, etc. This raised several problems through intensifying intergroup and interregional inequalities, but it enabled India to meet the foodgrains requirements of its growing population without imports, by the middle of the 1970s. The events of the earlier period are a grim reminder of what could have happened to the Indian economy in the absence of this happy realisation. Statutory rationing in metropolitan and extremely food-scarce areas to ensure foodgrains at reasonable prices to the population and to cordon them off so that they do not drain the surrounding areas of their food supplies, compulsory procurement or monopoly procurement by state agencies, priority in procurement and transport movement control, an extensive public distribution system, and attempts at the nationalisation of wholesale trade were all tried with varying but very limited success. The only relief came with the building up of substantial public stocks out of imports, and voluntary procurement of all wheat and rice that was offered at support prices, which were quite reasonable. No price change was of much help. Only a change in technology could restore the long-term equilibrium. In spite of a relatively low price rise in wheat and in rice, wheat and rice production grew at a rapid rate. Pulses and groundnut

Table 4.4 Availability of foodgrains: 1951 to 1986 (million tonnes)

Year	Net production (1)	Net imports (2)	Change in government stocks (3)	Net availability (= +2−3) (4)	Issuances through public distribution system (5)	Internal procurement Million tonnes (6)	Internal procurement As % of gross production (7)
1951	48.1	4.8	+ 0.6	52.3	8.0	3.8	6.9
1952	48.7	3.9	+ 0.6	52.0	6.8	3.5	6.3
1953	54.1	2.0	− 0.5	56.6	4.6	2.1	3.4
1954	63.3	0.8	+ 0.2	63.9	2.2	1.4	1.9
1955	61.9	0.5	− 0.7	63.1	1.6	0.1	0.1
1956	60.7	1.4	− 0.6	62.7	2.1	–	–
1957	63.4	3.6	+ 0.9	66.1	3.1	0.3	0.4
1958	58.3	3.2	− 0.3	61.8	4.0	0.5	0.8
1959	69.0	3.9	+ 0.5	72.4	5.2	1.8	2.3
1960	67.5	5.1	+ 1.4	71.2	4.9	1.3	1.7
1961	72.0	3.5	− 0.2	75.7	4.0	0.5	0.6
1962	72.1	3.6	+ 0.4	76.1	4.4	0.5	0.6
1963	70.3	4.5	–	74.8	5.2	0.8	1.0
1964	70.6	6.3	− 1.2	78.1	8.7	1.4	1.7
1965	78.2	7.4	+ 1.1	84.5	10.1	4.0	4.5

1966	63.3	10.3	+ 0.1	73.5	14.1	4.0	5.5
1967	65.0	8.7	− 0.3	74.0	13.2	4.5	6.1
1968	83.2	5.7	+ 2.0	86.9	10.2	6.8	7.2
1969	82.3	3.8	+ 0.5	85.7	9.4	6.4	6.8
1970	87.1	3.6	+ 1.1	89.6	8.8	6.7	6.7
1971	94.9	2.0	+ 2.6	94.3	7.8	8.9	8.2
1972	92.0	− 0.5	− 4.7	96.2	10.5	7.7	7.3
1973	84.9	3.6	− 0.3	88.8	11.4	8.4	8.7
1974	91.6	5.2	− 0.4	97.2	10.8	5.7	5.4
1975	87.4	7.5	+ 5.6	89.3	11.3	9.7	9.6
1976	105.9	6.9	+10.7	102.1	9.2	12.9	10.7
1977	97.3	0.5	− 1.6	99.4	11.7	10.0	9.0
1978	110.6	− 0.6	− 0.3	110.3	10.2	11.1	8.8
1979	115.4	− 0.2	+ 0.4	114.8	11.7	13.8	10.5
1980	96.0	− 0.3	− 5.8	101.5	15.0	11.2	10.2
1981	113.4	0.7	− 0.2	114.3	13.0	13.0	10.0
1982	116.6	1.6	+ 1.3	117.5	14.8	15.4	11.6
1983	113.3	4.1	+ 2.6	111.8	16.2	15.7	12.1
1984	133.3	2.4	+ 7.1	128.6	13.3	18.7	10.6
1985	128.0	− 0.3	+ 0.7	127.0	15.4	20.0	13.2
1986*	127.0	− 1.5	+ 2.7	122.8	20.0	20.0	13.8

* = CMIE estimates
Source: CMIE, *Basic Statistics Relating to the Indian Economy, vol.I: All-India* (Bombay) August 1986.

Table 4.5 Gross domestic capital formation: 1950–51 to 1984–85
(Rs crores in 1970–71 prices)

Year	Public sector	Private sector	Total	As % of GNP at market prices			Rs crores		
				Public sector	Private sector	Total	Public sector	Private sector	Total
1950–51	260	694	954	2.7	7.3	10.0	648	1 731	2 379
1951–52	304	884	1 188	3.0	8.9	11.9	718	2 086	2 804
1952–53	257	515	772	2.6	5.3	7.9	612	1 226	1 838
1953–54	293	616	909	2.8	5.9	8.7	686	1 441	2 127
1954–55	436	634	1 070	4.5	6.6	11.1	963	1 400	2 363
1955–56	498	971	1 469	4.8	9.5	14.3	1 127	2 196	3 323
Average 1951–56	*358*	*724*	*1 082*	*3.5*	*7.2*	*10.7*			
1956–57	666	1 293	1 959	5.6	11.0	16.6	1 452	2 819	4 271
1957–58	833	1 010	1 843	7.0	8.4	15.4	1 848	2 240	4 088
1958–59	815	970	1 785	6.1	7.2	13.3	1 544	1 838	3 382
1959–60	900	1 096	1 996	6.5	7.8	14.3	1 687	2 054	3 741
1960–61	1 141	1 402	2 543	7.6	9.4	17.0	2 029	2 494	4 523
Average 1956–61	*871*	*1 154*	*2 025*	*6.6*	*8.8*	*15.4*			
1961–62	1 147	1 291	2 438	7.2	8.1	15.3	1 948	2 192	4 140
1962–63	1 445	1 471	2 916	8.5	8.7	17.2	2 383	2 525	4 808
1963–64	1 681	1 585	3 266	8.6	8.1	16.7	2 615	2 465	5 080
1964–65	1 948	1 787	3 735	8.5	7.8	16.3	2 911	2 670	5 581
1965–66	2 216	2 174	4 390	9.3	9.0	18.3	3 115	3 055	6 170
Average 1961–66	*1 687*	*1 662*	*3 349*	*8.4*	*8.3*	*16.7*			
1966–67	2 135	3 302	5 437	7.8	12.0	19.8	2 621	4 054	6 675
1967–68	2 332	3 003	5 335	7.3	9.4	16.7	2 684	3 455	6 139
1968–69	2 168	2 946	5 114	6.6	8.9	15.5	2 442	3 316	5 758
Average 1966–69	*2 212*	*3 084*	*5 296*	*7.2*	*10.1*	*17.3*			

1969–70	2 259	4 026	6 285	6.2	11.0	17.2	2 400	4 277	6 677
1970–71	2 773	4 404	7 177	6.9	11.0	17.9	2 773	4 404	7 177
1971–72	3 165	4 821	7 986	7.3	11.2	18.5	2 957	4 599	7 556
1972–73	3 607	4 523	8 130	7.6	9.5	17.1	3 135	3 995	7 130
1973–74	4 814	7 010	11 824	8.2	11.9	20.1	3 738	5 359	9 097
Average 1969–74	*3 324*	*4 957*	*8 281*	*7.2*	*10.9*	*18.1*			
1974–75	5 664	7 715	13 379	8.2	11.1	19.3	3 517	4 727	8 244
1975–76	7 677	7 134	14 811	10.4	9.6	20.0	4 433	4 030	8 463
1976–77	8 513	8 208	16 721	10.6	10.3	20.9	4 920	4 396	9 316
1977–78	7 450	11 315	18 765	8.3	12.6	20.9	4 184	6 023	10 207
1978–79	9 649	14 625	24 274	9.9	15.0	24.9	5 012	7 296	12 308
Average 1974–79	*7 791*	*9 799*	*17 590*	*9.5*	*11.7*	*21.2*			
1979–80	11 816	13 467	25 283	11.0	12.5	23.5	5 309	5 717	11 026
1980–81	13 926	17 259	31 185	10.9	13.5	24.4	5 564	6 547	12 111
1981–82	17 528	18 957	36 485	11.9	12.9	24.8	6 101	6 507	12 608
1982–83	20 047	19 764	39 811	12.2	12.1	24.3	6 201	6 454	12 655
1983–84	21 773	23 575	45 348	11.3	12.2	23.5	6 121	7 370	13 491
1984–85 (quick estimates)	26 772	23 009	49 781	12.6	10.9	23.5	7 325	6 296	13 621
Average 1980–85	*20 009*	*20 513*	*40 522*	*11.8*	*12.3*	*24.1*			

Source: CMIE, *Basic Statistics Relating to the Indian Economy, Vol.1: All-India* (Bombay) August 1986.

Table 4.6 Production, productivity and price increases of some
agriculture products

	Production: annual growth rate between 1949–50 & 1984–85 (%)	Productivity: annual growth rate between 1950–51 & 1984–85 (%)	Prices: annual growth rate between 1950–51 & 1984–85 (%)
Rice	2.5	2.1	5.4
Wheat	6.0	3.1	4.1
Jowar	1.4	1.9	3.4
Gram	–	0.8	6.9
Maize	2.7	2.2	4.9
Sugarcane	3.1	1.9	4.1
Groundnut	2.0	0.7	6.3
Cotton	2.4	1.8	5.0
Tea	2.5	1.8	5.4
Rapeseed & mustard	3.3	1.6	5.2
Pulses	0.5	0.6	7.1

Source: CMIE, *Basic Statistics Relating to the Indian Economy, Vol. 1: All-India* (Bombay) August 1986.

production increased at a slower rate though their prices rose much more (Table 4.6). This can only be explained by the fact that the Green Revolution made such a substantial difference to wheat and rice productivity that even at constant prices their cultivation became attractive and higher prices of other crops where no productivity increase had taken place could not compensate for this.

Indian post-Independence price history registers the effects of all these factors at work. From 1964 onwards agricultural prices rose fast. In spite of high foodgrain imports with very bad monsoons the terms of trade greatly moved in favour of agriculture till 1967—68. The mid-1970s saw the movement reverse itself (Table 4.7).

Are foodgrain stocks likely to be exhausted in the future causing India to face a food crisis? For some years the production has been higher than the population increase (Table 4.8) and the foodgrains supplies are in excess of the demand as seen from the increase in stocks in spite of their use for NREP and RLEGP. The reasonableness of stocks has to be judged in relation to the needs they are to serve. On the basis of procurement and the public offtake records,

Table 4.7 Terms of trade between agriculture and non-agriculture:
1960–61 to 1982–83
(1970–71 = 100)

	Relative price of foodgrains and manufacture	Ratio of implicit deflators: agr. v. non-agr.	Thamarajakshi series	Kahlon and Tyagi series
1960–61	82.9	83.6	78.5	–
1961–62	80.4	84.2	79.1	–
1962–63	81.2	85.6	77.8	–
1963–64	83.9	92.1	76.5	–
1964–65	100.6	97.2	85.4	–
1965–66	100.3	103.7	89.9	–
1966–67	106.0	114.3	96.7	–
1967–68	119.1	114.6	98.2	115.6
1968–69	104.7	107.9	91.4	105.1
1969–70	108.2	106.4	98.7	101.8
1970–71	100.0	100.0	100.0	100.0
1971–72	94.4	98.4	94.6	97.5
1972–73	98.0	108.8	97.2	103.6
1973–74	101.7	120.6	105.3	108.3
1974–75	116.0	108.8	102.3	99.6
1975–76	101.7	86.6	92.4	84.6
1976–77	87.2	90.4	90.9	89.3
1977–78	95.1	97.9	95.1	90.8*
1978–79	96.2	84.6	91.0	85.4*
1979–80	85.9	88.1	87.3	88.6*
1980–81	84.4	86.2	81.6	87.5*
1981–82	87.7	82.5	81.8	–
1982–83	91.5	82.4	83.4	–

* Updated by Tyagi.
Sources: Thamarajakshi (1977), Kahlon and Tyagi (1983), Thamarajakshi (1985) and National Accounts. Quoted by Isher J. Ahluwalia, 'Inter-Relationships Between Agriculture and Industry', *Indian Economic Association Conference Volume*, Ahmedabad, 28–30 December 1985, part II, p. 12.

the stocks can easily serve violent seasonal fluctuations for two years. Considering the possibility of obtaining foodgrain imports in extreme situations, this should be considered safe enough. There is, however, one thought which is baffling. According to the Planning Commission estimates at the end of the Sixth Plan, 37 per cent of the population was below the poverty line. By definition, therefore, they did not have sufficient purchasing power to buy enough calories of foodgrains

Table 4.8 Gross per capita annual consumption of foodgrains
(Per capita per annum kgs)

Period	Kilograms
1951–53	164.64
1954–58	181.80
1959–67	184.87
1968–75	185.41
1976–83	185.18

Source: Dandekar, 'Agriculture, Employment and Poverty', *Economic and Political Weekly* (Bombay) 20–27 September 1986, p. A–91.

to keep body and soul together. This may not be reflected in the per capita availability of calories, as some people may take more calories. There is no conceivable means short of monopoly procurement of production and complete rationing to achieve consumption equality. Let us assume the poor were short of foodgrains by an average 10 per cent. If a key was discovered to make them rise above the poverty line, the demand for foodgrains may substantially increase by nearly 6 million tonnes. The situation will imply a considerable reorganisation of the public distribution system. It may also call for a change in the structure of agricultural production. The population increases at the rate of 2.2 per cent per annum and the growth may not rapidly slow down. After the 1960s, food production increases have mainly come from productivity increases (Table 4.9) and fodder and commercial crops are competing with foodgrains for land. Production increase have come in spurts. The Green Revolution is exhausting itself; it does not spread itself to other regions and crops. This can be done in a number of ways. To name just a few: (a) while it has been proved that the new water-seed-fertiliser technology is scale-neutral, access to credit, extension services and information remains restricted in practice for the marginal or small farmer. Unlike, therefore, under the old technology, his land productivity remains less than that of the medium or large farmer. If with improved organisation of credit, information dissemination and extension services it can be improved, the scope for production improvement will be enhanced; (b) there are several important parts of eastern India like Bihar, West Bengal and Assam, where the new technology has not spread because of tenure systems, absence of sufficient incentives, etc. If these obstacles can be removed, agricultural production can

Table 4.9 Area, productivity and production

Triennie ended	% increase			Index of per capita production
	Area	Productivity	Production	
1951–52 & 1964–65	1.7	1.4	3.2	1.1
1964–65 & 1985–86	0.3	2.0	2.6	0.4
1951–52 & 1985–86	0.9	1.7	2.8	0.6

Source: CMIE, *Basic Statistics Relating to the Indian Economy, Vol.1*: *All-India* (Bombay) August 1986.

grow fast; (c) a predominant portion of the land in India is unirrigated and depends on the rains. Because of the great pressure to increase food production and the immediate promise that irrigated land offered, resources and research were concentrated on them and dry land cultivation was ignored. If now more attention is devoted to developing dry farming, even with moderate success in it, a new dimension will be opened; (d) owing to the spread of minor irrigation through tubewells, new problems in optimum use of groundwater have arisen. If these are properly tackled, land productivity will substantially increase. If these four possibilities are well explored, foodgrains production can be no bottleneck to industrial growth.

While it is obvious that there is no foodgrains constraint on economic growth, is there a shortage of mass consumption agricultural goods – wage goods – which is acting as a check? While this plea is often advocated, the meaning of mass consumption goods and the way they are acting as a restraint is not made clear. If one is to judge by the per capita consumption, quite a few food items have shown a favourable turn. Milk, eggs, fish, sugar etc. belong to this category. Pulses for the rural masses, however, seem to present problems of scarcity and it seems difficult to increase their supplies. Fuel is another instance of an allied scarce commodity.

The slowing down of the rate of industrial growth after the 1970s has naturally raised the question of the responsibility of low agricultural growth for this. As we have argued before, given the relative demand elasticities, agricultural growth slower than industrial growth in the higher ranges is to be expected; and within agriculture the demand is likely to shift to superior cereals, milk and other dairy products, fruits and vegetables. This is already taking place to some extent in India. While certainly there is scope for accelerating agricultural growth in certain directions, one cannot say that by all prevalent standards, agricultural growth has been sluggish over the plan period. At the same time, consumption goods account for half of the value added by industry; and for many of these goods rural areas are very important markets. If agricultural incomes have not risen, the demand for many of the industrial goods will have a narrow market. One must, however, be clear on two points. Is one talking of an increase in the overall rate of growth or a change in its composition? What holds good of the one may not hold good of the other. The reciprocal demand-supply relationship dictates a certain ratio between the two: if the overall rate has to be increased, the problem of overall resources has to be squarely faced. Is it mainly lack of demand that has held up industrial development? The reasons for slow industrial growth may lie more on the supply side – the absence of sufficiently strong-based economic infrastructure like power, communications, and transport, unhealthy industrial relations, antiquated technology, management failures, inertia of entrepreneurs, etc.

We have hitherto spoken of agriculture and industry as a whole, where the broad interconnections are limited. There are, however, certain specific parts of both agriculture and industry which are more intimately related. An input-output matrix can give an idea of the relative dependence of agriculture on industry and of industry on agriculture, and if available at different points of time can give idea of the changes that have occurred over a period. We are fortunate in having such input-output tables for India (see Table 4.10). Table 4.11 shows that in dividing the economy into three sectors – agriculture, manufacturing and others – agriculture depended less on manufacturing (15 per cent) than manufacturing on agriculture (25.9 per cent).

While the food crops are mainly consumption goods or goods used within the agricultural sector, animal husbandry etc., commercial crops, and to some extent plantations, belong to a different category. They form raw materials for the industrial sector. It is the growth of the user industries that determines the demand for them. There thus develops a closer link between them and the specific industries like the agro-based industries. Such industries now constitute about one-third of the value added in the industrial sector (Table 4.12). The more important individual industries in this group are textile, cotton and jute, sugar, grain mill products, oil and tea. Most of these industries have, however, specific constraints independent of the domestic supply of raw materials. The supply of both cotton and jute

Table 4.10 Inter-industry transactions: 1973–74
(Rs crores)

Sector	Agriculture	Manufacturing	Others	Total inter-mediate use
Agriculture	1 867.12	4 217.64	2 511.78	8 596.54
	(21.72)	(49.06)	(29.22)	(100.00)
Manufacturing	736.19	8 032.34	3 991.28	12 759.81
	(5.77)	(62.95)	(31.28)	(100.00)
Others	2 183.98	4 045.17	6 530.65	12 759.80
	(17.12)	(31.70)	(51.18)	(100.00)
Total input	4 787.29	16 295.15	13 033.71	34 116.15
	(14.03)	(47.76)	(38.21)	(100.00)

Note: Figures in parentheses are percentages to total intermediate use.
Source: R.K. Patel, P.K. Sardana and S.D. Chamola, 'Resource Flows Between Agriculture and the Manufacturing Sectors in India', *Indian Economic Association Conference Volume*, Ahmedabad, 28–30 December 1985, part II, p. 70.

Table 4.11 Percentage distribution of inputs

Sector	Agriculture	Manufacturing	Others	Total inter-mediate use
Agriculture	39.00	25.88	19.27	25.20
Manufacturing	15.38	49.29	30.62	37.40
Others	45.62	24.83	50.11	37.40
Total input	100.00	100.00	100.00	100.00

Note: Derived from Table 4.10.
Source: R.K. Patel, P.K. Sardana and S.D. Chamola, 'Resource Flows Between Agriculture and the Manufacturing Sectors in India', *Indian Economic Association Conference Volume*, Ahmedabad, 28–30 December 1985, part II, p. 71.

---

were adversely affected at the time of partition, but both the raw materials have responded to the new demand. The development of the cotton textile industry had been more influenced by the unregulated growth of the power loom industry, the restrictions put on the mill industry to benefit the hand loom industry and the poor consumers, the growth of the synthetic fibre industry, smuggling and tax structure. A new textile policy has just been framed to stimulate the industry. The jute industry is more dependent on world demand and

Table 4.12 Development of some agro-based industries

Value of output 1973–74 (Excluding excise duties) Rs. crores (1)	Code no. (2)	Industry	Value of output (excluding excise duties) 1981–82		Rate of increase 1973–74 and 1981–82	
			Rs. crores (3)	As % of total output (4)	Total (5)	Per annum (%) (6)
2 051	231	Cotton textiles	4 372	5.9	113	9.9
713	206	Refined sugar	1 967	2.7	176	13.5
611	204	Grain mill products	1 965	2.7	222	15.7
408	247	Spinning, weaving and finishing of other textiles, synthetic fibres, rayons, nylons, etc.	1 864	2.5	357	20.9
735	211	Edible oils	1 509	2.0	105	9.4
329	212	Tea	882	1.2	168	13.1
197	201	Dairy products	865	1.2	339	20.3
362	210	Vanaspati	842	1.1	133	11.1
367	251	Jute and mesta	642	0.9	75	7.2
185	230	Cotton ginning & processing	434	0.6	135	11.3
92	232	Printing and dyeing of cotton textiles	411	0.6	347	20.6
41	264	Readymade garments	362	0.5	783	31.3
77	241	Wool spinning, weaving & finishing	355	0.5	361	21.1
77	226	Bidi	348	0.5	352	20.8
65	207	Indigenous sugar, boora, khandasari, gur, etc.	329	0.4	406	22.5
151	225	Processing of raw leaf tobacco	322	0.4	113	9.9
86	219	Food products not elsewhere classified	301	0.4	250	17.0
92	260	Knitting mills	277	0.4	201	14.8
77	205	Bakery products	262	0.4	240	16.5
40	248	Printing, dyeing and bleaching of synthetic textiles	257	0.3	543	26.2
150	227	Cigars, cigarettes, tobacco, etc.	217	0.3	45	4.7
76	214	Cashewnuts	168	0.2	121	10.4
35	203	Fish products	168	0.2	380	21.7

has been adversely affected by the development of synthetic substitutes. Sugar partially controlled has to compete with gur and khandsari which are left free to bid for sugarcane supplies. The states' advice to sugar factories to give more than the centrally fixed minimum prices have led to a chaotic situation. The oil industry has suffered from the heavy fluctuations of oilseed supplies, but the quixotic resolve of the government to keep vegetable oil prices stable at a level unrelated to oil-prices has led to difficulties.

Regarding the change over a period of time, agriculture progressively increased its dependence on industry. Per unit of output, it purchased more of fertilisers, pesticides, diesel oil, electricity and agricultural machinery, oil engines and pumps, etc. (Table 4.13). The government has taken many measures to promote and stimulate these improvements. As a result, purchases by agriculturists from non-agriculture increased more than sales.

The mechanism of state fiscal and regulatory powers can be used to make transfers from one sector to another. Such transfers may be necessary to provide the fast-growing industrial sector with the necessary capital for ready growth. Both the Japanese and Russian economic history give examples of the large transfers made through public finance and compulsory procurement of foodgrains at low prices from the farming community to others. Though absence of detailed statistical information makes it difficult to be precise, as far as India is concerned, the picture seems to be different. There is an attempt to do quite the reverse, at least as far as the tax aspect is concerned. This may be ascribed to the democratic regime in India with the predominance of the agricultural and rural representatives who are becoming quite conscious of their strength and power, or simply to the logic of rural poverty.

The Indian fiscal system is marked by two special features:

(i) As far as direct taxation is concerned, the authority to tax is divided between the Union Government and the States. The former has the power to levy tax on non-agricultural incomes and property, the latter on agriculture and agricultural land. Even if the states levy an exactly similarly-structured tax on agricultural incomes as the centre on non-agricultural incomes, if an agriculturist has agricultural property in more than one state and/or has non-agricultural income, he will be relatively lightly taxed. There was at one time a hope that the states would in due course impose a separate progressive agricultural income tax and/or make their land revenues more progressive and more income and price elastic over time. But these expectations

Table 4.13 CSO's estimates of gross value of output and inputs in 1970–71 and 1985–86

Items	1970–71		1985–86	
	Rs crores	As % of value of output	Rs crores	As % of value of output
A. *Gross value of output*	17 531	–	63 899	–
B. *Value of inputs*	4 512	25.7	22 655	35.5
1. Feed of livestock	2 169	12.3	7 160	11.2
2. Seed	695	4.0	2 316	3.6
3. Chemical fertilisers	344	2.0	3 397	5.3
4. Organic manure	292	1.7	1 215	1.9
5. Diesel oil	226	1.3	4 200	6.6
6. Electricity	59	0.3	387	0.6
7. Irrigation charges	52	0.3	198	0.3
8. Pesticides & insecticides	40	0.2	351	0.6
9. Market charges	97	0.6	348	0.5
10. Consumption of fixed capital	424	2.4	2 463	3.9
11. Current repairs, maintenance of fixed assets & other operational cost	114	0.6	620	1.0
C. Net value added (A – B)	13 019	–	41 244	–
D. Factor incomes (Labour, rent and interest) paid out	4 863	–	18 606	–
E. Net income left with the farmers (C – D)	8 156	–	22 638	–

Note: Value of output is exclusive of the cost of operation of government irrigation system.
Source: CMIE, *Basic Statistics Relating to the Indian Economy, Vol. 1: All-India* (Bombay) August 1986.

have been belied. Agricultural income tax has been levied only by a few states; it is mainly confined to plantations; the presumptions made about the relationship of agricultural income to land revenue or land holding are very liberal. It, therefore, yields only a small part of agricultural taxation (Table 4.14). Land revenue, the other direct tax

Table 4.14 Taxation of agriculture: 1951–52 to 1985–86
(Rs crores)

Year	Taxes on agriculture			Total tax revenues of Central and State Governments	Col. (3) as % of col. (4)
	Land revenue	Agricultural income-tax	Total (1+2)		
	(1)	(2)	(3)	(4)	(5)
1951–52	48	4	52	741	7.0
1961–62	95	9	104	1 537	6.8
1962–63	120	10	130	1 855	7.0
1963–64	123	9	132	2 313	5.7
1964–65	120	11	131	2 585	5.1
1965–66	112	10	122	2 902	4.2
1966–67	90	11	101	3 240	3.1
1967–68	99	12	111	3 423	3.2
1968–69	114	10	124	3 736	3.3
1969–70	103	14	117	4 185	2.8
1970–71	113	11	124	4 735	2.6
1971–72	101	13	114	5 568	2.1
1972–73	93	12	105	6 433	1.6
1973–74	157	12	169	7 368	2.3
1974–75	161	14	175	9 206	1.9
1975–76	230	29	259	11 155	2.3
1976–77	183	35	218	12 294	1.8
1977–78	166	62	228	13 215	1.7
1978–79	188	80	268	15 491	1.7
1979–80	152	58	210	17 645	1.2
1980–81	146	46	192	19 793	1.0
1981–82	205	38	243	24 067	1.0
1982–83	189	30	219	27 175	0.8
1983–84	213	44	257	29 535	0.9
1984–85 (RE)	282	54	336	34 117	1.0
1985–86 (BE)	327	57	384	37 994	1.0

Source: CMIE, *Basic Statistics Relating to the Indian Economy, Vol.I: All-India* (Bombay) August 1986.
Notes: RE Revised Estimats
BE Budget Estimates

on agriculture, at best intended to be a proportional tax, is based on land settlements held decades back. It takes no account of the great changes in the facilities and techniques nor of price changes since then. A few *ad hoc* changes made suffer from the defects of their base. In some of the more prosperous agricultural states the per hectare land revenue is less than in the backward states. As a broad summary of the sort of discrepancy in direct taxation between the two sectors, it may be pointed out that agricultural taxation yielded 0.6 per cent of agricultural incomes compared with 2 per cent of non-agricultural incomes yielded by the general income tax. A logical solution of the problem will be to extend the scope of the general income tax through a constitutional amendment or agreement with the states to agricultural incomes also, but this demand is not likely to be conceded. The only concession by the Central Government so far has been to take into account agricultural incomes also for the purpose of determining general income tax rates, but not the amount. Increasingly the Central Government has been making clear its resolve to exempt agriculture from the ambit of its general tax measures. Agricultural wealth, for instance, is not liable to the wealth tax; the gift tax does not cover gifts of agricultural land, etc.

(ii) It must be recognised in fairness that there are fundamental features of agricultural incomes which make their identical treatment with non-agricultural incomes difficult. Agricultural incomes are subject to great seasonal fluctuations whose impact is very unevenly distributed over different agriculturists. Land ceiling laws have ensured that only a few of them will be apparently above the present liberal income tax exemption level. To yield the same proportion of agricultural income by way of tax revenue as the general income tax of non-agricultural incomes, land taxation may need drastic remodifications. But a continuance of the present system is highly inequitous and invites widespread evasion of non-agricultural incomes assuming the garb of agricultural incomes.

(iii) As compared with direct taxation where the formal tax structure is different, the rates and structure of indirect taxation, customs, excise and sales, are the same for the rural and urban groups. This is of great significance in India, where commodity taxation yields four-fifths of tax revenues. The payment and consumption habits of the rural masses are different from those of their urban compeers. More of their consumption is in kind, and the goods they consume are subject to less heavy tax rates. Successive incidence studies have found that the tax burden on rural groups as a percentage of their

Table 4.15 Tax burden indirect taxes, 1973–74
(per cent)

Expenditure group (Rs)	Rural	Urban	All
0– 15	2.91	3.63	2.96
15– 28	3.33	6.31	3.63
28– 43	4.45	7.36	4.89
43– 55	6.18	9.66	6.85
55– 75	6.71	11.86	7.92
75–100	10.02	14.80	11.40
100 and above	*16.17*	*30.19*	*21.96*
All households	8.05	*17.96*	10.54

Source: Government of India, Ministry of Finance, Report of the Indirect Taxation Enquiry Committee, (Mimeo) part I, p. 21 (New Delhi) October 1977.

expenditure is less than that on parallel on urban expenditure groups (Table 4.15). Since rural incomes and expenditures on an average are less than urban incomes and expenditure, and since tax burden income-wise or expenditure-wise is progressively distributed, the tax burden as percentage of rural income or expenditure is less than in the case of urbanites. The only exception may be the non-income-tax-paying urbanites who may be paying less than some rural marginal farmers because of land revenue burden which is quixotic in its character.

This naturally raises the question of whether a part of the burden of development that should be borne by the agricultural sector is transferred through the mechanism of taxation to industry. It would be unfair to pronounce any final opinion on this question before taking up the distribution of public expenditure. If agriculture is both relatively undertaxed and underspent than industry, the right remedy may not only be to tax it more but also to spend more on it. Very limited information, however, is available on benefits aspect. The benefits of a significant part of the expenditure such as that on defence, law and order, are indivisible; the rural-urban break-up of many items of expenditure cannot be obtained. Many of the facilities of higher education, better medical facilities, etc. are concentrated in urban areas, but are availed of by rural people also. The NSS Surveys, which serve the basis for tax incidence studies, furnish little helpful data for determining the public expenditure benefits the beneficiaries obtain. Ever since the mid-1960s there have been persistent efforts to ensure the spread of all state services and facilities to rural areas. Looking, however, to the location of elementary facilities and their quality it cannot be gainsaid that the advantage obtained from revenue expenditure is much more in urban areas. A few items are, however, exceptions. A large amount of money – Rs 20 500 millions and Rs 16 500 millions in 1985–86 – is spent on fertiliser subsidies and foodgrains subsidies respectively and in both cases there are controversies on their unduly benefiting the farmers.

Fertiliser subsidies are meant to keep fertiliser prices low and encourage their use, to increase agricultural production. The fertiliser factories are paid different prices according to their assumed costs of production but fertiliser is sold at less than average cost price to farmers. By now the use of fertilisers is well known, and price lowering may not be the best device to encourage their further use. An educational campaign and extension service may, by better use of fertilisers, improve their use and productivity and yield better results. A temporary excess supply may put some pressure on the producers to improve their marketing methods. Lower fertiliser prices will reduce the cost of cultivation of all crops using fertilisers, but these will not generally be passed on in lower product prices. The better off farmers using more fertilisers will get an advantage. Foodgrain subsidies keep the prices of foodgrains sold through the public distribution system low. In a way they represent a part of the interest cost of public distribution inventories. It is the price for acting in an anti-market way – selling when the commodity is scarce and buying when it is plentiful at the same price. There is, however, also a subsidy on distribution; a part of this covers the higher cost of public over private distribution. The public distribution system, however, distributes mainly rice and wheat; the inferior cereals, millets, etc. are mainly not dealt with. Also, the spread of the public distribution system is greater in urban than in rural areas, partly because of its less scattered population and partly because of the larger proportion dependent on the market. There is no doubt that the public distribution system is valuable to the urban poor and to the scarcity areas, but the per capita benefits of the food subsidy are certainly less in the rural than the urban areas. In the rural areas it is the non-agriculturists who gain more.

Wherever agriculture is provided with commercial services by the state, there is a tendency to levy the charges at less than commercial rates containing a high element of subsidy. The water rates for irrigation are now not sufficient even to pay for the maintenance charges of the canals, and the interest costs are entirely subsidised. Attempts have sometimes been made to recover a part of the costs through the betterment levy on newly-irrigated land but, as a result of resistance were later on abandoned. It has been pointed out that for purchase of water from neighbouring tubewells farmers have paid more. It must in fairness be pointed out that in certain parts of the canal, and in certain seasons, supply of irrigation water has its problems, whereas tubewell water is generally provided in required volume at required times. Sometimes, low charges, poor quality services and high resistance to charge increases become a vicious circle difficult to break. Just like water charges, electricity rates for agriculture are subsidised, sometimes by the Central Government through the Rural Electrification Corporation, sometimes by the state government compensating the State Electricity Board, and in places by the State Electricity Board itself. The subsidy takes its worst form of benefiting the large farmers and leading to waste when metering is dispensed with. Loans for agricultural pumps, tractors, etc. are given at specially low interest rates.

While agriculture has grown at a slower rate than either industry or the tertiary sector, we have already seen that it has changed its character and increased its dependence on the manufacturing sector. This is also true of its dependence on other sectors which has been greater. In the pre-Independence period, the transport, communications and banking services were so built up as to facilitate movement of export crops and imports via port towns. Interior areas and rural roads had no significance *per se*. Agriculture had, therefore, to be built on new lines after independence. Regional specialisation in crops had to be encouraged after the first phase of self-sufficiency in foodgrains was over. Commercial and plantation crops had always been meant for the market. Allied agricultural products like dairying and poultry, fruits and vegetables which are expected increasingly to contribute to income and employment, depend on the urban market. Realising these facts, the Planning Commission tried to direct more resources into the rural sector so that development could take place. The private services and industry sector had, with notable exceptions earlier, devoted their efforts to the industrial and urban sectors so that power, capital markets, better educational and medical facilities were available only there. With the predominance of the public sector in these spheres a deliberate effort had been made to shift the balance. Some idea of the proportion of resources spent on

Table 4.16 Plan outlay on agriculture and industry

| Sector | Third Plan: 1961–66 | | | | Annual Plans: 1966–69 | | | |
| | Outlays | | Actuals | | Outlays | | Actuals | |
	Rs crores	% of total	Rs crores	% of total	Rs crores	% of total	Rs crores	% of total
Total	8 099	100.0	8 577	100.0	6 757	100.0	6 625	100.0
of which:								
Agriculture and allied activities	914	11.3	1 089	12.7	839	12.4	1 107	16.7
Irrigation and flood control	837	10.3	665	7.8	784	11.6	471	7.1
Industry & minerals	1 883	23.2	1 726	20.1	1 575	23.4	1 510	22.8
Village and small industries	264	3.3	241	2.8	144	2.1	126	1.9

Source: CMIE, *Seventh Five Year Plan: 1985–90: A Comparative Picture* (Bombay) November 1985.

agriculture and industry can be obtained from the public investment figures on the plans (Table 4.16). In reading the table, however, some cautions must be exercised. The broad sectoral expenditure heads are not fully indicative of agriculture or industry purposes. A part of industrial investment may be spent on the fertiliser industry, whose direct benificiary is agriculture. Power, transport, communications, trade are for both agriculture and industry. It is difficult to allocate their proportions except in power.

Apart from the direction of public sector activities to agriculture and rural areas, the government has made special arrangements for agricultural finance through the NABARD, the regional rural banks and cooperative institutions. Agriculture is also treated as a priority subsector for which 40 percent of priority bank credit has been earmarked. Statistics regarding the allocation of credit show that this guideline in complied with. They also show a general shift against big industry and in favour of agriculture (Table 4.17), but the big bank borrowing sectors like trade are a mixture of both.

A wider question may be raised at this stage. Besides tax-expenditure, the state acts on agriculture in various ways through movement restrictions, compulsory procurement, export-import control, etc. The Indian Government has resorted to all these devices at some stage. While this is no time to examine the various steps taken and the consequences in detail, a few general observations may be in order. Whatever the compulsions exercised in the past, at present

| Fourth Plan: 1969–74 | | | | Fifth Plan: 1974–79 | | | | Sixth Plan: 1980–85 | | | |
| Outlays | | Actuals | | Outlays | | Actuals | | Outlays | | Actuals | |
Rs crores	% of total	Rs crores	% of total	Rs crores	% of total	Rs crores	% of total	Rs crores	% of total	Rs crores	% of total
15 902	100.0	15 779	100.0	39 303	100.0	39 426	100.0	97 500	100.0	109 951	100.0
2 175	13.7	2 320	14.7	4 205	10.7	4 865	12.3	12 539	12.8	14 638	13.3
1 641	10.3	1 354	8.6	4 479	11.4	3 877	9.8	12 160	12.6	10 981	10.0
3 338	21.0	2 864	18.2	9 660	24.5	8 989	22.8	13 237	13.6	14 697	13.4
293	1.8	243	1.5	535	1.4	593	1.5	1 780	1.8	1 830	1.7

there is no coercion on the farmers either to cultivate certain crops only or to sell to certain parties. There is no acreage or output restriction. To encourage production and see that it is not discouraged by violent price fluctuations, a support price is fixed for foodgrains at which the government guarantees to purchase all the quantities that are offered. These amount to only a part of the marketable surplus. The farmers are free to keep foodgrains for themselves or sell them to private parties. But the measures to encourage foodgrains production along with the announcement of a minimum support price fixed on the recommendation of the Commission for Agricultural Costs and Prices have succeeded so well that at the commencement of the marketing season the Food Corporation of India is offered large quantities in surplus areas, which are sufficient, even without help from imports, to build up large stocks, besides meeting the legitimate claims of distribution to card-holders. There is, therefore, no question of any state policy to lower the terms of trade against agriculture. If the terms are still adverse, it is the result of market forces following from abundance of foodgrains produced at low costs. Parity of prices may demand higher foodgrains prices, but left to the market the likely immediate consequence is further price fall. An attempt to raise prices may mean more stocks without chances of market disposal. In the case of commodities like pulses, the market forces only decide the price. They are much above the support prices, and no sizeable quantities are sold to or through the

Table 4.17 Sectoral pattern of gross bank credit: March 1977–March 1985 (for 50 major banks)

	Outstanding as on last Friday of March 1977 (Rs crores)	Outstanding as on last Friday of March 1985		Variation between March 1977 & March 1985		
		Rs crores	% share	Rs crores	% change	% share
A. Priority sector	3 382	18 407	38.4	15 025	444.3	43.4
Agriculture	1 343	7 657	16.0	6 314	470.1	18.3
Small scale industries	1 403	6 608	13.8	5 205	371.0	15.0
Other priority sectors	636	4 142	8.6	3 506	551.2	10.1
B. Directly identifiable public sector agencies	2 374	6 212	13.0	3 838	161.7	11.1
Public food procurement credit	2 190	5 827	12.0	3 637	166.1	10.5
Cotton corporation	132	103	0.2	−29	−22.0	−0.1
Food corporation (fertilizers credit)	23	166	0.4	143	621.7	0.4
Jute Corporation	29	116	0.2	87	300.0	0.3
C. Other trade (mainly private)	815	2 266	4.7	1 451	178.0	4.2
D. Industry (medium & large) including autonomous public sector undertakings	5 539	15 948	33.2	10 409	188.0	30.1
E. Other sectors	1 247	5 120	10.7	3 873	310.5	11.2
Bank credit for 50 banks (A + B + C + D + E+)	13 357	47 953	100.0	34 596	259.0	100.0

Note: These data are available from the Reserve Bank of India and relate to 50 banks which together account for 95% of the gross bank credit.

Source: CMIE, Basic Statistics Relating to the Indian Economy, Vol. 1: All-Indian (Bombay) August 1986.

government. The support prices fixed for cotton and jute are much less effective in maintaining stable prices. For export and import commodities trade controls are used to regulate prices but this policy is for both agricultural and industrial products. As a part of the foreign trade policy of the country, both exports and imports are controlled and they have their impact on prices. Generally in case of import crops, the effect of the policy of import restrictions is to push domestic prices above world prices. In the case of agricultural commodities, however, there is a greater concern to prevent large price rises. The general policy is to encourage exports, but in the case of essential agricultural commodities like cotton and tea, exports of which would much raise domestic prices or starve the home market, are guarded against. As a smaller proportion of industrial commodities would be regarded as essential, their imports would be discouraged and exports stimulated more unreservedly.

It is in the competition of scarce natural resources that the picture of agriculture versus industry emerges. By and large there is no competition in the demand for unskilled labour where there are plentiful resources. Land has hitherto been the main preserve of agriculture, though the widespread demand for conversion of agricultural land into non-agricultural and the use of many dubious devices for this purpose near urban complexes show the likely conflicts ahead. Forests and their right use are becoming an area of struggle between industrialists and environmentalists interested in the future of agriculture. In areas where power is short and industries cannot resort to independent means of power generation, agriculture and industry fight for power in busy seasons. Water may soon come in this category once the dangers of private ownership of means of water supply are recognised. Regeneration of scarce natural resources like water, land and power may be called for. In the early stages of planning round about the Third Plan, the question of agriculture versus industry was sharply raised. With the better recognition of interdependence the controversy was stilled. It is now likely to be raised in another form. Means should be found to settle it in an expanding horizon.

Note

1. My grateful thanks are due to my colleagues at the Centre for Monitoring Indian Economy for their help in preparing this lecture.

5 Relationship between Rural and Industrial Development

Oleg T. Bogomolov

INSTITUTE FOR THE SOCIALIST WORLD ECONOMIC
SYSTEM OF THE ACADEMY OF SCIENCES OF THE
USSR, MOSCOW

As the last lecturer on today's agenda, I have not to be very eloquent and I'll try to keep myself from speaking too long. What we heard yesterday and today facilitates my task. Some of my conclusions were anticipated by other speakers. I was especially stimulated by the inaugural address by Professor Rao.

Let me now explain in a rather general way the attitude of Soviet scholars to the main issue of our Congress.

The development of agriculture historically served as the springboard of industrial progress. The separation of handicrafts from agriculture and their growth into manufacturing industries gave rise to further major shifts in the social division of labour. Its continuous development is resulting today in high technology industries, the sphere of production and social services playing an ever greater role. Agriculture, though remaining in the orbit of these changes, has found itself, nevertheless, in the group of 'old' branches of the economy whose share is diminishing. This has its own sociopsychological repercussions. Thus, modern conceptions of socioeconomic progress, strengthening of the national economic potential and improvement of the national economic well-being are associated with industrialisation. Indeed, with the exception of New Zealand, it is difficult to find an example of how a country drawing mainly upon its agriculture and the processing of its products could reach the level of per capita national income of the industrially developed countries of the West. Does this mean that agriculture has lost its exceptionally important role in the present-day economy? In my opinion, successful development of agriculture even today is one of the indispensable preconditions of general economic progress. This holds true for all groups of countries, irrespective of the level of their development and social organisation. Half the world population still lives on income from agriculture, while in developing states this proportion is considerably higher (FAO, 1982, p. 1). Providing the world population with foodstuffs, and industry with agricultural raw materials, has become one of the most acute global problems of our times, whose solution calls for internationally co-ordinated efforts and determines, in a large measure, the prospects of human civilisation.

Technological progress is making rapid inroads in agricultural production. Many countries, including India, have felt the beneficial effect of the Green Revolution. Despite this, however, the agrarian sector of the economy nearly everywhere exhibits considerably less dynamism and greater conservatism in its structures as compared to industry. In most cases it has a lower level of labour productivity than in industry, less concentration of production and a smaller output per unit of capital investment. It is becoming ever more evident that industrial progress by polluting the environment and by reducing the productive farm areas hampers the growth of the production of foodstuffs. Coupled with this is the great dependence of agriculture on climatic conditions and the instability of agricultural markets. Are not these the reasons responsible for the fact that in many developing countries and in some socialist states the agrarian sector is the 'bottleneck' in the economy, and that in the industrially developed countries of the West the high level of agrarian production is based to a great extent on enormous state subsidies?

What should be the balance between industry and agriculture in our day? The contemporary world is multi-faceted and the levels and conditions of development of individual countries generally differ. It is impossible therefore to answer this question unambiguously. It is clear that on the global level there is no balance. In the past few decades the annual increase in food production only insignificantly surpasses the growth rate of population. Starvation and malnutrition of hundreds of millions of people in some parts of the planet are combined with 'overproduction' of foodstuffs in other areas. The above-mentioned balance is absent in many cases on a national level too.

The general dependence between the economic growth of a country and the development of its agriculture are well known today and mathematically described, thanks first of all to the works of Professor S. Kuznets (Kuznets, 1964). The development of the non-agricultural sector of the economy usually rests upon expansion of domestic agricultural production as regards both the provision of the urban population with foodstuffs, and light industries and food industries with raw materials. The agrarian sector in the course of its development increases its demand for industrial goods, and thus provides an additional impetus to industrialisation. It also releases additional manpower for industry and can serve as a source of capital investment in other sectors (especially for primary accumulation in the industry); thanks to exports, it can secure the necessary revenues in foreign currencies, thus making possible, in particular, imports of modern technology and equipment.

All this would speak of the inadmissibility of industrialisation to the detriment of the progress of agriculture. Nevertheless, historical experience shows that the general trend of diminution of the agrarian sector's share in the economy over a long period, prevailed in a number of developing and socialist countries in the selection of the strategy of their development. As has been noted by S. Ghatak and K. Ingersent in their book *Agriculture and Economic Development*, these countries found themselves in a kind of a trap because they underestimated the 'critical importance of domestic agriculture's product contribution to the maintenance of an adequate rate of economic growth' (Ghatak and Ingersent, 1984, p. 31).

Still another lesson could be drawn from historical practice. A certain surplus of supplies of foodstuffs and agricultural raw materials over the demand serves, all other conditions being equal, as a factor of dynamic economic growth and imparts a greater stability to it.

Especially sensitive points in establishing an optimal interrelationship between agriculture and industry at the initial stage of industrial development are the overspill of a part of accumulation and of the labour force from the agrarian into other sectors of the economy and, at later industrial stages, state subsidising of agriculture. Extremes and exaggerations of any kind in this matter can bear heavy consequences.

The specific character of agriculture makes the stimulation of production, the enhancement of its efficiency and the application of modern machinery and technology often more complicated than in other sectors. In this connection a number of circumstances can be mentioned: the presence, for example, in many countries, of a large traditional sector oriented to self-reliance, side by side with the modern agricultural sector which is market oriented. Because of its fragmentation and underdevelopment the former sector displays a strong inertia with regard to social and technological transformations. The progress of agrarian production can be hindered by the system of land ownership, a low level of education and culture of farmers, their poor knowledge of the achievements of modern agricultural technology and unwillingness to take the risk of its application. It is also hampered by a lack of, or shortage of, investments and energy, the more so as modern production systems in agriculture are very capital- and energy-intensive. There are also data showing that expenditure on R&D in the agro-industrial complex of many industrialised countries is inferior to the corresponding expenditure in industry; it is also insufficient in developing countries (Gabor and Colombo, 1981, p. 157).

Reaching an optimum in the balance between agriculture and industry presupposes implementation of such measures of the agrarian policy as land reform, encouragement of the cooperative movement in its most diverse forms, creation of state farms, well-thought-out and flexible taxation policy, implementation of state programmes of irrigation and land improvement, control of erosion, stimulation of the industry processing agricultural products and supplying it with machinery, fertilisers and various chemicals. State support has greatly contributed to the successful development of agriculture in a number of countries of South-East Asia and Latin America. This is illustrated by the example of India.

Former concepts of the relationship between the agrarian and industrial sectors of the economy are changing today due to the ongoing process of integration of both sectors and the formation of national agro-industrial complexes. It is noteworthy that scientific farming is increasingly assuming the features of industrial technologies. Agricultural production is combined with its processing, transportation, construction and repair jobs. This ensures employment of the released (fully or partly) rural population and increases incomes of agricultural enterprises and families. As a result, the state's agrarian policy becomes enriched in its content and it begins to cover the most important links in the entire agro-industrial complex.

World practice knows not a few examples of both successful and insufficiently effective agrarian policies. The experience of many socialist countries is also instructive in this respect.

In the Soviet Union the basic mass of agricultural production is in the public socialist sector (collective and state farms) – about 100 per cent of grain, cotton, beet, sunflower, about 70 per cent of meat, milk, eggs and 40 per cent of potatoes. The rest is obtained from peasants' personal plots. Gross agricultural output by 1985 had grown, as compared to the pre-war year 1940, by 2.7 times and productivity of labour in this sector by 4.6 times. Industrial output for the same period grew by 25 times and productivity of industrial labour by 9 times, (Narodnoe, 1986, pp. 34–5).

The comparison of these figures does not show an optimal balance between agriculture and industry. Despite big capital investments in the agro-industrial complex, its efficiency increased but insufficiently. For this reason, the task of accelerating agrarian development and improving its efficiency is an especially urgent one. During the period 1986–90 it is planned to more than double the increment of production as compared to the previous five-year period.

To this end, institutional unity is being ensured in the management of the agro-industrial complex at both the state and the regional levels, the effectiveness of economic levels of management (price, taxes, self-financing) is being broadened and improved, greater independence is being given to industrial enterprises and industrial technologies are being applied in various branches of agriculture (CPSU, 1986, pp. 30–32).

The governmental organ 'Agroprom', newly-created in the USSR, has to co-ordinate and harmonise the agricultural and industrial development within the agro-industrial complex. In this connection, several ministries dealing with agriculture itself, processing of its products, supplying it with machinery and so on were shut down. We are trying to make a better use than before of the potential of co-operative forms of agricultural production and of peasants' personal plots. We started introducing 'family accord' in some cases in order to increase incentives for a greater output in animal breeding and in some other branches of agriculture. New industrial technologies are being ever more broadly applied for grain production and so on.

These guidelines of agrarian policy are also characteristic for other socialist countries. They have proved their effectiveness in Hungary, the GDR, Czechoslovakia and Bulgaria. In these countries the successful development of agriculture makes a great contribution to general economic growth and gives stability to the entire economy. Czechoslovakia, for example, has reached self-sufficiency in basic foodstuffs, the GDR has considerably reduced imports of grain, while Hungary has become a major exporter of agricultural products. During 1970–84 the crop yield in Hungary increased from 24.9 to 53.0 centners per hectare, meat – from 101 to 173 kg. per capita, the milk yield per cow – from 2.2 to 4.5 tons (CMEA, 1985, p. 218). These figures are about one and a half to two times the growth rates in other European socialist countries. It should also be noted that intensification of agriculture in Hungary, where a great role had been played by industrial production systems, was carried out with a satisfactory efficiency of capital investments (their share in the total investments in the national economy decreased).

As a result of the intensive development of the agro-industrial complex in the GDR and Czechoslovakia, a high level of living standards is ensured, sizeable currency and material resources are being saved and switched over to the needs of the structural reorganisation of industry (CMEA, 1988, pp. 206, 218, 222; Bogomolov, 1984, pp. 132, 141–2, 165–6).

The experience of China is interesting. As a result of giving up administrative methods of management and switching over to economic ones, and encouraging the economic interests of peasants, it has become possible to increase sharply, within less than ten years, the productivity of labour and agricultural output on the old, practically unchanged, technical base of the agrarian sector. The released labour force is partly employed in the local industry of rural areas processing agricultural products, producing agricultural implements, construction materials, and so on. Grain imports have been substantially reduced, while China's agro-industrial exports have considerably increased the foreign currency earnings which are being invested in a further modernisation of agriculture and the food industry and in the development of other industries of the national economy.

In resolving the question of the relationship between agriculture and industry, many countries proceed from the concept of self-sufficiency in basic foodstuffs. Despite the deepening international division of labour, this concept has its own justification. The land – the main factor of agricultural production – must be productively used everywhere to feed the population. Besides, strong dependence on imports of foodstuffs, even given certain comparative advantages, always contains more elements of risk than provision from domestic sources. The same applies to export in comparison with sales in the domestic market.

The policy of self-sufficiency, nevertheless, does not exclude, but often goes with, a desire to expand exports of agricultural products. Agricultural export plays a very considerable role in the economic and, in particular, industrial progress of many countries of the world. It enables the developing countries to pay for the import of investment equipment and for many other commodities indispensable for stable economic growth. Export specialisation in agricultural products for the production of which a given country has considerable comparative advantages can contribute to raising the productivity of national labour, to the growth of living standards of the population, and to the accumulation of funds for industrial development. This can be easily exemplified by the group of both developing states and industrialised countries of the West, as well as by socialist states. The import of foodstuffs and agricultural raw materials by industrially-developed states simultaneously creates demand for their manufactured goods on the part of agrarian suppliers. In short, in determining the optimal balance between the agrarian and industrial sectors of the national economy, the growing role of the world market cannot be left out of account.

In the opinion of many experts, world trade in agricultural products is currently experiencing a dangerous crisis. It is manifested in enormous surpluses, very low prices caused, to a considerable extent, by overproduction and export subsidies in industrialised countries, as well as in growing protectionism. According to statistical data published in the USA, international trade in agricultural products in the years 1981–85 declined by 12 per cent from $233 to $206 bn (Bureau of the Census, 1986, p. 47).

The price drop hit the developing countries especially hard. Their export prices in real terms during the period 1980–85 dropped by more than 30 per cent, while for the US farmers this reduction was only 12 per cent and in the EEC the prices remained substantially unchanged (UNCTAD, 1986, p. 39).

Prices are pulled down by the export subsidies introduced in the USA for wheat, cotton, sugar, rice and other commodities (over $2 bn). The US budget expenditures for maintaining farmers' incomes and prices, as well as for the programme of reducing the sowing area, are close to $35 bn. From a wheat importer, the EEC has become a major exporter to a considerable extent, owing to agrarian protectionism and subsidies on wheat prices. In the EEC the total volume of agricultural subsidies in recent years was 60–70 bn ECU including 8 bn ECU for wheat (Far Eastern Economic Review, 1986). Japan also ranks among the world's major importers of foodstuffs, but its domestic agriculture is protected more strongly than in any other Western country, except Switzerland.

All this incurs enormous losses for the countries exporting agricultural products, including some socialist states. The undermining of the world agricultural market can bring heavy consequences for industrialisation of the Third World countries; it can also make the crisis of indebtedness even more acute. Thus the problem of balance between the two sectors of the economy takes on an important global aspect. The imbalances are revealed not only in the enormous surplus of foodstuffs in the USA and EEC and absolute shortages in many countries of Africa and Asia, but also in the impossibility of expanding agrarian export in those countries where it remains the main source of technological modernisation of the economy.

To attain a more balanced industrial and agricultural development on both national and global levels, a far greater degree of co-ordination of state policies and actions is required now than before.

The Soviet Union, aware of the growing threat of the imbalance of the world economy now facing the international community, emerges as the initiator of concrete steps on arms control and the reduction of military arsenals which would not only remove the threat of war, but also free mankind of the enormous burden of non-productive spending; would make it possible to render effective assistance to the developing countries in overcoming their economic lag; and would facilitate major additions to the goods and services in international exchange. The Soviet Union also calls for the elaboration of measures ensuring economic security of countries by means of joint control over dangerous tendencies in international economic development, elimination of protectionist and discriminatory measures, rejection of economic pressure and blackmail with strict adherence to the principles of equality and mutual benefits. Moreover, building their international co-operation on the principles of consistent democratism and comradely solidarity, the Soviet Union and other socialist countries are accumulating valuable experience in organising international economic life on a planned crisis-free basis.

References

Bogomolov, O.T. (ed.)(1984) *Agrarian Relations in the Socialist Countries (Agrarnye otnosheniya v stranakh o Soksializma)* (Moscow: Nauka).

Bureau of the Census (1986) *Report on International Agricultural Trade* (Washington DC: US, Dept. of Trade).

CMEA (1985) *Statistichesky ezhegodnik stran-chlenov SEV, 1985 (Statistical Yearbook of CMEA Member Countries for 1985)* (Moscow: Finance and Statistics).

CPSU (1986) *Materialy XXVII S"yezda KPSS (Documents of the 27th Congress of the CPSU)* (Moscow: Politizdat).

FAO (1982) 'Food and Agriculture Situation and Issues', World Food Day Colloquium, Background Paper (Rome: Food and Agriculture Organisation of the United Nations).

Far Eastern Economic Review, 11 September 1986.

Gabor, D. and Colombo, U. (1981) *Beyond the Age of Waste: A Report to the Club of Rome* (New York: Pergamon Press).

Ghatak, S. and Ingersent, K. (1984) *Agriculture and Economic Development* (Brighton: Wheat Sheaf Books).

Kuznets, S. (1964) 'Economic Growth and Contribution of Agriculture' in Eicher, G.K. and Witt, L.W. (eds) *Agriculture in Economic Development*, (New York: McGraw Hill).

Narodnoe khozyaistvo SSSR v 1985 g (*USSR National Economy in 1985*) (Moscow: Statistika 1986).

UNCTAD (1986) *Trade and Development Report 1986* (New York: United Nations).

6 Problems of Late Industrialisation: an Asian Perspective*

Shigeru Ishikawa

AOYAMA GAKUIN UNIVERSITY, TOKYO

This summer, quite unexpectedly, I received a request from Professor Kenneth Arrow, President of the International Economic Association and Professor Sukhamoy Chakravarty, President of the Indian Economic Association to make a Plenary Session address at the 8th World Congress of IEA in New Delhi. After much hesitation, I finally accepted the invitation with a sense of great honour and sincere thanks. With regard to the topic, after some thought I have chosen the one in my title. This is a topic about which I have been recently very much concerned, and it also relates closely to the common theme of this Congress.

1 ON THE 'LATENESS' AND 'ASIAN PERSPECTIVE'

First, let me comment on two terms in my title; namely 'lateness' and 'Asian perspective'. In connection with the former, the dual impact, both favourable and unfavourable, exerted by the technological gap between the early-comers and the late-comers upon the economic development of the latter has long been noted à la Gerschenkron (1961). This impact, particularly in its unfavourable aspect, is much greater now than before, as the technological gap after the Second World War has become enormous. Secondly, the population explosion which occured after the end of the Second World War is crucially related to it. As a result, unemployment and underemployment issues in the developing countries have been increasingly serious, often aggravated by an accompanying issue of income inequality. I once thought that a conventional method of solving the issue by industrialisation was not sufficient to cope with it, and that it should be tackled squarely by devising measures for increasing labour absorption at the place of origin of underemployment; namely, the agricultural production sector (Ishikawa, 1978). The policy suggestion is, however, still inoperative. It may be that the conventional method through industrialisation should be again emphasised as the only effective one.

As a third characteristic of 'lateness', I wish to note that the economic system upon which the contemporary late-comers are developing is very different from those of the early comers of the West. Typically in the latter the market economy developed on the basis of the ruins of the village communities (or customary economy). The Industrial Revolution was an event that took place on this basis. In the contemporary developing economies, however, industrialisation has proceeded on the two bases of an insufficiently developed market economy and of village communities which more or less remain in place. In addition, the nature and the function of the state differ. While it is not easy to specify the difference, it is at least clear that there is in today's developing countries no government of the Western pattern which emerged as a result of the bourgeois revolutions, and whose intrinsic role is to protect the market economy and compensate for its failure.[1]

Next, the words 'Asian perspective' will provide a more particular characterisation of the economic system of contemporary developing countries. Four points can be made.[2]

First, it is important to note that the primary foundation of the livelihood of Asian people is monsoon-based rice culture. It provides for the existence and survival of the farming families at a subsistence level, even in the stage of early technological development. However, such families are eager to acquire security for their survival. This is the basic behaviour of low-income families which seek institutionalised mutual relief within the face-to-face groups of small localities. On the other hand, monsoon-based agriculture, in particular in its technologically higher development stage, requires institutional arrangements for making possible basic infrastructure construction and maintenance for flood control and irrigation, joint water management and co-operative operation in certain processes of current production.

These three factors necessitate the institutionalisation of village communities within the scope of natural villages (corresponding more or less to the basic unit of common water utilisation), as the foundation of monsoon-based agriculture. (Parenthetically, a community is defined as a territorial group in which the activities of the families residing in a small locality are determined, not only for the purpose of maximising their own individual welfare, but allowing in addition for the increased welfare of their fellow families. Customary practices of work-sharing and income-sharing typically result.) With the enlargement of the basic units of common water utilisation, the territorial scope of the community tends to expand by formation of inter-village associations, which require the support by the public power of the State.[3]

Secondly, the increased demand for agricultural outputs due to population increase or increased requisition is met, unless the land frontier is easily expanded, by strengthening the working of the above factors on the basis of monsoon-based agriculture. Namely, on the one hand there are seen intensified flood control and irrigation and, as a result, more a labour-intensive production method leading to output increase. On the other hand this is systemically accompanied by the strengthening of community-type activities and of their support by the state power. (This is nothing more than 'involution', as developed by Clifford Geertz, 1963).

Thirdly, the development of commerce and industry in the non-farm sector exerts various impacts upon the farming communities. These impacts are not limited to the conventional pattern in which the communities tend to be replaced by markets. When commercial development penetrates into the communities to an extent and in a way that threaten the subsistence and its security of community members, it often happens that the communities counteract this threat by commercialising themselves, e.g., by organising themselves into market-type co-operatives. In this way the communities may become prime movers of the market economy development. It is easy for the state to become a guardian of the communities in this effort.

Finally, these community-characteristics of the farm sector tend to have a variety of reflections in the intra- and inter-firm organisations of the non-farm sector. To the extent that this is actually the case, the modern firms in Asia are exempt from the market-type competition.

2 THE AIM OF THIS DISCUSSION

The aim of the present discussion is to explore the processes of structural transformation, in particular industrialisation, of the Asian economies after the end of the Second World War, and also, to investigate the kind of impact which the above characteristics of contemporary late-comers in Asia exert in the process of structural transformation.

First some preliminaries and qualifications should be described. I classify the countries in Asia into three groups, in terms of characteristics of structural transformation.

The first two groups consist of the countries in which structural transformations are currently in some critical stage. The countries of the first group include India and China, and are defined in terms of their initial conditions for development as 'old-established low-income countries in which population was dense, natural resources were poor, but there was already established a certain industrial base, albeit small'. I myself consider that the process of structural transformation of this group could be approximated by the familiar dual economy development model of W.A. Lewis (1954). This theory suggests that the process of transformation in these countries was not, until the recent past, a success story in which intersectoral flows of labour and of wage goods (i.e., agricultural products) were proceeding smoothly, and in which the economy is moving steadily in the direction of Lewis's 'turning point'. It was rather a case in which such transformation was obstructed mainly by the constraint placed by the limited supply of 'wage goods' from agriculture and the economy was in constant danger of being caught in the 'Ricardian Growth Trap'.[4] In India this trap is often seen as reflected in an industrial stagnation after the mid-1960s.[5] In China the trap had arisen at least twice by the early 1970s, and after that it was evaded by the strict enforcement of regulations restricting labour migration from the rural to the urban sector (Ishikawa, 1984).

I do know that in both these countries gross agricultural production increased significantly after the end of the 1970s, and the possibility for the economy finally to get rid of the Ricardian Growth Trap may soon be in sight. But I do not know whether such a production increase has been accompanied by organisational arrangements in the vast agricultural region that assure continuous investment in agricultural infrastructure and the continuous realisation of technological progress in current production. In China's case, as is widely observed, the recent output performance has been largely due to the incentive effect of the sweeping organisational reform of the Rural People's Communes, reactivating family farms in effect. In any case, this classification is one which is made leaving aside the appraisal of the most recent agricultural changes in both countries.

The second group consists of the ASEAN countries. This group is defined in terms of initial conditions as 'newly-developed countries in which natural resources were rich but population was sparse and which were specialised as primary-export economies'. I consider that while their economic growth process could until recently be approximated by Hla Myint's Vent-for-Surplus Model (Myint, 1958), some of them are at present caught in what may be characterised as 'Vent-for-Surplus Growth Trap', which will be explained shortly. They are pursuing industrialisation in varying forms in attempts to avoid this trap, but the final outcome is yet to be seen.

It should be noted that once the countries of these two groups are trapped in either form, the issues of open and disguised unemployment and of the accompanying income-inequality tend to be further aggravated. As is widely discussed, the issue is widespread over Asia, but appears most explicit and acute in India (Barker and Herdt, 1985, pp. 134–5; Dantwala, 1986, p. 111).

The third group consists of countries which, after successful graduation from the stage of Ricardian and Myint models of development, either have already got into, or are getting into, a steady industrialisation stage. For the former we have as typical cases Japan and the Republic of Korea, and for the latter, Taiwan.

Now I would like to discuss the process of structural transformation, mainly in connection with the first group of countries and mainly in connection with the rural and agricultural sector. I should especially mention that I have reserved the long-term assessment of the recent increases in agricultural production in India and particularly in China for future study. Including these, my study of the overall topic is preliminary and includes conjectural elements.

3 STRUCTURAL MECHANISM OF THE RICARDIAN GROWTH TRAP

Let me first discuss in greater detail how I have approximated the structural transformation in India and China until recent years by the Ricardian Growth Trap Model. There are in these countries two basic relationships which combine to bring about such a trap:

1. In the agricultural sector, cultivable but uncultivated land is no longer left. While it is possible to increase real agricultural output either by additional investment or by technological progress, its

rate of increase is not much different from that of the agricul-
turally-employed population. Hence, a significant increase in agricultural output per unit of agricultural labour force has not yet
arisen. (This implies that the possibility for the agricultural sector
to increase the marketed ratio of its output is small.)

2. The rate of increase in employment in the non-agricultural sector,
   which is required by the policy-induced real rate of growth in that
   sector, is significantly larger than the rate of increase in the supply
   of wage goods from the agricultural sector.[6]

In the 1960s and 1970s both of these relationships arose in the two
countries. The structural transformation therefore was very slow. In
both countries the proportion of employment in the agricultural
sector did not change significantly between the early 1950s and the
present time.[7]

Why do such outcomes emerge? There are many factors in the
production structure which are directly or indirectly related to this
question. They may be classified into two kinds – factors which relate
to the production structure in individual agricultural and non-
agricultural sectors, and factors which relate to resource transfers
between the sectors.

To begin with the second set of issues, inter-sectoral resource
transfers in the process of structural transformation take place in
various forms: products, inputs, labour and capital. Studies have thus
far been conducted for each individual form in isolation. A more
crucial determinant of structural transformation seems to be the
interrelation between the resource transfers in these forms. Two
points are worthy of note in actual context:[8]

1. In both countries, labour generally migrated from agriculture to
   the industry. This was not accompanied by any parallel movement
   of wage-goods (agricultural products) in a quantity sufficient to
   feed the migrated labour force. This was true even when imported
   food grains were added in the 1950s and later. For this reason, the
   inter-sectoral commodity terms of trade moved against industry.
   A tendency of increasing real wage costs and declining profit ratios
   emerged in industry.
2. In the area of interaction between the transfer of savings and
   income and the transfer of products, the issue is this: given the
   initial low-accumulation level in monsoon-based Asian agriculture, it is essential for overcoming the basic relation of the Ricar-

dian Growth Trap that there is a prior net outflow of funds in the combined invisible-current and capital accounts from industry to agriculture. This net outflow then finances the net export surplus of commodity trade from industry to agriculture mainly in the form of agricultural-input and capital goods. (Parenthetically, I have continuously argued, in the Asian context, against the commonplace proposition that early industrialisation should be financed by 'primitive accumulation' in agriculture.) However (Ishikawa, 1967, chapter 4, 1986), the direction of the net flow was a net outflow from agriculture in India until the mid-1960s (Mundle, 1981). In China, the direction of the net flow was the one we consider desirable. In order to obtain this result, however, severe exploitation of agriculture by use of agricultural price regulation took place. Incentives for the producers to increase output were thus reduced. The realised agricultural import surplus was not sufficiently large to offset the unfavourable incentives.

Turning to the changes in the production structure in each individual sector, the decisive problem in agriculture seems to be determination of the mode of irrigation and the choice of appropriate techniques in current production on the irrigated land. One typical set of alternatives is a combination of community-based minor irrigation, higher-yielding crop varieties, and multiple cropping (and labour-using mechanisation), and the other is a combination of privately-based tubewell irrigation, higher-yielding varieties, and labour-saving mechanisation. In India the second set of alternatives has been preferred (Ishikawa 1967 and 1978). This choice tended to neglect opportunities for community-based minor irrigation. The desirable amounts of income and saving transfers to agriculture seem to have been large to that extent. However, such expectation was not satisfied, and no fundamental improvement of agricultural productivity came from this source. In China, the choice was apparently on the former set of alternatives. A huge expansion of agricultural infrastructure investments was brought about which, however, does not seem sufficient to counterbalance the disincentive effect derived above.

Discussions on the role of the industrial sector to cope with the Trap are only brief. First, it should be noted that the Ricardian Trap can be brought about in the agricultural sector alone, provided that the rate of population explosion is sufficiently high. However, the decisive factor was the rate of growth of the industrial sector, which was far above that of the agricultural sector. This high rate of industrial growth was created deliberately. Family farm agriculture in Asia is basically labour-intensive, and the linkage effect of the intermediate goods demand transmitted from agriculture to industry is very small. In the period of systematic introduction of high-yielding varieties of rice, agriculture's demand for chemical fertilisers, chemical insecticides and tractors increased side by side, which had an effect of increasing the linkage effect.[9] But linkage is still far from comparable to the significant effect observed in the capital-intensive agriculture in the countries in the New Continent. The final demand effect also cannot be significantly large in the low-income stage of development.

Therefore, in the case where industrialisation in fact took place in the countries of Asia, the pressure for it usually came from export promotion, import substitution or deliberate investment allocation among domestic sectors. India and China have chosen the latter two courses in combination. The resulting growth rate of industrialisation was excessive relative to that of agriculture.

We also comment on issues of structural transformation in the countries under the Vent-for-Surplus Trap. The essence of the Vent-for-Surplus Model is a process of economic growth of the countries of our second group in which large surplus land (cultivable land) and underutilised labour force are utilised more fully for export production under the stimulus of emerging foreign demand for the potential products of the land. The resulting growth is a widening process without significant technological accompaniment. Therefore, once a stage comes in which no additional cultivable land is left, the growth process ends, and a growth trap results. When population explosion occurs, it becomes necessary for underutilised resources to be spent not only for export production, but for feeding an increased portion of population. Hence the trap arrives more quickly than otherwise.

The Vent-for-Surplus Trap had arrived in Indonesia toward the end of the nineteenth century. No cultivable land was then said to exist any longer in Java (van den Meer, 1986). In Thailand and the Philippines it arrived during the 1950s (Ishikawa, 1970).

As a strategy for getting rid of the Vent-for-Surplus Trap, these countries have thus accorded the highest priority to industrialisation, and debates have been going on as to the choice of a specific form of industry (e.g., from among the industry processing agricultural resources, the labour-intensive light industries, and the capital-goods industry with a higher forward-linkage effect), or as to the choice of specific method (e.g., growth by import substitution or by export promotion). From somewhat different points of view, there are also issues as to how to raise entrepreneurship, government technocrats or professional and technical manpower. Recently, however, the crucial importance, even in the primary export economies, of raising the technological and productivity levels of foodgrain production by family farms is again being emphasised as a prerequisite for getting rid of the Growth Trap through industrialisation in whatever form.[10] It appears that in this regard the ASEAN countries are still searching for the effective course for solution.

4   SUCCESSFUL TRANSFORMATIONS

In searching for ways to get rid of either the Ricardian or the Vent-for-Surplus Growth Trap, one clue at least is provided by the experiences of the Asian countries which graduated from the development paths each involving the risks of the respective Traps. In connection with the Ricardian Growth Trap we have the experience of Japan from the 1860s to the 1940s, or even to the 1970s. In connection with the Vent-for-Surplus Growth Trap, there is the experience of Taiwan from the period of Japanese occupation up to the present.[11]

In Tokugawa Japan, a considerable amount of prior investment had taken place from the non-agricultural to the agricultural sectors (mainly by big merchants and local clans). As a result, about half of the total area of rice fields was equipped with facilities for flood control and irrigation at an elementary level. After the Meiji Restoration, Japanese agriculture benefited from steady increases in both output per hectare of land and output per agricultural worker. The market ratio of agricultural products also increased steadily. The outcome was that the Japanese agricultural sector was able to export to the industrial sector all of the annual natural increment of their labour force. Industrialisation became steady after the end of the First World War.

The factors differentiating the performance of structural transformation in Japan from those of India and China are many. One should also remember the significant difference in the initial levels of economic development, measured in terms of per capita GNP or of progress in the social division of labour. What concerns me here is a strong possibility that the inter-country differences in the economic system affect these preference patterns for technology and the mode of production, thus resulting in differential performances.

In Japan, the village community system functioned throughout the course of economic development. It facilitated the choice of techniques of the pattern that combined minor irrigation, higher-yielding varieties and multiple cropping (with labour-using mechanisation), and promoted further organisational changes in farm management toward a market orientation. The community survived even in the 1970s, playing a positive role in co-operativisation and co-ordination, on the natural village level, of production and management of individual farm families, in the post-war context of new technology development.

However, in India and China, for different reasons and accompanied by significant regional differentials, the village communities appear generally to have disintegrated prematurely, as judged by income levels and the degree of social division of labour. The resultant vacuum was filled by the yet-immature resource allocation system of the market economy. The causes behind the disintegration of the village communities in India appear to be complicated, but it is claimed that the age-old practices of village-level irrigation management, which provided strong support for the community formation, were administratively abolished by the British Colonial Government, and that irrigation management, nominally transferred to the jurisdiction of the local governments, was in actuality neglected (Sengupta, 1985). The causes behind the typical Indian choice of techniques in agriculture today, a combination of private-based tubewell irrigation, higher-yielding varieties and labour-saving mechanisation, may be traced back to this historical event. In many areas, decision-making by the upper-strata farmers is taking the place of the community's collective decisions.

In North China, the disintegration of the village communities was brought about by the destruction of the invading northern tribes. Behaviour patterns maximising private individual interest emerged and persisted for hundreds of years. It is interesting that under the organisational set-up of 'production teams' in the People's Communes, the community-type behaviour of the member families often appears to have revived (in the form which we call pseudo-community) (Ishikawa, 1983). The weakness of this set-up was its ease of subjugation to state intervention. It is for this reason that, while the choice of techniques in China was similiar to that of Japan, the overall outcome in terms of production and management was disappointing, as described above.

Four items are worthy of note among the functions which the village community has played in the course of economic development:

1. It becomes an agent of construction and maintenance of agricultural infrastructure investment and of water management.
2. It takes initiatives for conducting co-operative and/or collective farming operations, as well as commercial activities by the village members.
3. It arranges institutions of work-sharing and income-sharing, and sponsors relief undertakings when necessary.
4. It promotes the emergence of innovators for introducing and creating those types of technologies which increase the welfare of the village members.

It seems almost obvious that these functions helped direct the choice of techniques in basic investments and current production toward the patterns indicated above. I wish particularly to note the following two points: as a result of the working of these functions, technologies developed such that the most abundant factor of the community, i.e., labour, was most intensively used and the scarce factors, land and capital, were economised. This took place directly or indirectly by the initiatives of the villagers themselves. Also, in the same way, it was easier to provide some security at the minimum subsistence level for the lower income working people who constituted the majority of the community.

There are a few points about which caution is necessary. First, it is possible for the village community to take a number of sociological forms. Secondly, there are different types of community: hierarchical type and equal-partner type. In Japan, the village community prior to the Second World War was a hierarchical community in which village leaders and innovators were landlords, who themselves cultivated their land of 4 to 5 hectares with the aid of a few agricultural labourers. (The rest of the land was lent out to tenants, living mostly in the same village.) However, during and after the First World War rising industrial wages reacted on the rural sector, so that the direct management of farms by the cultivating landlords was no longer feasible. Yet this did not mean the disintegration of the village community. While 'cultivating' landlords were converted into 'parasitic' ones, the community did re-emerge in a new form, in which customary practices of mutual aid among working peasants (of approximately equal social standing) expanded, and horizontal solidarity of the villagers replaced the previous hierarchical relations. The new leaders and innovators were a group of middle-sized owner- and half-owner-cultivators. As carriers of the innovations village-based agricultural co-operatives, called Minor Co-operatives, were organised all over the country during the 1920s.

It should be noted that, in different terms, there is a variation of the community forms, from a territorial and pseudo-familial organisation of the Japanese type to a kinship (consanguineal) organisation as found in many regions of South-East Asia.

Next, with regard to the commercialised activities of the villages, it may not be appropriate to regard them as an indication that the village community or its resource allocation principle is disappearing. Japanese experience shows that it is quite possible that the village as an organic unit requires its members to increase the collective happiness of the village members, while permitting or even encouraging them to seek private profit or welfare in their dealings with outsiders. The community principle also provides an ideological motive for commercialisation of the village economy as a whole. There is indeed evidence that the village communities continued to exist even in the rapid growth period of the 1970s.[12]

Taiwan, on the other hand, appears to have been facing the danger of a Vent-for-Surplus Growth Trap toward the end of the nineteenth century, at the beginning of Japanese colonisation. During the colonial days Taiwan got out of the trap by developing export production of *japonica* rice and crude sugar, and at the same time by raising the productivity of *indica* rice for domestic consumption. After decolonialisation, it went on to industrialise successfully.

Behind this success story the development path of the Vent-for-Surplus Growth Model was in practice the role of village community in Taiwan. Although my knowledge of the Taiwanese village community is poor, it is possible to say that the Movement for Production Increase of rice since 1920, and the accompanying projects for irrigation, would have been much less successful if there had not been a successful introduction of terminal water utilisation since 1930 (construction and maintenance of the terminal waterways connecting the distribution channel to the farmer's field and related water management). And the success of the terminal water utilisation was made possible on the basis of the Minor Co-operatives of Water Utilisation organised all over Taiwan since around 1930, which were in fact communities of the cultivating peasants. The activities of these Minor Co-operatives were further strengthened after the Second World War (Chen, 1972).

5 HOW ALIVE IS THE VILLAGE COMMUNITY?

Although located similarly in Monsoon Asia, why do the village communities in Japan and Taiwan differ so decisively from those in India and China? And what about conditions in other Asian countries? In connection with these questions, it may be pointed out that, as a result of new research conducted recently in a growing number of countries, and mainly on the basis of field studies, the village communities remaining in various localities in Asia are found to be much more numerous and active than we once supposed them to be.

On the Indian subcontinent, field studies by Nirmal Sengupta in Bihar and Tamil Nadu have taught us that most traditional terminal irrigation areas in the three-level river irrigation system, and most traditional minor irrigation systems, had been considered to be obsolete as the British Colonial Government removed them from the local-community jurisdiction. Nevertheless, many of them are in fact found surviving and in operation through community work and community management. It is suggested that traditional irrigation systems, and side by side with them village communities, continue to be in extensive operation in other parts of India too. A model of 'a self-contained village community in India' developed by Ashok Rudra seems in a sense to be a summary of his extensive field studies on villages of the eastern zone of India (Rudra, 1984). It vividly describes the process of direct transactions between a small number of landholders and the majority of landless labourers within a closed and isolated system of villages, and together with it patron-client relationship working inside the villages. The issue is how prevailing the state described by this model actually is, even restricting our scope to eastern India. S. Hirashima (1977) described the existence of a similar relationship in rural Pakistan in the form of the *seyp* system, which is a hereditary system of mutual-help relations between the cultivators and the artisans in a village, and is called in India *jajmani*.

Village communities in China are conjectured, as we stated earlier, to have re-emerged as informal organisations parallel to the 'production teams' of the People's Communes, in reaction of the subsistence farmers in small localities to serious outside pressure. To extend this conjecture somewhat further – in order for the pseudo-community to expand its control area beyond the range of single villages, a mutual trust relationship must have been established in advance between the local government officials (or local party cadres) and the community members. The agricultural stagnation which occurred in China in the 1970s seems to have been caused by the disappearance of such mutual trust relationships in the Chinese countryside (Ishikawa, 1983).

Recent researchers on the countries of South-East Asia, particularly those of Hayami and Kikuchi, indicate that village communities and their functions exist much more extensively than we had previously surmised.[13] Many of these researches were initiated by serious concern about the impact which the advent and diffusion of the Green Revolution might exert upon the agrarian society, particularly its class structure. Hayami and Kikuchi's case studies in the Philippines and Indonesia indicate that the serious impact of development of the market economy due to the Green Revolution on agrarian structure, such as 'bipolarisation', tended to be ameliorated and averted in the areas where community relations remain to operate. This is because such actions of the landlords or rich farmers as eviction of tenants and the arbitrary denial of the customary privileges given to the low-income group of the village (for example, the privilege to participate in the harvest labour in any fields in the villages) are avoided in these areas. However, generally in these studies, the re-evaluations of the village communities are made at the same time as the identification of tendencies in which the area dominated by community relations is becoming smaller side by side with the Green Revolution.

I think that the existence and functioning of the village community, which has as its base communal irrigation, should be studied intensively. In this connection, special attention should be paid to the question of how the village community (or customary economy) interrelates with the market economy, *both* in connection with the working of its static resource-allocation principle *and* in connection with its dynamic functions promoting commercialisation and innovation.

6 THE STUDY OF THE DEVELOPMENT OF THE MARKET ECONOMY

In the above sections I have studied the process of structural transformation in the industrialisation phase in an Asian perspective. I have seen that at least one factor determining the success or failure of industrialisaton lies in whether or not the community relations of the customary economy are allowed to play a positive role in the structural transformation process. But, by saying this, I have no intention to deny the crucial importance of the development of the market economy, or to reverse the existing attempts at economic and social reforms in any reactionary direction.

Rather I have intended to argue that when the economy is in a low-income stage with the majority of the people living at a subsistence level and leaving no appreciable personal savings, the market economy tends to be underdeveloped. Also, no market yet exists to insure the poor against unemployment and the risk of losing a minimum-subsistence income. Under these conditions, the customary economy, which ensures every member family against these risks, plays a vital role of motivating the working people to work. It is even possible for the community to generate the motive power for the market-economy type of development (Ishikawa, 1985). I also wanted to argue that the sole abundant factor of production in this stage of the economy, which is labour, is provided with substantial employment opportunities under the customary economy. For all these desirable functions, the village communities which we suppose are still in operation in many areas of Asian countries, still constitute the most natural and spontaneous organisation to perform them.

In this discussion we have not been able to discuss the functions of the customary economy in the industrial sector. It may be pointed out, however, that in a low-income development stage, there seems to be a tendency for individual enterprises, public bodies, government offices, and even universities in the modern sector, to convert themselves into units of small self-reliant communities, as far as the private lives of the employees are concerned (Ishikawa, 1985). If this conversion is handled skilfully, it can have the positive effect of providing to those working in those units the strength and vigour for the work, as it assures them and their families the security of subsistence. This effect is likely to be greater than the loss of efficiency that results from this conversion, which will admittedly eliminate competition among the working people.

It will probably take a fairly long time before the market economy will develop to an extent sufficient to take over all these roles which the customary economy is currently playing. Therefore, the functions of the village communities, as we have seen, are by no means trivial.

These arguments have some connection with the recent debates on the subject of the role of development economics and its importance as a separate sub-discipline of economics. In connection with these debates, I would only like to point out the following impressions. Development economics will have to study the characteristics of the customary economy as a particular system of resource allocation, and the mechanism in which this system actually works. This would constitute a part of study of the state of underdevelopment of the market economy, which I presume is a crucial characteristic of contemporary developing countries. The study should also include the dynamic aspects. We wish to know the process of development of the market economy, with the changes in the customary economy as an integral part. It is my sincere hope that while continuing the debate on development economics, these issues will be seriously taken up, although until now they have been by-passed.

Notes

* I wish to thank Professors K. Arrow, M. Bronfenbrenner and Y. Hayami very much for their useful comments. I also appreciate the assistance of Professor Bronfenbrenner in kindly correcting and improving my English.

1. Three kinds of studies might be referred to which relate in some way or other to the observations made in this paragraph: Hicks (1969), Moore (1966), and a series of attempts of 'New Political Economy' to explain the determination of the economic policy of the developing countries by the motivaton of the state, which is quite different from that run by Western democracies (see, for example, Lal, 1984, and Findlay, 1986).

2. Most of the discussion on the first three points is made in Ishikawa (1967) chapters 1 and 2, and Ishikawa (1975).

3. I am not assuming here the familiar Wittfogel's theory of 'hydraulic agriculture' or 'hydraulic society' (Wittfogel, 1957). Basically it is a theory explaining the agricultural society based on large-scale irrigation in the arid or semi-arid regions which can be constructed and managed only by strong, authoritarian states. In the area under monsoon, as observed by Wittfogel himself, agriculture based on small-scale irrigation that can be constructed and managed on an individual locality basis is more normal, i.e., 'hydroagriculture' in his terminology. My argument is based on the observations of these more normal conditions that exist in Asia.

4. This term may more properly be changed to 'Lewisean Growth Trap'. But the present term is used as it is well known. The following point should be kept in mind, however. Lewis's dual economic development model comprises two different types of economy; first a classical type in which the capitalist sector produces wage goods for its own consumption, and the subsistence sector supplies to the capitalist sector labour only; and secondly an Asian type in which the subsistence sector supplies to the capitalist sector both wage goods and labour (although his main discussion was with regard to the latter type). Now strictly the 'Ricardian Growth Trap' is a phenomenon specific to the former type of economy. It emerges when, due to economic growth, the demand for wage goods increases, but diminishing returns to labour in capitalist agriculture bring about the increase in the share of land rent and the decrease in the share of profit in agricultural output. The result is that the profit ratio in the industry subsector falls closer to zero. In the Asian context, the Ricardian Growth Trap should be reinterpreted as one arising as a result of interaction between the subsistence sector including agriculture and the capitalist sector, or, in short, between agriculture and industry.

5. The most explicit assessment of the situation along these lines is in Mellor (1979).

6. The employment elasticity of output in the non-agricultural sector is in both countries much less than unity.

7. The proportion of the labour force engaged in agriculture in India is estimated by a working group headed by S. Chakravarty to have remained at over 72 per cent throughout the period of planning (Dantwala, 1986, p.111). The same proportion in China was 88 per cent in 1952 and 76.1 per cent in 1978 (Research Group in China's Rural Development, 1986).

8. These two points are discussed in Ishikawa (1986).

9. I have in mind here the nature and role of wheat production in the final phase of economic development as postulated in the Staple Theory (Watkins, 1963; McCarty, 1964). Wheat production tends to have strong effects of both forward and backward linkages (as well as a final demand effect). When after the successive switching of individual export staples the economy finds yet another export staple, it becomes possible for the economy to enter into a self-sustained growth process due to these linkage effects. This is what actually happened in such colonies or settlements as the USA, Canada and Australia (see North, 1955).

   In other countries in similar colonies of settlements staples with such strong linkage effects were never found. Industrialisation of these countries had to depend upon some other separate courses from the one approximated by the Staple Theory.

10. Lele (1986). Also see a discussion on the Green Revolution in Myint (1972).

11. Most of the discussion in this section are based on Ishikawa (1975).

12. Government of Japan, Ministry of Agriculture and Forestry (1972) is particularly useful for observing this evidence.

13. To cite only a few, Hayami and Kikuchi (1981), Taylor and Wickham (1976) and Sengupta (1985).

References

Barker, R. and Herdt, R. W. (1985) *The Rice Economy of Asia* (Baltimore: Johns Hopkins University Press).

Chen, R. T. (1972) 'Rice Farming and Irrigation in Taiwan: Minor Cooperatives for Water Utilization and Water Utilization Teams', *Ajia Keizai* (Asian Economy), vol. 13, no. 3 (March), vol. 13, no. 4 (April).

Dantwala, M. L. (1986) 'Technology, Growth and Equity in Agriculture', in Mellor, J. and Desai, G. M. (eds) *Agricultural Change and Rural Poverty: Variations on a Theme by Dharm Narain* (Delhi: Oxford University Press).

Findlay, R. (1986) 'Trade, Development and the State', a paper presented at Yale University Economic Growth Center's 25th Anniversary Symposium on the State of Development Economics, Progress and Perspectives, 11–13 April.

Geertz, C. (1963) *Agricultural Involution: The Process of Ecological Change in Indonesia* (Berkeley and Los Angeles: University of California Press).

Gerschenkron, A. (1961) *Economic Backwardness in Historical Perspective* (Cambridge, Mass.: Belknap Press of Harvard University Press).

Government of Japan, Ministry of Agriculture and Forestry (1972) *1970-nen Sekai Nōringyō Sensasu: Nōgyō Shūraku Chōsa Hōkokusho* (1970 World Agricultural and Forestry Census: Report on the Survey of Agricultural Hamlets) (Tokyo: Ministry of Agriculture and Forestry).

Hayami, Y. and Kikuchi, M. (1981) *Asian Village Economy at the Crossroads* (Tokyo: University of Tokyo Press).

Hicks, J. (1969) *A Theory of Economic History* (Oxford: Oxford University Press).

Hirashima, S. (1977) 'Zamindars and Kammees in the Punjab: An Economic Analysis of Non-farm Households in the Pakistan Punjab', in Hirashima, S. (ed.) *Hired Labor in Rural Asia* (Tokyo: Institute of Developing Economies).

Ishikawa, S. (1967) *Economic Development in Asian Perspective* (Tokyo: Kinokuniya).

Ishikawa, S. (1970) *Agricultural Development Strategies in Asia: Case Studies of the Philippines and Thailand* (Manila: Asian Development Bank).

Ishikawa, S. (1975) 'Peasant Families and Agrarian Community in the Process of Economic Development', in Reynolds, L. G. (1981) (ed.) *Agriculture in Development Theory* (New Haven: Yale University Press); also in Ishikawa (1981) ch. 3.

Ishikawa, S. (1978) *Labour Absorption in Asian Agriculture: An 'Issues' Paper* (Bangkok: ILO-ARTEP (Asian Regional Team of Employment Promotion); also in Ishikawa (1981) ch. 1.

Ishikawa, S. (1981) *Essays on Technology, Employment and Institutions in Economic Development: Comparative Asian Experience* (Tokyo: Kinokuniya).

Ishikawa, S. (1983) 'Agriculture and Agrarian Problems in Economic Development in China and Japan: A Comparison', a paper presented at the 31st International Congress of Human Sciences in Asia and North Africa, Tokyo, 1–3 September.

Ishikawa, S. (1984) 'Medium- and Long-term Prospects for the Chinese Economy' in Ishikawa, S., Kojima, R. and Sekiguchi, S. (eds) *chūgoku Keizai no Chū-Chōki Tembō* (Medium- and Long-term Prospects for the Chinese Economy) (Tokyo: Nicchū Keizai Kyōkai).

Ishikawa, S. (1985) 'Socialist Economy and the Experience of China: A Perspective on Economic Reform', The Alexander Eckstein Memorial Lecture, University of Michigan Center for Chinese Studies, 18 March.

Ishikawa, S. (1986) 'Patterns and Processes of Inter-sectoral Resource Flows: Comparison of Cases in Asia', a paper presented at Yale University Economic Growth Center's 25th Anniversary Symposium on the State of Development Economics, Progress and Perspectives, 11–13 April.

Lal, D. (1984) 'The Political Economy of the Predatory State', World Bank discussion paper no. DRD 105.

Lele, V. (1986) 'Comparative Advantage and Structural Transformaton: A Review of Africa's Economic Development Experience; a paper presented at Yale University Economic Growth Center's 25th Anniversary Symposium on the State of Development Economics, Progress and Perspective, 11–13 April.

Lewis, W. A. (1954) 'Economic Development with Unlimited Supplies of Labour', *Manchester School of Economic and Social Studies*, no.22 (May).

McCarty, J. W. (1964) 'The Staple Approach to Australian Economic History', *Business Archives and History*, vol. 4 (February).

Meer, C. L. V. van den (1986) 'A Comparison of Factors Influencing Economic Development in Thailand and Indonesia 1820–1940', in Maddison, A. and Prince, G. (eds) *Economic Growth and Social Change in Indonesia 1820–1940* (Leyden: KITLV).

Mellor, J. (1979) 'The Indian Economy: Objectives, Performance and Prospects' in Mellor, J. (ed.) *India, a Rising Middle Power* (Colorado: West View Press).

Moore, B. (1966) *Social Origins of Dictatorship and Democracy: Lord and Peasant in the Making of the Modern World* (New York: Penguin Books).

Mundle, S. (1981) *Surplus Flows and Growth Imbalances: The Inter-sectoral Flow of Real Resources in India 1951–71* (New Delhi: Allied Publishers Privated Ltd).

Myint, H. (1958) 'The "Classical Theory" of International Trade and the Underdeveloped Countries', *Economic Journal*, vol. 68 (June).

Myint, H. (1972) *Southeast Asia's Economy: Development Policies in the 1970s* (Harmondsworth: Penguin Books).

North, D. C. (1955) 'Location Theory and Regional Economic Growth', *Journal of Political Economy*, vol. 63.

Research Group in China's Rural Development (1986) 'Study on Structural Change in the National Economy', *Jinji-Yanjiu* (Economic Research), vol. 5 (May).

Rudra, A. (1984) 'Local Power and Farm-level Decision-making', in Desai, M., Rudolph, S. H. and Rudra, A. (eds) *Agrarian Power and Agricultural Productivity in South Asia* (Berkeley: University of California Press).

Sengupta, N. (1985) 'Irrigation: Traditional and Modern', *Economic and Political Weekly*, Special No. 1985, pp. 20–47.

Taylor, D. C. and Wickham, T. H. (1976) *Irrigation Policy and the Management of Irrigation Systems in Southeast Asia* (Bangkok: The Agricultural
Development Council).

Watkins, M. H. (1963) 'A Staple Theory of Economic Growth', *Canadian
Journal of Economic and Political Science*, vol. 29 (May).

Wittfogel, K. A. (1957) *Oriental Despotism: A Comparative Study of Total
Power* (New Haven: Yale University Press).

7 Africa and India: what do we have to learn from each other?[1]

Amartya K. Sen

ALL SOULS COLLEGE, OXFORD AND WORLD
INSTITUTE OF DEVELOPMENT ECONOMICS
RESEARCH, HELSINKI

There is a great deal that can be learnt from the respective successes and failures of Africa and India in different fields.[2] This lecture is concerned with some of these lessons. Time will not permit more than a few of the issues being discussed. I shall concentrate on some elementary matters of life and death.

1 FAMINES AND FOOD AVAILABILITY

There are many important lessons in the Indian experience in famine prevention. Sub-Saharan Africa has been plagued by recurrent famines in recent decades, affecting many countries including Ethiopia, Somalia, Sudan, the Sahel countries (Chad, Niger, Mali, Burkina Faso, Mauritania, Senegal), and others. In contrast, despite the continuing poverty, there has been no famine in India since Independence.[3] The last one was in 1943 – the so-called 'Great Bengal Famine' in which three million people died.[4]

This contrast is often explained in terms of India's alleged success in raising food output per head dramatically, through such things as the Green Revolution. There has indeed been some rise in the per capita output of food in India, and this does certainly contrast with the experience of some parts of Africa.[5] But food availability in India has not, by any means, gone up dramatically. The growth rate of food output over the decades has been modest, and even on generous assumptions amounts to no more than a half per cent per year on average.[6]

More importantly, food output per head in India is still lower than in many sub-Saharan countries. In fact, in terms of the supply of calories per head, India still has a lower availability than a majority of the sub-Saharan economies (see Table 7.1). In particular, the per capita food availability in India, measured in terms of calories per head, is lower than many of those sub-Saharan countries that have experienced substantial famines in recent years, or are experiencing such famines now. A greater general availability of food is certainly not the reason behind India's success in famine prevention.

India's success in famine prevention is related much less to the production side of the story than to the distributional side, especially public intervention in precarious situations. This should come as no surprise if famines are not seen as being invariably related to food availability, but being caused by the inability of large sections of the population – usually belonging to a few occupation groups – to command food (see Sen, 1977, 1981).

There are many different causes that can lead to the decline of a particular occupation group's entitlement to food within the system. For example, in a market economy, increased unemployment or lower wages or higher food prices may undermine the wage-earner's ability to establish ownership over food. Similarly, a particular occupation group may be unable to command food if the product it sells suffers from a decline in demand, and if the members of the occupation group find it hard to move into other occupations rapidly enough. Famines can occur even in situations of a boom rather than a slump if some occupation groups are *relatively* left behind, when others are experiencing enhanced purchasing power. In the battle for food, the Devil takes the hindmost. If famines are analysed in terms of variations of entitlements of specific occupation groups, it can be seen that neither food output nor food supply can provide an adequate understanding of the causation of famines. In fact, many major famines have taken place without any decline in food availability per head.[7]

2 INTERVENTION AND CASH RELIEF

If famines are caused by entitlement failures, one way of averting famine is to recreate the lost food entitlements of the affected occupation groups. Creating purchasing power is an obvious and immediate way of achieving this. One of the big differences between

Table 7.1 Comparative food availability per head 1983 in sub-Saharan Africa

Country	Daily calorie supply per head
Less than India	
Ghana	1 516
Mali	1 597
Chad	1 620
Mozambique	1 668
Benin	1 907
Kenya	1 919
Zambia	1 929
Guinea	1 939
Zimbabwe	1 956
Burkina Faso	2 014
Nigeria	2 022
Cameroon	2 031
Angola	2 041
Central African Republic	2 048
Somalia	2 063
Sierra Leone	2 082
India	*2 115*
More than India	
Sudan	2 122
Zaire	2 136
Botswana	2 152
Togo	2 156
Ethiopia	2 162
Malawi	2 200
Mauritania	2 252
Niger	2 271
Tanzania	2 271
Rwanda	2 276
Uganda	2 351
Liberia	2 367
Lesotho	2 376
Burundi	2 378
Congo	2 425
Senegal	2 436
Ivory Coast	2 576

Source: *World Development Report 1986*, Table 28.

the nature of famine relief in India and that typically used in Africa is the much greater reliance on cash distribution in India. Famine relief efforts in India often take the form of paying cash wages for work. If the dispossessed find temporary employment and cash income, their ability to command food in the market is enhanced, and even if food is not brought to the famished by vehicles owned or requisitioned by the government, food does move in response to the enhanced demands. The crucial issue for government policy is to recreate the entitlement of those who have lost their means of support (for whatever reason, e.g., loss of employment connected with a drought or a flood, loss of agricultural output whether of food or of cash crops, and so on).

The failure of a person to command food in a market economy can arise from one of two different dysfunctions.[8] There is a 'pull failure' if the person loses his ability to demand food in the market, e.g., through loss of employment and the resulting loss of purchasing power. On the other hand, if there is no such change, but the person's ability to command food collapses because of supply not responding to the market demand, then this is a case of a 'response failure'. This can possibly occur as a result of market disequilibria, or monopolistic imperfections, e.g., the cornering of the market by some manipulative traders. The rationale of cash relief rests on the assumption that 'pull failure' is the main thing to worry about, and the problem of 'response failure' is secondary, if at all present.

Famine relief in most African countries has typically tended to take the form of food being actually carried over and physically handed over to the destitute.[9] Given the geographical spread, this has often involved enormous logistic problems for the government bureaucracy in getting the necessary transport vehicles and the organisational set-up to carry the food from the points of supply to the points of distribution. The underlying belief in such a strategy may be partly based on taking a rather literal view of 'food relief', or on being deeply suspicious of distributing cash, but it may also – more reasonably – relate to the fear of systematic 'response failure'.

It is certainly true that the promptness and adequacy of the market's response to effective demand will vary with the nature of the market mechanism.[10] The possible problems of passively non-responsive traders, or of actively manipulative ones, may indeed have to be carefully watched, but there is no general presumption for assuming a systematic response failure. Indeed, the Indian experience indicates that the possibility of manipulation by private traders can be systematically dealt with by regular participation of the government in trading activities, and by having a sizeable stock of foodgrains in the public sector, without insisting that the entire delivery system of food be done through bureaucratic control. It is a question of choosing the particular role of the government in re-establishing the lost food entitlements of the potential famine victims, and in the Indian context this has often taken the form of the government concentrating on remedying the 'pull failure' through cash-for-work programmes. While food-for-work has also been frequently used, and also food handouts and direct feeding, the distinctive use of cash-for-work is certainly extremely important in Indian famine evidence. Threatened famines have been averted in different parts of the country in different years using employment schemes, often paying for work in cash (e.g., in Maharashtra in 1973; also in Bihar in 1967, in West Bengal in 1979, and so on).

The reliance of famine relief systems on cash disbursements has the advantage of quickness which is particularly noteworthy in the light of the much-discussed delays in the relief system in the case of some recent African famines, e.g., in Ethiopia, Sudan and Somalia. The provision of cash income leads to giving aid to the potential famine victims immediately. It also helps in food being pulled into the famine affected region in response to market demand, supplementing food movements by the government itself.

Furthermore, the cash distribution system also helps to prevent the widely observed phenomenon of 'food counter-movement' (see Sen, 1981). Food often moves *out of* the famine-stricken regions in the case of a 'slump' famine (e.g., from the famine-affected Wollo province in Ethiopia in 1973, from famine-struck Ireland during the notorious famines of the 1840s), since the non-famine regions (namely, Addis Ababa and Asmara in the case of the Wollo famine, and England in the case of Irish famines) with greater purchasing power, tend to attract food away through the market mechanism from the famine regions (even though they have less food per capita than the non-famine regions). By providing cash income and by enhancing the purchasing power in the famine regions, food counter-movement can be resisted, along with positively pulling more food into the famine regions from elsewhere.

Emergency relief in Indian famine management has usually taken the form of temporary employment schemes. This employment can be used for improvement of productivity in the future through, say, such counter-drought measures as the digging of wells, or by contributing to the social infrastructure in the form of the making of roads. Sometimes these investments have indeed been productive. even though the success here has been very mixed.

More immediately, the requirement of working as a condition for getting a wage income has had the affect of serving as a *selection mechanism* for identifying the needy. Even though there is something rather contrary in making people do work at a time when there is deprivation of food and of calories, the selection mechanism involved in giving relief only to those who are ready to work has an important role in targeting the relief to those who need it really badly.[11]

The system of cash relief also has the advantage of supporting (and in some cases, regenerating) the infrastructure of trade and transport in the economy (through increased demand and more economic activities), with lasting benefits to the economy, rather than spending resources in setting up *ad hoc* and transitory arrangements for transport and distribution through bureaucratic channels. Furthermore, since the distribution of food to the destitute usually requires the setting up of 'relief camps', the system of direct feeding can be very disruptive to normal family life as well as to pursuing normal economic activities, e.g., cultivating land. In contrast, cash relief can be provided without making people leave their homes, and it can take the form of the potential famine victims working in particular employment projects, without disrupting family lives or indeed the continuation of other economic activities that may survive the onslaught of the threatening famine.[12]

Any decision on the balance between cash relief and food relief must, obviously, be determined on pragmatic grounds, rather than on the basis of some general principles. However, in so far as one can judge from Indian success in famine relief, the strategy of paying cash wages for employment does seem to have much to commend it.[13] In so far as cash relief has been tried in Africa, that too seems to have had a fair amount of success. This applies, for example, to an innovative 'cash for food' project sponsored by UNICEF in Ethiopia, explicitly aimed at dealing with entitlement failures of vulnerable occupation groups, leaving the problem of the 'response' to the market (Bjoerck, 1984; Kumar, 1985 and Padmini, 1985).

There have been, of course, a number of cases of very successful famine relief in Africa as well. To take one example – the relief system set up in response to drought in Botswana during 1983–85 was clearly a major success. There were a number of innovative features in that system, including complementing a feeding programme (both direct and supplementary) with an employment-based relief system, and it is estimated that this employment programme had the effect of replacing about a third of the incomes lost as a result of the drought.[14]

One of the important features in Indian famine relief policy is the efficiency of the administrative structure. There have been, of course, tales of failures and horrors as well. But these are relatively rare compared with the enormity of the task. The point is sometimes made that the lessons from the Indian experience in famine relief cannot be applied to Africa because of the limitation of its administrative structure. There are, of course, variations in the nature of the administrative structures in different countries in the world. But a simple generalisation of the kind quoted would be hard to defend. A number of African countries have had relatively successful relief programmes and food administration, including Botswana, Kenya, Tanzania, Zimbabwe, and others, with varying degrees of success.

Some of the relief programmes carried out in Africa have involved extremely elaborate administrative actions. Furthermore, a number of African countries have had interventionist programmes of highly ambitious forms in other fields. An example is the Tanzanian crash programme of expanding primary education and literacy, which – despite its difficulties and limitations – did achieve a much higher level of literacy than in, say, India (the adult literacy rate around 1980 was estimated to be 60 per cent in Tanzania as opposed to 36 per cent in India (World Bank, 1983, p. 148).

In fact, the concentration on income creation, rather than on directly feeding the destitute through government channels, is itself one reason for the administrative success of famine relief in India, since it limits the necessary activities of the government in quite a major way. The tasks involved in purchasing, acquiring or requisitioning transport vehicles so that the government can itself move foodgrains, and the organisation involved in the delivery of food to the destitute, are quite exacting. If the administrative structure is limited, that surely is a strong argument *in favour of* concentrating on remedying the main problem (namely, loss of purchasing power) that cannot be left to the private sector.

Creating income for those who have lost their sustenance through drought, flood, or unemployment caused by other factors, is not something that the private sector can be relied on to do on its own. Obviously, no private entrepreneur has any particular interest in giving jobs to destitutes on a large scale to dig wells or build roads, irrespective of private profit. On the other hand, once such employment has been created and incomes have been generated, private traders do have an incentive in meeting the newly-created market demand, with the revived destitute now being able to pay cash for the food they need. The consideration of administrative deficiencies is, in fact, an argument in *favour* a limited but active programme concentrating on what the government can do best (and possibly can do uniquely). Thus the distinction between giving the destitute the *ability* to command food, and actually feeding the destitutes, is an important one in this context.

3 FOOD SUPPLY AND FAMINE RELIEF

The magnitude of the achievement of the relief system against threatened famines in India can be appreciated by looking at the comparative picture of food production and availability in famine-threatened situations in India *vis-à-vis* those in the Sahel countries. The comparative figures are presented in Table 7.2, with 182 kg per capita per annum standing for 100. The figures cover 1966 to 1974. This period includes the threatened Bihar famine in 1967, and the threatened Maharashtra famine during 1971, 1972 and 1973. It also includes the Sahel famine of the early 1970s.

It may be noted first that the Sahel region had higher food availability than India as a whole throughout the period except for 1972. More importantly, the collapse of food production and food availability in the famine-threatened years in Bihar (1967) and in Maharashtra (1971–73) is very much sharper than in the Sahel countries. While in the Sahel the food production figures go down to the index value of 75 and 78 in 1972 and 1973 respectively, and the availability figures have the values 76 and 85 respectively for those years, the index value of food production in Bihar in the famine-threatened year of 1967 is just 35, and even the food availability index is only 45. Similarly in Maharashtra, in the famine-threatened years of 1971, 1972 and 1973, the food production figures are 51, 46 and 27 respectively, and the corresponding food availability figures are 55, 57 and 46.

Even if the food availability figures for the different Sahel countries are considered separately for 1966–74, none of the Sahel countries among the six (i.e., Chad, Mali, Mauritania, Niger, Burkina Faso, and Senegal) had as low a food availability in any year as Bihar in 1967, nor as low as Maharashtra in 1973 (Drèze, 1986, Table 2.2b).

Table 7.2 Food production and availability in famine-affected Sahel and famine-threatened India, 1966–74
(100–182 kg per capita per annum)

Year	Production				Availability			
	Sahel	India	Bihar	Maharashtra	Sahel	India	Bihar	Maharasthra
1966	113	69	63	49	105	72	62	
1967	124	72	35	62	115	73	45	
1968	126	88	75	68	118	81	85	75
1969	116	87	79	67	111	80	75	74
1970	98	90		63	93	81		68
1971	102	96		51	101	84		55
1972	75	92		46	76	84		57
1973	78	83		27	85	76		46
1974	115	88		62	120	82		73

Source: Drèze (1986). Tables 2.2a and 2.2b.

The fact that the threatened famines in India could be averted despite the much more severe food-availability situation in those famine-threatened states than in the Sahel countries during their famines is a considerable tribute to the relief system.

In interpreting the figures presented in Table 7.2, it should be noted that the availability figures in the famine-threatened states are consistently higher than the production figures. This reflects inter-state food movement in the right direction (and not 'food counter-movement'), and this was undoubtedly helped by the enhancement of the purchasing power in the famine-threatened states through employment projects and the creation of wage incomes (buttressing planned transfers of food from the central government's stocks). But it should also be noted that even after the inter-state transfers, the total food *availability* (not just *production*) in the famine-threatened states in India were extraordinarily low – much lower than in the Sahel countries.[15] Despite that, the threatened famine did not, in fact, occur, and this is because the *inter*-state redistribution of foodgrains was supplemented by an enormous *intra*-state redistribution, with the potential famine victims being able to command a higher share of the food of the state with the enhanced purchasing power generated by the relief system.[16]

In the famine relief programmes in Maharashtra, nearly five million people were being given cash wages for employment in relief schemes. With their dependents, the five million beneficiaries would have represented a very substantial section of the population indeed. Undoubtedly, this gigantic project saved many millions of people from starvation, and protected a very large number from premature mortality.

4   POLITICS AND THE NEWS MEDIA

While the form of the famine relief in India (e.g., government stocks, relief employment and cash wages) is a matter of economic decision, the success of this type of intervention depends on the alertness of the information system and speedy public response, both of which involve factors that go well beyond pure economics. I have tried to argue elsewhere that both the informational alertness and the quickness of public response are sharply enhanced by the role of the news media and the pressures generated by the opposition parties in India.[17] It is the news media that make it impossible for the governments – at the centre and at the state – to ignore a threatening famine. While on the one hand it provides a government with valuable early information (an active news media is perhaps the best 'early warning system' that a country can have), it also, on the other hand, makes it imperative for the government to take some countermeasures to the threatening famine to avoid embarrassment in public and losing credibility (and perhaps the following election). The success of the Indian anti-famine policy cannot, therefore, be discussed without going into the social and political features involved in the active roles of the news media and the opposition parties.

Many features of Indian famine relief policies do, in fact, go back to the Famine Codes formulated during the last part of the nineteenth century. Indeed, the Famine Commission of 1880 provided a very enlightened analysis of the causation of Indian famines (stressing, *inter alia*, the connection of famine mortality with the decline of purchasing power of particular occupation groups). The British Indian administration's record in famine prevention in India was not particularly praiseworthy in much of the nineteenth century and earlier, but after the Famine Code was adopted in the 1880s there was potentially an effective and efficient system of famine relief in India. Indeed, the famine relief policies pursued in India in the post-Independence period can be seen as extensions and refinements of policies that were worked out in the late nineteenth century British

India. Even the policy of employment creation at cash wages was among the means of famine relief explicitly discussed and commended in the Famine Code.

The problem with the Famine Codes is, however, a political one. When they were invoked and put into practice in an active way, famine relief was indeed easily achieved. But often the Famine Codes were invoked too late. Sometimes they were not invoked at all. For example, during the Great Bengal Famine of 1943, the Famine Code was *never* invoked.[18] The politics of colonial rule in India made this possible, since there was no powerful democratic pressure that could force the government to invoke the Famine Code despite its unwillingness to do so. This did, however, require suppressing the press, and in 1943 this was particularly easy, both because of the colonial administrative powers and because of the priorities of the Second World War. It is interesting that even when the British-Indian government was forced to intervene belatedly and very weakly (without invoking the Famine Code) in the Bengal famine of 1943, a lot of the forcing came from the powerful news coverage and the crusading editorials in the newspapers, particularly in the influential Calcutta paper, *The Statesman*.[19]

In post-Independence India, the role of the news media is, of course, much more explicitly recognised and accepted. The speed is also much greater. The crusading editorials in *The Statesman* came only in the middle of October 1943, after the famine had been raging for about five months and after the death toll in the city of Calcutta itself had risen to about 38 000 per week. The current response of Indian newpapers to threatening famine situations tends to be, of course, very much quicker and pervasive. This is, in fact, one of the positive sides of the nature of Indian democracy. In each of the threatening famines, whether in Bihar in 1967, or Maharashtra in 1971–73, or in West Bengal in 1979, the press has played a major part in making the facts known and forcing the hands of the respective state and central governments. The political pressures from opposition parties forcing the governments to act have tended to follow news reports in the press.

Africa has been, in general, less fortunate in terms of the press and the news media, and also there tends to be typically rather less political plurality within each country. The indigenous and collaborative attempts at developing a powerful news media in Africa, using aggressive journalism, has been thwarted by domestic as well as international politics. The latter includes big-power rivalries, giving neither side any noticeable inclination to support diversification of political power and the control of news. In this respect, both the 'free market' West and 'socialist' East seem to support similarly monolithic political structures in Africa (paying more attention to the loyalty of the government in question than to the respective big powers). One of the important aspects of anti-famine policy is to make the threatening famine visible by spotting early signs and by demanding counteracting actions. This has, in many ways, proved to be a harder thing to achieve in Africa than in India, and the weakness of the news media has contributed to this.

I should mention that even in India there is much scope for political pressure to achieve *more*, especially in tackling non-famine, persistent hunger. One of the extraordinary aspects of the food problem in India is that endemic hunger and malnutrition seem to be tolerated rather quietly, without pressures from newspapers or opposition parties demanding fast remedial action. The clear visibility of deaths due to starvation – even when it takes place in relatively small numbers – seems to contrast with the hidden nature of extensive endemic hunger. The former gets media attention immediately; the latter hardly ever. The suffering and the enhanced morbidity and mortality connected with widespread endemic hunger in the regular existence of the rural poor turns out to be easier to ignore as a feature of the economy than the more manifest early signs of starvation indicating a threatening famine. There is certainly very considerable opportunity in India of reaping more from enhanced alertness and involvement on the part of the news media and political opposition in dealing with endemic hunger.

However, as far as famines are concerned, the India news media and political opposition already do achieve a very great deal. In Africa there is much more scope for the press to do more in tackling the problem of famine, over and above that of regular undernourishment. The social and political problems involved in news distribution and party politics are important subjects to study for effective famine relief in Africa, and for a greater contribution to the reduction of endemic hunger both in Africa and in India.[20]

5 SEX RATIO AND THE GENDER BIAS

So far I have been dealing with a subject, namely famine prevention, in which India has achieved a fair amount, and from the experience of which something can be learnt that is of interest to Africa. There is a great deal to learn from Africa on the part of India as well. I have already referred earlier to examples of activism of some African governments, e.g., the speedy enhancement of literacy and primary education in Tanzania. The continuing low level of literacy in India indicates a governmental failure and also public apathy on the subject.[21] On matters of political determination and public activity there are many things that India can learn from a number of African countries.

However, in the rest of this paper I am going to concentrate on a problem in which the exact role of public action is hard to disentangle, and in which economic, political and cultural matters are all relevant. I refer to the problem of gender bias or sexual inequality. The nature of this bias is reflected even in such crude statistics as the so-called 'sex ratio', i.e., the number of females per males in the population.[22]

In the richer and economically more advanced countries, the number of women per 100 men in the total population tends to be around 105 or 106 (apparently because of certain biological advantages of the female in survival, especially at higher ages). In much of Asia, in sharp contrast, the number of women is substantially *lower* than the number of men in the population. India and the other countries in South Asia have among the lowest sex ratios in the world. In contrast, in Africa the number of women considerably exceeds the number of men. Though the ratio is not as high as in Europe or America, nevertheless the African ratio of 1.015 is much closer to the value in the richer, developed countries than the Asian ratio of 0.953, and the Indian one of 0.931. Even in the Third World, India lies very much at one extreme, along with Pakistan and Bangladesh, and Africa lies at the other end of the range, with a sex ratio considerably higher than unity.

In Table 7.3 the sex ratios in 1980 for different regions of the world are presented, calculated from demographic tapes provided by the United Nations. So are the estimated life expectancy ratios for 1980–85. Virtually everywhere in the world the life expectancy of the female at birth is considerably higher than that of the male. Even in China, with a very low over-all sex ratio (0.941), the life expectancy ratio is considerably higher than unity (1.034). On the other hand, in India, Pakistan and Bangladesh the life expectancy ratios are respectively 0.993, 0.961, and 0.979. These countries are altogether exceptional in having a lower expectation of life at birth of women than of men, even in the last census.

Table 7.3 Sex ratio and life expectancy ratio (female/male)

Region	Sex ratio 1980	Life expectancy ratio 1980–85
World	0.990	1.047
Western Europe	1.064	1.104
Eastern Europe	1.056	1.098
United States	1.054	1.106
Latin America	0.999	1.078
Asia	0.953	1.022
of which:		
India	0.931	0.993
Pakistan	0.929	0.961
Bangladesh	0.939	0.979
Western Asia	0.940	1.052
Eastern & South-Eastern Asia	1.008	1.066
China	0.941	1.034
Africa	1.015	1.065
of which:		
Northern Africa	0.986	1.050
Non-Northern Africa	1.024	1.071

Source: Calculated from the tapes of the United Nations' (1985) 'Estimates and Projections of Population', as assessed in 1984. Note that 'Eastern and South-Eastern Asia' excludes China and Japan.

6 MISSING WOMEN: INDIA AND CHINA

It is interesting to calculate the number of women we would expect to have in India, given the number of men, if the African sex ratio were to hold in India. At the African ratio, there would have been nearly 30 million more women in India than actually live today. This number is calculated by taking the number of Indian males, multiplying it by the sex ratio in Africa, and then comparing the derived would-have-been number of Indian women with the actual number. In Table 7.4, the percentages as well as the absolute numbers of 'missing women' are given for India, Pakistan, Bangladesh, and China. The number of 'missing women' is proportionately comparable in Pakistan and Bangladesh to that in India, even though in absolute numbers they are much smaller, namely, 3.8 million and 3.5 million respectively.

Table 7.4 Missing women (at African female-male ratio)

	Percentage	Number of women missing (millions)
India	8.4	29.9
Pakistan	8.6	3.8
Bangladesh	7.6	3.5
China	7.4	38.2

Source: Derived from Table 7.3.

In China the number of 'missing women' is even larger than in India, namely, more than 38 million, even though in percentage terms it is a little smaller than in India. However, the Chinese situation is made more tolerable by the fact that the expectation of life at birth of the female is now significantly longer than that of the male, conforming to the pattern in the rest of the world. The Chinese sex ratio, which is still very considerably below unity, can be expected to adjust correspondingly in the African direction. In India such a shift was not yet clearly observed in the last Census in 1981, even though there is some indication that the cross-over might be taking place at about this time.[23]

7 GENDER BIAS AND WOMEN'S PLACE IN PRODUCTION

It is not easy to find an agreed explanation of the lower level of gender bias in Africa compared with Asia, especially India and the Indian subcontinent. There are many economic, political and cultural factors involved in gender bias.

There are considerable differences of views as to how the observed gender bias in mortality is brought about in South Asia. There is some evidence of inequalities in the nutritional status of girls *vis-à-vis* boys, with girls more undernourished, in observations made in different parts of India and Bangladesh (see, for example, Chen, Huq and D'Souza, 1981; Sen and Sengupta, 1983; Taylor and Faruque, 1983; Hassan and Ahmad, 1984; Sen, 1984a; Agarwal, 1986; Bhuiya *et.al.* 1986). There is some historical and anthropological evidence suggesting inequalities in the division of food between boys and girls (see, for example, Miller 1981). But the empirical evidence is not by any means unambiguous, and there seem to be considerable variations, both between regions (e.g., between North and South India, on which see Pranab Bardhan 1974, 1982; Miller 1981), and also within the same region (e.g., the sharp difference between the levels of observed sex bias in nutritional status of children in Kuchli *vis-à-vis* Sahajapur, two villages close to each other in the same district of West Bengal, studied by Sen and Sengupta, 1983). There also exist some observations contrary to anti-female bias in the divisions of nutrients (on which see, for example, Wheeler, 1984; Harriss, 1986b; Kakwani, 1986: Alaka Basu, 1987).

There is also evidence in favour of the hypothesis that girls receive less health care and medical attention (see, for example, Chen, Huq and D'Souza 1981, related to Bangladesh, and Kynch and Sen, 1983; Taylor and Faruque, 1983: Das Gupta, 1987, related to different parts of India). Indeed, while studies in this field have been less plentiful (partly because of difficulties of observation as well as of interpretation of the observed data in terms of relative health needs and fulfilment), there seem to be greater agreement among writers in this field on the existence of a sex bias in the division of *health care* than on the prevalence of a sex bias in the distribution of *food*. In fact, some authors entertain the hypothesis that the inequality in question may perhaps come almost entirely from medical inequality rather than food inequality.

Much more empirical work has to be done to arrive at a more definitive picture regarding the exact mechanics underlying the unusual sex bias in mortality in India and South Asia. However, a couple of general points may be worth making here to clarify the nature and import of these debates.

First, the inequalities in observed *nutritional levels* of boys and girls (e.g., in the village surveys of Sen and Sengupta, 1983) must not be interpreted, as they sometimes have been, as clear evidence of inequalities in the division of food itself. Even if there were no discrimination in food intakes, but girls received systematically less medical attention and health care than boys, the nutritional levels of girls would tend to be lower than those of boys. The achievement of nutrition (i.e., the 'functioning' of 'being well-nourished'), in terms of any reasonable health criterion (e.g., weight for age, as in Sen and Sengupta, 1983, could be expected, under the circumstances specified, to be higher for boys than for girls, e.g., due to a higher incidence of parasitic diseases among girls. The nutritional status of a person is not the same thing as the food intake of the person. Rather, being nourished is a state of being of the person influenced by many factors of which food intake is one (undoubtedly an important one!).

Secondly, it is not at all clear that the objectives of the family heads can be best understood in terms of any intrinsic gender bias regarding *inputs* of food, health care, etc., rather than that regarding *functionings* of the people involved. That is, if the family head is more worried about the illness or undernourishment of boys than of girls, then this bias regarding desired functioning achievements will be reflected, in a *derivative* way, into biases in the division of food, health care, etc., without these latter – derived – biases being the primary concerns of the decision-takers. If the problem is seen in this light, it seems, on the one hand, a little unlikely that the instrumental biases could be, in general, confined exclusively to some inputs (e.g., health care), without applying to the others (e.g., food).

On the other hand, it may not in fact always matter precisely how this functioning-bias is brought about (the exact process will depend presumably on contingent circumstances of the respective situations), and the more basic parameter to wrestle with would be the desire for, or the tolerance of, these functioning biases involving nourishment, morbidity, mortality, and so forth.[24]

Thirdly, the desire for, or tolerance of, gender-related functioning inequalities may itself derive from other – more basic – objectives, such as economic success (the family head's economic future may depend more on the survival of boys than on the survival of girls), social standing (the 'mother of a successful son' may have more status), or some perceptions of 'legitimate' order (more favourable to the males) influenced by prevailing cultural values. If public policy is to be geared towards eliminating or reducing sex bias in the 'well-being and survival' of girls *vis-à-vis* boys, and of women *vis-à-vis* men, then we may sensibly focus attention primarily on these underlying deeper causes, rather than starting off with the exact details of the instrumental choice (e.g., divisions of food or medical facilities) in the generation of sex bias in morbidity or mortality.

The relative earning powers of men *vis-à-vis* women have received attention in some of the recent literature (see particularly Rosenzweig and Schultz, 1982; Behrman, 1986; Bardhan, 1987). From the point of view of the family head, the return to rearing boys successfully may well be greater than doing the same for girls.

But the family decisions relevant to sex bias in well-being and survival cannot be seen as being arrived at by exactly *one* adult decision-taker deciding on who gets what, since there are also problems of division of labour and benefits *among the adult members* as well, on which different adult members may each have some say. This in turn may influence the relative treatment of girls and boys also. The perpectives of the 'bargaining problem', and more generally of 'co-operative conflicts', have been invoked in the context of sexual divisions by a number of authors recently (see, for example, Manser and Brown, 1980; Sen, 1985), and while any such 'bargaining' may be largely implicit rather than explicit, the problems of combining co-operation with resolving conflicts may well be particularly relevant in understanding the nature of household equilibria.[25] In particular, it is useful to consider the nature of the 'breakdown point', related to the understanding of what each party can respectively do on its own, which is central to the formulations of the standard bargaining problem by Nash (1950) and others. It is also central to understanding the nature of the 'extended entitlements' involved in notions of legitimacy regarding who has 'contributed' how much to the family opulence and thus who 'deserves' what in the division of the jointly begotten cake.[26]

These considerations can be expected to apply to sexual divisions in all the different societies, in different parts of the world, but they may not apply in the same way given the objective differences in the circumstances of the different societies (e.g., in terms of economic roles as well as cultural values). One of the factors that may be parametrically relevant in understanding the contrast between Africa and India is the extent of female participation in the so-called 'gainful activities' – earning an outside income or producing a tangible good outside the home. Ester Boserup (1970) referred to this in the context of studying Africa, and the contrast has been used to understand the problems of Indian women and the regional differences *within* India (see, for example, Bardhan, 1974, 1982, 1984, 1987; Miller, 1981, 1982, 1984; Bennett, 1983; Bardhan, 1985, among others).[27]

It is important to recognise that outside earnings not only provide a basis for the adult heads to estimate 'rates of return' from *raising* boys and girls respectively, but they are also relevant for the nature of the freedom, power and status that *adult women* may enjoy *vis-à-vis adult men*, since they will – *inter alia* – influence 'breakdown points' as well as the perceptions of who is 'contributing' how much to the family.[28] In fact, the existence of a partly independent life outside the home also has social effects that may be no less important than the purely economic ones in terms of earnings or support. From many different points of view, the issue of outside activities may, thus, be quite a useful one to examine in trying to understand the differences in sex bias in different broadly-defined cultures.

Do the differences in the so-called 'activity rates' between India and Africa, and other such broad regions, throw any suggestive light on sex bias in well-being, and specifically on the differences in mortality and life expectancy of men and women in these different regions of the world? Indeed, the relative activity rates of women are considerably higher in Africa than in Asia, in a similar way to sex ratios and life expectancy ratios. But there are variations also *within* Africa and *within* Asia, even between the broad regions, such as South Asia (including India) and Eastern and South-Eastern Asia. Within Africa there are considerable variations between Northern Africa and the rest of Africa. In Table 7.5 these activity rates are presented for five major regions in Africa and Asia, namely, Northern Africa, Non-Northern Africa, Western Asia, Southern Asia, and East Asia and South-Eastern Asia.

As mentioned before, Southern Asia has the lowest sex ratio, closely followed by Western Asia and then Northern Africa. All these regions have sex ratios below unity. On the other side of the line we find Non-Northern Africa, and East and South-Eastern Asia.[29]

While the sex ratio reflects the overall results of *historical* differences in mortality rates over the potential lifetimes of people, the calculation of life expectancy ratios is based on *current* mortality rate for each age group. The figures for life expectancy ratios are also given in Table 7.5, revealing a slightly different ranking from the sex ratios. In particular the relative positions of Western Asia and Northern Africa are reversed, with no other difference.

It is interesting that the activity rate ratios (female activity rate divided by the male activity rate) has a ranking that is extremely similar to the female-male life expectancy ratios. In fact the rank order of the different regions are exactly the same, with only one exception (the relative positions of Southern Asia and Northern Africa are reversed). I am not sure that a great deal of importance should be attached to this close coincidence of the two sets of ratios, but it is possible to argue that the higher female activity rates (*vis-à-vis* the male rates) go with social and economic structures that are more favourable to the position of women, acting against gender bias.

Table 7.5 Gender bias in survival and female earning activity

Regions	Sex ratios 1980 (female/male)		Life expectancy ratios 1980–85 (female/male)		Activity rate ratios 1980 (female/male)	
	Values	Ranks	Values	Ranks	Values	Ranks
Non-Northern Africa	1.024	1	1.071	1	0.645	1
East and South-Eastern Asia	1.008	2	1.066	2	0.610	2
Western Asia	0.940	4	1.052	3	0.373	3
Southern Asia	0.935	5	0.989	5	0.336	4
Northern Africa	0.986	3	1.050	4	0.158	5

Notes: Calculated from the United Nations' (1985) tapes on 'Estimates and Projections of Population', as assessed in 1984, and from ILO (1986). All the countries for which data are given in these sources are covered in the aggregative picture presented in this Table. Northern Africa includes Algeria, Egypt, Libya, Sudan and Tunisia, while Non-Northern Africa includes the rest of the African countries. Western Asia includes Bahrain, Cyprus, Iraq, Israel, Jordan, Kuwait, Lebanon, Oman, Qatar, Saudi Arabia, Syria, Turkey, United Arab Emirates, Yemen and Yemen PDR. East and South-Eastern Asia includes Burma, Hong Kong, Indonesia, Kampuchea, Korea, Korean PDR, Laos PDR, Malaysia, Mongolia, Philippines, Singapore, Thailand and Vietnam (but not China). Southern Asia includes Afghanistan, Bangladesh, Bhutan, India, Iran, Nepal, Pakistan and Sri Lanka. Activity rate ratios, taken from ILO (1986), are defined in terms of the population involved in so-called 'economic' (or 'gainful') activities, as percentages of total population of each sex respectively.

It is difficult to decide what the units of analysis should be. Some influences are supposed to operate at very much the individual level, e.g., the influence on decisions of family heads on the different future earning potentials of female *vis-à-vis* male children, viewed as a purely economic calculation (see, for example, Rosenzweig and Schultz, 1982). On the other hand, if the nature of female activity and participation in earning influences the over-all standing and power of the female in the general culture, and through that affects notions of 'legitimate inequalities' and the nature of gender bias, one would not expect this to be adequately reflected in individual decisions taken in isolation.

The approach pursued here takes more the latter line than the former. This raises the question as to what the boundaries of social and cultural influences may be taken to be. The broad categorisation presented in Table 7.5 relates to a correspondingly wide view of cultural influences. For example, the distinction between Northern Africa and Non-Northern Africa has some substance at a general cultural level, especially in terms of the impact of the Middle East, but obviously overlooks a great many distinctions that would operate within each region, varying from country to country. Even if a finer classification of cultures were sought, it is not obvious that the countries would provide the best basis of study, since some of the political divisions between one country and another happen to be quite arbitrary, imposed by the nature of western political dominance and the historical division of Africa among the erstwhile colonial powers. Be that as it may, the nature of the relationships observed in Table 7.5 must be seen to be no more than something suggestive about the link between female earning activity and gender bias in survival.

There are other complications in viewing the relationships in these terms. For example, the influence of female earning activity may depend not merely on activity rates, but also on actual earnings and the nature of the jobs held.[30] Even if the activity rate has an influence, it must be only one influence among many, and the nature of the relationship studied in Table 7.5 should not make us think that somehow 'the central influence' on gender bias in survival 'must have been' unearthed.

Coming back to the question as to what India has to learn from Africa in this field, there are some things that can be more easily said than others. First of all, the distressingly low sex ratios in India contrast sharply with that of Africa in general, and particularly with Non-Northern Africa. The estimates of 'missing women' is a presentational device to bring out the orders of magnitudes of the differences involved. 30 million 'missing women' in India is a quiet statistic, which express a terrible story of remarkable inequality and relative neglect. It is the systematic excess of age-specific female mortality rate over male mortality rate in India (going all the way up to the age of the late thirties) that has led over time to the observed differences in sex ratios, and the deficit of women in the Indian population. No matter what causal analysis we eventually come up with to explain this difference, it can hardly be denied that a comparison with Africa brings out the extraordinary nature of Indian (and in general South Asian) gender bias reflected in the elementary statistics of lower female survival (see also Kynch and Sen, 1983, and Sen, 1984a).

Secondly, in so far as the activity rate contrast brings out anything, it seems to indicate that the higher female participation in earning activities in Non-Northern Africa may well be a considerable influence against some of the extreme forms of gender bias, unlike in many other parts of the Third World and especially in India and the rest of South Asia. As was mentioned earlier, this influence must be one among many,[31] even though the pattern of over-all regional contrasts is not negligible. Also, the sharp contrast *within* Africa – between Northern Africa and Non-Northern Africa – is quite consistent with a story relating activity rates to gender bias and survival (see Table 7.5). Here, too, there is a tentative lesson which would have to be taken seriously and examined.

8 CONCLUDING REMARKS

In this paper I have discussed some possible lessons that can be learnt by Africa and India from the experience of each other. As far as lessons from India are concerned, I have discussed the relative success of India in the prevention of famines since Independence, and have tried to relate it both to the nature of the relief provided (especially the use of government stocks, employment schemes and cash wages), and to the political and social systems of news distribution and of opposition pressures on the nature of government action. The contrast between India and Africa is not, of course, a clear-cut one, and considerable variations can be found within Africa in terms of success in famine prevention. As it happens, the particular lessons learnt from India appear to be consistent with these contrasts.

The enormity of India's success in famine prevention can be fully appreciated only if the precarious nature of the food availability situation in various threatened famines in India is closely examined and contrasted with actual famines in Africa, revealing the fact that the food availability situation was very often remarkably *more* adverse in India than in Africa. Even today, the Indian availability of food per capita, measured in terms of calories, is no higher than in much of Africa, and indeed considerably lower than that in many countries in sub-Saharan Africa which have experienced famines recently. The absence of famines in India is to be traced, therefore, to factors other than food availability, and in this context some of the economic, political and social factors involved in the contrast have been examined.

On the other side, I have tried to analyse the differences in gender bias in India *vis-à-vis* Africa, pointing to the excess of female mortality over male mortality rates in India compared with that in Africa.[32] The figure of 30 million 'missing women' in India (at the African sex ratio) is just a presentational device to bring out the extraordinary magnitudes involved in differential survival rates. It can scarcely be doubted that the nature of gender bias in India is remarkably sharper than in Africa in some matters of life and death, and this fact in itself is an issue to which Indian economists and other social scientists must pay attention. It is one thing for a poor, Third World country like India to have a lower sex ratio than Europe or America, but it is quite another to see how the India picture contrasts with that of Africa, which also belongs to the Third World in much the same way.

Aside from taking full note of the differences in sex ratios and life expectancy ratios and the corresponding magnitudes of 'missing women' in India, there are also some causal factors that need investigation. One particular influence that was briefly examined relates to the differences in the ratio of female and male activity rates between India, on the one hand, and Africa, on the other (especially non-Northern Africa). The original Boserup (1970) hypothesis that a lower relative involvement of the females in 'productive' or 'gainful' activities may be an influence in favour of gender bias gets some tentative confirmation on the basis of broad interregional contrasts among different parts of Asia and Africa.[33] Even the contrast between Northern Africa and Non-Northern Africa tends to confirm the hypothesis. There are perhaps some lessons to be learnt here for further research and eventual use in actual policy making, and more generally in working for political and economic change.

There are indeed a great many lessons to be learnt by India and Africa from the experiences of each other. The two issues that I have discussed here relate to crude matters of life and death. There are many subtler lessons and finer questions to be discussed. But the crude issues do have some immediate importance, since millions of lives are involved. The terrible facts of continuing famines in Africa and enormous gender bias in India command our attention. I have tried to discuss some directions in which such attention may be fruitfully channelled.

Notes

1. This is a slightly revised version of my C. N. Vakil Memorial Lecture at the Eighth World Congress of the International Economic Association, at New Delhi, in December 1986. The paper has benefited greatly from my collaborative work with Jean Drèze, and from his many fruitful ideas and suggestions. I am most grateful to Jocelyn Kynch for computational assistance and for helpful comments, and to the Leverhulme Trust for providing this research support. For helpful editorial suggestions I am indebted to Professor Kenneth Arrow and Dr. Patricia Hillebrandt.
2. This question has been addressed from different perspectives by Clay (1986), Drèze (1986), Harriss (1986a), McAlpin (1986), Sen (1986), Swaminathan (1986) and Mellor, Delgado and Blackie (1987), among others.
3. Swaminathan (1986) notes the 'irony' in the fact that even two decades ago, many predictors expected famine and hunger to intensify in India, but not in Africa (see, for example, Paddock and Paddock 1967).
4. The official estimate of famine deaths in the Bengal Famine of 1943 was 1.5 millions (see Famine Inquiry Commission, 1944). For the statistical basis of the three-million estimate, and the procedures used in deriving that figure, see Sen (1981).
5. For some general analyses of the problems of food production and security in Africa, see Kates (1981), Eicher (1982), Svedberg (1985), Glantz (1987), Ghai (1987), Mellor, Delgado and Blackie (1987), and Rukini and Eicher (1987), among others.
6. Scrutinising the composition of the food output and the distributional aspects of food consumption would seem to indicate an even more modest assessment. For example, Ramachandran (1987) finds that a detailed study of 'food consumption in rural Indian households' leads to the following conclusion: 'these three-year moving averages do not lend any support to the conclusion of increasing trends of calorie intake in any State except possibly in Gujarat in a small way . . . In any case, there is no evidence in these data of an increasing secular trend in the average calorie intake of the lowest income groups' (p. 3).
7. On the nature of the 'entitlement approach' to famine analysis see Sen (1977, 1981). For discussions of the main aspects of the entitlement approach, see Arrow (1982), Desai (1984), Solow (1984), Tilly (1985). Devereux and Hay (1986), Ravallion (1987), and Vaughan (1987) among others. On related matters, see also Reutlinger and Selowsky (1976), Taylor (1977), Alamgir (1980), Oughton (1982), Bongaarts and Cain (1982), Eicher (1982), Leibenstein (1982), Richards (1983), Appadorai (1984), Bush (1985a, 1985b), Crow (1985), Khan (1985), Ravallion (1985), Snowdon (1985), Svedberg (1985), Vaughan (1985), Chakravarty (1986), Desai (1986), Tilly (1986), among others.
8. I have discussed this distinction (and the policy issues involved) in my Elmhirst Lecture to the International Association of Agricultural Economists in 1985 (see Sen, 1986).
9. There are two distinctions here, namely, (1) payment of cash for work

versus food for work, and (2) food for work *versus* food hand-outs (or direct feeding). Many of the African famine relief efforts seem to take the form of hand-out (or feeding) and thus they differ from food for work as well as cash for work. A further possible contrast in policy composition concerns merely *selling* food in the famine region as opposed to giving it away free. On these issues see also Coate (1987).

10. See Harriss (1982). Sometimes state intervention in the structure of private trade may actually act in favour of monopolies, by suppressing 'technically illegal' competitive firms. Harriss emphasises the need to make sure that the effect of state intervention is not that of 'exacerbating what it intervenes to restrain' (p. 90). It is important to assess objectively the actual effects of indirect as well as direct intervention of the state in the pattern of trading, without being guided by political presumptions one way or the other.

11. This type of relief does not, however, help much the ill and the disabled among the needy. In fact, the employment schemes connected with famine relief are best seen as *replacements* for the lost employment and activities associated with the causation of the famine. The ill and the disabled who would have had difficulty in finding employment anyway (whether or not there is a famine) are not well protected by this mechanism. Dealing with disability calls for much finer tuning, and provides a ground for the belief that no matter how successful the employment scheme might be, in order to prevent famine deaths altogether, something else is needed to supplement payment for employment. A more comprehensive scheme of social security is of obvious relevance to this problem.

12. On these issues, see Sen (1986).

13. See particularly Jean Drèze's (1986) major study of 'famine prevention in India'. These and related issues have also been discussed by Basu (1981, 1984), Clay (1986), Harriss (1986a), McAlpin (1986), among others. See also Berg (1972), Singh (1975), Subramanian (1975), and Oughton (1982).

14. See Morgan (1985, 1986). On a general assessment of the relief programme in Botswana, see Hay, Burke and Dako (1985 on f.202).

15. The availability was much lower also than in Ethiopia during the famines of 1973 and 1974; on this see Sen (1981), pp. 92–3.

16. Drèze (1986) discusses how the enhanced purchasing power of the vulnerable groups as a result of the relief system in Maharashtra did *inter alia* have the effect of reducing the consumption of the richer sections of the population, thereby releasing a larger relative share of the total food availability for the use of the potential famine victims.

17. See Sen (1983, 1986). Ram (1986) has studied the problem in much greater depth, with extensive empirical studies of the response patterns of the Indian press.

18. The Governor of Bengal, Sir T. Rutherford, explained in a letter to the Viceroy that it was a part of a deliberate decision not to invoke the Famine Code; see document 158 in Mansergh (1973), p. 363.

19. *The Statesman* was a British-owned paper, edited by a remarkable journalist called Ian Stephens. Excellent accounts of this battle can be

found in his autobiographical writings, entitled *Monsoon Morning* and *Unmade Journey* (Stephens, 1966, 1977).

20. This is discussed in Sen (1983) and Ram (1986). See also George (1976) and Sobhan (1979, 1986) on other political aspects.

21. On this the press and the other news media in India have shown relatively little interest and involvement.

22. The sex ratio is sometimes defined as the number of females per male, and sometimes as the number of males per female. I shall use the former convention, which is the one standardly used in Indian demography.

23. It is interesting to ask whether the differences in sex ratio are primarily reflections of differences in sex-specific mortality rates, and whether differences in sex ratio at birth may play a substantial part in explaining the lower sex ratio in India compared with that elsewhere in the world. This question has been addressed effectively by Visaria (1961), demonstrating that the difference is primarily related to mortality rates rather than to the especially low birth ratios of the female *vis-à-vis* the male in India.

24. One of the variables that has received some serious attention in the context of India (see, for example, Bhatia, 1978) is the desire for *having* male children – in the sense of giving birth to them and taking special care to make them survive. This preference for having sons may, of course, in its turn be influenced by other variables, but it may be an important link in the chain, influencing the contingent choice of instrumental divisions of food, medical care, and so on. On this, See Das Gupta (1987).

25. On the relevance of this type of consideration in interpreting historical developments, see Tilly (1986).

26. The concept of 'extended entitlements' of members of the family, and its relation to both the over-all entitlements of the family, and divisions within the family, are discussed in Sen (1985). See also Sen (1984a, 1984b).

27. On related matters, see Chakravarty (1986). Ruth Dixon (1983) has provided an interesting analysis of international contrasts of women's involvement in agriculture.

28. On this, see Sen (1985). That paper also refers to various empirical micro-studies relating women's status to the nature of their work activities (such as Bhatty, 1980; Mies, 1982). It must be noted that the standard ideas of 'gainful activity' or 'productive work' are themselves extremely biased, since these activities are, in fact, parasitic on other types of activities (such as housework, cooking, rearing children, etc.) being performed. This type of perception of what is 'gainful' and what is 'productive' tends to militate against giving an appropriate value to women's work in traditional societies, and this bias may lead to severe underestimation of women's work, both inside and outside the home (on this see Beneria, 1981; Bryceson, 1985; Jain and Banerjee, 1985). While the 'perception bias' should be subjected to severe scrutiny and criticism, and this might have an important role in creating the conditions for the removal of sex bias (see Sen, 1985), nevertheless in *explaining* the interregional variations, the bias in the perspective has to be explicitly

recognised (and related to observed differences in causal influences and results).

29. It should be noted that China has not been included in the latter group.
30. The fact that this can make a difference is brought out in the context of inter-state contrasts within India, on which see Bardhan (1987). Tilly (1986) has discussed in a historical context the importance of the nature of respective types of work and rewards, and the varying social arrangements that go with them. See also Sen (1985).
31. Indeed, the combination of a lower activity rate ratio for Northern Africa than for Southern Asia and its somewhat higher sex ratio (and life expectancy ratio) indicates that there must be other factors to be looked at.
32. There are also sharp differences *within* India in the gender bias in survival, among the different states. On this see particularly Miller (1982) and Bardhan (1987). It may be noted that the only state with a higher sex ratio than unity in India is Kerala, which has, in fact, a higher sex ratio (1.032) than non-Northern Africa itself. Since Kerala is a state with a great deal of public intervention in health and education (and a much higher female literacy rate than in the rest of India), the role of such activities may well be fruitfully examined.
33. China is, however, an exception to the relationship that can be read from Table 7.5. The Chinese sex ratio is indeed very low, namely, 0.94, much the same as that of Western Asia and its life expectancy ratio is also very low (1.034), lower than for every region covered in Table 7.5 with the exception of Southern Asia. On the other hand, the activity rate ratio in China is very high (0.808), reflecting a part of the political policy of the Chinese leadership. This high activity ratio is of relatively recent origin, and the age specific activity ratio declines rather sharply in China as we move to higher ages. It has been speculated that the governmental policy of limiting the family has tended to strengthen the nature of the gender bias in survival, given the pre-existing cultural influence in favour of boys. There are many particular issues to be studied in fully appreciating the nature of the Chinese experience in this field, and I have not attempted to go into this question here.

References

Agarwal, B. (1986) 'Women, Poverty and Agricultural Growth in India', *Journal of Peasant Studies*, vol. 13.

Alamgir, M. (1980) *Famine in South Asia – Political Economy of Mass Starvation in Bangladesh* (Cambridge, Mass.: Oelgeschlager, Gunn and Hain).

Appadorai, A. (1984) 'How Moral Is South Asia's Economy? – A Review Article', *Journal of Asian Studies*, vol. 43.

Arrow, K. J. (1982) 'Why People Go Hungry', *New York Review of Books*, vol. 29 (15 July).

Arrow, K. J. and Hahn, F. (1971) *General Competitive Analysis* (San

Francisco: Holden-Day; republished, Amsterdam: North-Holland, 1979).

Bardhan, K. (1985) 'Women's Work, Welfare and Status, *Economic and Political Weekly*, vol. 20 (21–28 December).

Bardhan, P. (1974) 'On Life and Death Questions', *Economic and Political Weekly*, vol. 9 (Special Number).

Bardhan, P. (1982) 'Little Girls and Death in India', *Economic and Political Weekly*, vol. 17 (4 September).

Bardhan, P. (1984) *Land, Labour and Rural Poverty: Essays in Development Economics* (New York: Columbia University Press, and New Delhi: Oxford University Press).

Bardhan, P. (1987) 'On the Economic Geography of Sex Disparity in Child Survival in India: A Note', (Berkeley: University of California) mimeo.

Basu, A. M. (1987) 'Is Discriminaton in Food Really Necessary for Explaining Sex Differential in Childhood Mortality?' (New Delhi: National Council of Applied Economic Research) mimeo.

Basu, A., *et al.* (1986) 'Sex Bias in Intrahousehold Food Distribution: Roles of Ethnicity and Socioeconomic Characteristics', *Current Anthropology*, vol. 27.

Basu, K. (1981) 'Food for Work: Beyond Roads that Get Washed Away', *Economic and Political Weekly*, vol. 16 (3–10 January).

Basu, K. (1984) *The Less Developed Economy: A Critique of Contemporary Theory* (Oxford: Blackwell).

Behrman, J. R. (1986) 'Intrahousehold Allocation of Nutrients in Rural India: Are Boys Favoured? Do Parents Exhibit Inequality Aversion?' mimeo. *Oxford Economic Papers* (forthcoming).

Beneria, L. (1981) 'Conceptualizing the Labor Force: The Underestimation of Women's Economic Activities', in Nelson (1981).

Bennett, L. (1983) 'The Role of Women in Income Production and Intrahousehold Allocation of Resources as a Determinant of Child Health and Nutrition', mimeo, WHO/UNICEF Seminar on 'The Determinants of Infant Feeding Practices, Geneva, 5–9 December.

Berg, E. (1972) 'Famine Contained: Notes and Lessons from the Bihar Experience', *Tropical Science*, vol. 2; also in Blix *et al.* (1971).

Bhatia, B. M. (1967) *Famines in India* (Bombay: Asia Publishing House).

Bhatia, J. C. (1978) 'Ideal Number and Sex Preference of Children in India', *Journal of Family and Welfare*.

Bhatty, Z. (1980) 'Economic Role and Status of Women: A Case Study of Women in the Beedi Industry in Allahabad', ILO Working Paper.

Bhuiya, A. *et al.* (1986) 'Socio-Economic Determinants of Child Nutritional Status: Boys versus Girls', *Food and Nutrition Bulletin*, vol. 8.

Bjoerck, W. A. (1984) 'An Overview of Local Purchase of Food Commodities (LPFC)', mimeo. (Addis Ababa: UNICEF).

Blix, G., Hofvander, Y. and Vahlquist, B. (1971) *Famines: A Symposium Dealing with Nutrition and Relief Operations in Times of Disaster*.

Bongaarts, J. and Cain, M. (1982) 'Demographic Responses to Famine', in Cahill (1982).

Borton, J. (1984) 'Disaster Preparedness and Response in Botswana', mimeo. (London: Relief and Development Institute).

Boserup, E. (1970) *Women's Role in Economic Development* (London: Allen & Unwin).

Boserup, E. (1985) 'Economic and Demographic Interrelationships in Sub-Saharan Africa', *Population and Development Review*, vol. 11.

Bryceson, D. F. (1985) *Women and Technology in Developing Countries* (Santo Domingo: United Nations International Research and Training Institute for the Advancement of Women).

Burki, S. J. *et al.* (1976) *Public Works Programmes in Developing Countries: A Comparative Analysis*, World Bank Staff Paper, no. 224 (Washington, DC: World Bank).

Bush, R. (1985a) 'Briefings: Drought and Famines', *Review of African Political Economy*, vol. 33.

Bush, R. (1985b) 'Unnatural Disaster – The Politics of Famine', *Marxism Today*.

Cahill, K. M. (ed) (1982) *Famine* (Maryknoll, NY: Orbis).

Chakravarty, L. (1986) 'Poverty Studies in the Context of Agricultural Growth and Demographic Pressure (Case of Post Independence India)', mimeo. (Delhi: I.P. College).

Chaudhuri, P. (1982) 'Nutrition and Health Problems and Policies: Women and Children in India', mimeo. (University of Sussex).

Chen, L. C. (1986) 'Primary Health Care in Developing Countries: Overcoming Operational, Technical, and Social Barriers', *Lancet* (29 November).

Chen, L. C., Chowdhury, A.K.M.A. and Huffman, S.L. (1980) 'Anthropometric Assessment of Energy Protein Malnutrition and Subsequent Risk of Mortality among Preschool Aged Children', *American Journal of Clinical Nutrition*, vol. 33.

Chen, L. C., Huq, E. and D'Souza, S. (1981) 'Sex Bias in the Family Allocation of Food and Health Care in Rural Bangladesh', *Population and Development Review*, vol. 7.

Clay, E. J. (1986) 'Rural Public Works and Food-for-work: A Survey', *World Development*, vol. 14.

Coate, S. (1987) 'Cash versus Direct Food Relief', Center for Mathematical Studies in Economics and Management Science, Discussion Paper 724, Northwestern University.

Crow, B. (1985) *Famine and Plenty*, unit 24, *The Open University*.

Das Gupta, M. (1987) 'The Second Daughter: "Neglect" of Rural Children in Rural Punjab, India', mimeo. (New Delhi: National Council of Applied Economic Research).

Desai, M. (1984) 'A General Theory of Poverty', *Indian Economic Review*.

Desai, M. (1986) 'Economic Aspect of Famine', mimeo. London School of Economics.

Devereux, S. and Hay, R. (1986) *The Origins of Famine*, mimeo. (to be published) Queen Elizabeth House, Oxford.

Dixon, R. (1983) 'Land, Labour, and the Sex Composition of the Agricultural Labour Force: An International Comparison', *Development and Change*, vol. 14.

Drèze, J. (1986) 'Famine Prevention in India', WIDER conference paper (to be published in Drèze and Sen, 1987).

Drèze, J. and Sen, A. (eds) (1987) 'Hunger: Economics and Policy, World Institute of Development Economics Research (WIDER) report (to be published by Oxford University Press).

D'Souza, S. and Chen, L.C. (1980) 'Sex Differentials in Mortality in Rural Bangladesh', *Population and Development Review*, vol. 6.

Dyson, T. (1984) 'Excess Male Mortality in India', *Economic and Political Weekly*, vol. 19.

Dyson, T. and Moore, M. (1983) 'On Kinship Structure, Female Autonomy, and Demographic Behaviour in India', *Population and Development Review*, vol. 9.

Eicher, C. K. (1982) *Transforming African Agriculture* (San Francisco: The Hunger Project).

Eicher, C. K. and Baker, D. (1986) *Research on Agricultural Development in Sub-Saharan Africa: A Critical Survey* (Department of Agricultural Economics, Michigan State University, East Lansing).

El-Badry, M. A. (1981) 'Summary of Papers and Discussions', in *Population Projections: Methodology of United Nations* (New York: UN).

Famine Inquiry Commission (1944) *Report on Bengal* (New Delhi: Government of India).

Folbre, N. (1984) 'Cleaning House: New Perspectives on Household and Economic Development', mimeo. (New York: New School for Social Research).

George, S. (1976) *How the Other Half Dies: The Real Reasons for World Hunger* (Harmondsworth: Penguin Books).

Ghai, D. (1987) 'Successes and Failure in African Development: 1960–82', mimeo. OECD Development Centre.

Glantz, M. H. (ed.) (1987) *Drought and Hunger in Africa: Denying Famine a Future* (Cambridge: Cambridge University Press).

Harriss, B. (1981) *Transitional Trade and Rural Development* (New Delhi: Vikas).

Harriss, B. (1982) 'The Marketing of Foodgrains in the West African Sudano-Sahelian States: An Interpretative Review of the Literature', ICRISAT Progress Report, Patancheru, Andhra Pradesh, India.

Harriss, B. (1986a) 'Africa Post Famine', mimeo. London School of Hygiene and Tropical Medicine.

Harriss, B. (1986b) 'Intrafamily Distribution of Hunger in South Asia', WIDER conference paper (to be published in Drèze and Sen, 1987).

Harriss, B. and Watson, E. (1984) 'The Sex Ratio in South Asia', mimeo. London School of Hygiene and Tropical Medicine.

Hassan, N. and Ahmad, K. (1984) 'Intra-Family Distribution of Food in Rural Bangladesh', *Food and Nutrition Bulletin*, vol. 6.

Hay, R. W., Burke, S. and Dako, D. Y. (1986) *A Socio-Economic Assessment of Drought Relief in Botswana*, a UNICEF/UNDP/WHO report Government of Botswana, Gaborone.

Holm, J. D. and Morgan, R. D. (1985) 'Coping with Drought in Botswana An African Success', *Journal of Modern African Studies*, vol. 23.

ILO (1985) 'Women in the Labour Force', *World Labour Report*, chapter 13 vol. 2 (Geneva: ILO).

ILO (1986)*Economically Active Population Estimates and Projections, 1950–2025* (Geneva: ILO).

Jain, D. and Banerjee, N. (eds.) (1985) *Tyranny of the Household: Investigative Essays on Women's Work* (New Delhi: Vikas).

Jodha, N. S. (1985) 'Strategies to Mitigate the Impact of Drought in Africa', mimeo. ICRISAT, Patancheru, Andhra Pradesh, India.

Kakwani, N. (1986) 'Is Sex Bias Significant?' mimeo. WIDER, Helsinki.

Kates, R. W. (1980) 'Disaster Reduction: Links between Disaster and Development', in L. Berry and R. W. Kates (eds.) *Making the Most of the Least: Alternative Ways to Development* (New York : Holmes and Meier).

Kates, R. W. (1981) 'Drought Impact in the Sahelian-Sudanic Zone of West Africa: A Comparative Analysis of 1910–15 and 1968–74', mimeo. (Worcester, Mass: Clark University).

Khan, Q. M. (1985) 'A Model of Endowment-Constrained Demand for Food in an Agricultural Economy with Empirical Applications to Bangladesh', *World Development*, vol. 13.

Kumar, B. G. (1985) 'The Ethiopian Famine and Relief Measures: An Analysis and Evaluation', mimeo. (New York: UNICEF).

Kumar, B. G. (1986)'Ethiopian Famines 1973–85: A Case Study', WIDER conference paper (to be published in Drèze and Sen, 1987).

Kynch, J. (1985) 'How Many Women Are Enough? Sex Ratios and the Right to Life', *Third World Affairs 1985* (London: Third World Foundation).

Kynch, J. and Sen, A. (1983) 'Indian Women: Well-being and Survival', *Cambridge Journal of Economics*, vol. 7.

Leibenstein, H. (1982) 'Famine and Economic Development', in Cahill (1982).

McAlpin, M. B. (1986) 'Famine Relief Policy in India: Six Lessons for Africa', Working Paper 2, Center for the Comparative Study of Development, Brown University.

Manser, M. and Brown, M. (1980) 'Marriage and Household Decision-Making: A Bargaining Analysis', *International Economic Review*, vol. 21.

Mansergh, N. (ed.) (1973) *The Transfer of Power 1942–7*, vol.IV (London: HMSO).

Mazumdar, V. (1985) 'Emergence of Women's Question in India and Role of Women's Studies', mimeo. (New Delhi: Centre of Women's Development Studies.

Mellor, J. W., Delgado, C. and Blackie, M. J. (eds) (1987) *Accelerating Food Production in sub-Saharan Africa* (Baltimore: Johns Hopkins University Press).

Mies, M. (1982) *The Lace Maker of Narsapur: Indian Housewives Produce for the World Market* (London: Zed Press).

Miller, B. D. (1981) *The Endangered Sex: Neglect of Female Children in Rural North India* (Ithaca, NY: Cornell University Press).

Miller, B. D. (1982) 'Female Labour Participation and Female Seclusion in Rural India: A Regional View', *Economic Development and Cultural Change*, vol. 30.

Miller, B. D. (1984) 'Child Survival and Sex Differential in the Treatment of Children', *Medical Anthropology*, vol. 8.

Mitra, A. (1979) *Implications of Declining Sex Ratio in India's Population* (Bombay: Allied Publishers).

Morgan, R. (1985) 'The Development and Applications of a Drought Early Warning System in Botswana', *Disasters*, vol. 9.

Morgan, R. (1986) 'From Drought Relief to Post-disaster Recovery: the Case of Botswana', *Disasters*, vol. 10.

Mwaluko, E. P. (1962) 'Famine Relief in the Central Province of Tanganyika, 1961', *Tropical Agriculture*, vol. 39.

Nash, J. F. (1950) 'The Bargaining Problem', *Econometrica*, vol. 18.

Natarajan, D. (1982) *The Changes in the Sex Ratio: Census of India*, Census Centenary Monograph 6 (New Delhi: Office of the Registrar General).

Nelson, N. (1981) *African Women in the Development Process* (London: Frank Cass).

Oughton, E. (1982) 'The Maharashtrian Drought of 1970–73: An Analysis of Scarcity', *Oxford Bulletin of Economics and Statistics*, vol. 44.

Paddock, W. and Paddock, P. (1967) *Famine – 1975!* (Boston: Little, Brown).

Padmini, R. (1985) 'The Local Purchase of Food Commodities: "Cash for Food" Project, Ethiopia', mimeo. (Addis Ababa: UNICEF).

Ram, N. (1986) 'An Independent Press and Anti-Hunger Strategies', WIDER conference paper (to be published in Drèze and Sen, 1987).

Ramachandran, K. (1987) 'Food Consumption in Rural Indian Households: Has It Increased in Recent Years?' *NFI Bulletin*, vol. 8 (January).

Ravallion, M. (1985) 'The Performance of Rice Markets in Bangladesh during the 1974 Famine', *Economic Journal*, vol. 92.

Ravallion, M. (1987) *Markets and Famines* (Oxford: Clarendon Press).

Reutlinger, S. and Pellekaan, J. V. H. (1986) *Poverty and Hunger: A World Bank Policy Study* (Washington, DC: World Bank).

Reutlinger, S. and Selowsky, M. (1976) *Malnutrition and Poverty* (Baltimore: Johns Hopkins University Press).

Richards, P. (1983) 'Ecological Change and the Politics of African Land Use', *African Studies Review*, vol. 26.

Rosenzweig, M. R. and Schultz, T. P. (1982) 'Market Opportunities, Genetic Endowments, and Intrafamily Resource Distribution: Child Survival and Rural India', *American Economic Review*, vol. 72.

Rukini, M. and Eicher, C. K. (eds) (1987) *Food Security for Southern Africa* (Harare: University of Zimbabwe).

Sen, A. K. (1977) 'Starvation and Exchange Entitlements: A General Approach and Its Application to the Great Bengal Famine', *Cambridge Journal of Economics*, vol. 1.

Sen, A. K. (1981) *Poverty and Famines: An Essay on Entitlement and Deprivation* (Oxford: Clarendon Press).

Sen, A. K. (1983) 'Development: Which Way Now?', *Economic Journal*, vol. 93 (reprinted in Sen, 1984b).

Sen, A. K. (1984a) 'Family and Food: Sex Bias in Poverty', in Sen (1984b).

Sen, A. K. (1984b) *Resources, Values and Development* (Oxford: Blackwell, and Cambridge, Mass.: Harvard University Press).

Sen, A. K. (1985) 'Women, Technology and Sexual Divisions', *Trade and Development*, United Nations, vol. 6.

Sen, A. K. (1986) 'Food, Economics and Entitlements', *Lloyds Bank Review*, vol. 160.

Sen, A. K. and Sengupta, S. (1983) 'Malnutrition of Rural Children and the Sex Bias', *Economic and Political Weekly*, vol. 19 (annual number).

Singh, K. S. (1975) *The Indian Famine 1975: A Study in Crisis and Change* (New Delhi: People's Publishing House).

Snowdon, B. (1985) 'The Political Economy of the Ethiopian Famine', *National Westminster Bank Quarterly Review*, (November).

Sobhan, R. (1979) 'Politics of Food and Famine in Bangladesh', *Economic and Political Weekly*, vol. 14 (December).

Sobhan, R. (1986) 'Politics of Hunger and Entitlement', WIDER conference paper (to be published in Drèze and Sen, 1987).

Solow, R. M. (1984) 'Relative Deprivation?' *Partisan Review*, vol. 51.

Stephens, I. (1966) *Monsoon Morning* (London : Ernest Benn).

Stephens, I. (1977) *Unmade Journey* (London: Stacey International).

Subramanian, V. (1975) *Parched Earth: The Maharashtra Drought 1970–73* (New Delhi: Orient Longmans).

Svedberg, P. (1984) *Food Insecurity in Developing Countries: Causes, Trends, and Policy Options* (Geneva: UNCTAD).

Svedberg, P. (1985) 'The Economics of Food Insecurity in Developing Countries', Institute for International Economic Studies, University of Stockholm.

Swaminathan, M. S. (1986) *Sustainable Nutrition Security for Africa: Lessons from India* (San Francisco: The Hunger Project).

Taylor, C. E. and Faruque, R. (1983) *Child and Maternal Health Services in Rural India: the Narangwal Experiment* (Baltimore: Johns Hopkins University Press).

Taylor, L. (1977)'Research Directions in Income Distribution, Nutrition, and the Economics of Food', *Food Research Institute Studies*, vol. 16.

Thomas, J. W. *et al.* (1976) 'Public Works Programmes: Goals, Results, Administration, in G. Hunter, A. Bunting and A. Bottrall (eds) *Policy and Practice in Rural Development* (London: Croom Helm).

Tilly, L. A. (1985) 'Food Entitlement, Famine and Conflict', in R. I. Rotberg and T. K. Rabb, (eds), *Hunger and History* (Cambridge: Cambridge University Press).

Tilly, L. A. (1986) 'Sex and Occupation in Comparative Perspective', mimeo. (New York: New School for Social Research).

UNICEF (1987) *The State of the World's Children 1987* (New York: UNICEF).

Vaughan, M. (1985) 'Famine Analysis and Family Relations', *Past and Present*, vol. 108.

Vaughan, M. (1987) *The Story of an African Famine* (Cambridge: Cambridge University Press).

Visaria, P. (1961) *The Sex Ratio of the Population of India*, Monograph 10, Census of India 1961 (New Delhi: Office of the Registrar General).

Wheeler, E. F. (1984) 'Intra-household Food Allocation: A Review of Evidence', mimeo. London School of Hygiene and Tropical Medicine.

World Bank (1983) *World Development Report 1983* (Washington DC: The World Bank).

World Bank (1986) *World Development Report 1986* (New York: Oxford University Press for the World Bank).

8 Valedictory Address

Manmohan Singh
PLANNING COMMISSION OF INDIA

I am very grateful to Professor Kenneth Arrow for inviting me to deliver the Valedictory Address to such an august body as the World Economic Congress, attended by a galaxy of distinguished economists from all parts of the world. For your deliberations you have chosen an ancient theme which inspired the founding fathers of our discipline. The relationship between agriculture and industry in the process of economic development has a profound bearing on our understanding of the nature and causes of growth in income and wealth. At a time when the two-thirds of humanity which lives in the Third World is grappling with problems of poverty, underdevelopment and structural change, the importance of your deliberations can be hardly overemphasised.

In the post-war years, professional economists have made an immense contribution to promote a better understanding of the dynamics of social and economic change. However, there are still many unresolved puzzles, and in the last fifteen years there have been renewed doubts about the continued validity of several well-established propositions and policy prescriptions of mainstream economics. I do hope that out of these doubts and questioning will emerge a new spirit of enquiry leading to yet another creative and innovative phase in the growth of our discipline. Your deliberations thus represent an important milestone in our quest for more knowledge, knowledge which is both light bearing and fruit bearing.

I do not claim to have made an in depth scholarly analysis of the issues you have been debating this week. However, I have been involved in economic policy planning in India for nearly two decades and in this process I have gained some insights which may have some bearing on the problems of structural change, development strategies, policies and programmes which figure on your agenda. I, therefore, propose to share with you my thoughts born out of my experience in policy planning in my own country.

By the time India embarked on planned economic development in the early 1950s, both empirical analysis and theoretical work pointed to the following conclusions:

1. Meaningful solutions to the problems of underdevelopment in an over populated, predominantly agrarian society could not be found in the framework of a static occupational structure dominated by agriculture.
2. Structural change must involve a progressive diversification of the occupational structure and production structure with the secondary and tertiary sectors gaining in importance and the primary producing sectors losing their relative importance in the process of development. Since value productivity per worker in the secondary and tertiary sectors was much higher than in the primary sector, the shift in occupational structure would be associated with a rise in per capita income.
3. Although sustained industrial development must also be accompanied by some increase in agricultural production, a substantial increase in agricultural production in an over-populated country, characterised by extremely small and fragmented holdings, could come about only after a reorganisation of the production structure, made possible by reduced over-crowding of population in the agricultural sector.

In this analysis, industrialisation was to perform the role of the leading sector in the process of structural transformation. The work of authors like Allyn Young and Rosenstein-Rodan, with their emphasis on external economies and inter-sectoral linkages, reinforced the modernising role of industrialisation in the development process. In Latin America, the sharp decline in the terms of trade of the primary producing countries in the inter-war years, which has been emphasised in the writings of Raul Prebisch and H. W. Singer, contributed a great deal to weakening the case for continued specialisation in primary production derived from the classical theory of comparative advantage. However, this was not the dominant influence on Indian thinking as the latter emphasised not so much the limited international demand for primary commodities as the limitations on growth of output of agriculture in the framework of a static occupational structure. By the same logic, the work of Ragnar Nurkse which stressed the limited possibilities of growth of international trade in primary products also had no great influence on the planning of development strategy in India.

As to the pattern of industrialisation, factor endowments of a labour surplus economy and considerations of both income and employment growth would normally have led to a preference for a labour intensive pattern of industrialisation, starting from simpler consumer goods and moving gradually thereafter to intermediate and capital goods. By contrast, India decided to give priority to the development of capital goods and intermediate products at the very early stage of industrialisation. *Ex ante*, this decision could be justified for several valid reasons. First of all, consumer goods industries such as textiles and sugar had already witnessed substantial development in the pre-independence era, and it was felt that further growth along the traditional lines could not lead to the desired acceleration of the growth process. Secondly, there was a fear that too rapid an expansion of the modern factory sector in consumer goods industries would adversely affect employment in the traditional industries such as the handloom. Of course, the conflict between the income and employment objectives could be avoided if the modern consumer goods sector was sought to be developed with an eye on the export markets. However, Indian planners took a rather pessimistic view of export prospects for industrial consumer goods industries. Finally, another consideration favouring the development of an iron and steel industry and associated metallurgical industries was the availability in close proximity of the principal raw materials of these industries, so that their growth could be justified in terms of perception of long run comparative advantage.

Any review of India's industrial development must take note of the very substantial diversification of the industrial structure that has taken place in the regime of planned development. Indian industry is now able to meet 85 per cent of the total domestic demand for capital goods. There has also been a remarkable growth of industrial and managerial skills which has added very substantially to the country's absorptive capacity for investment. Subsequent events have not led to the questioning of the leading role of industrialisation in the social and economic transformation of an over-populated agricultural economy. All the same, it has to be admitted that the observed industrial growth rate which averages about 6 per cent per annum since the early 1950s cannot be considered as very impressive — more so since rapid industrialisation has been a major objective of Indian development policy since the mid-1950s.

There is by now a large mass of literature which seeks to explain this phenomenon. Most of the explanations point to the limitations and inefficiency of the import-substitution-based industrial development strategy. The coexistence of slow industrial growth, persistent balance of payments difficulties, the failure to achieve a sustained break-through in industrial exports and high costs and low quality of industrial products are undoubtedly well substantiated. However, I am convinced that simple-minded explanations which seek to categorise development strategies as import substitution and export oriented are not a very helpful guide to future policy planning. For one thing, one should not lose sight of the possibilities of converting at least some of yesterday's import substitutes into promising exports of tomorrow through a selective reform of domestic policies relating to supply of imported inputs, taxation of inputs, and introduction of a greater measure of competition in the domestic economy. In any case, at a time when prospects for the growth of international trade do not look particularly bright, and protectionist tendencies are gaining ground in the developed countries, a wholesale abandonment of the import substitution strategy cannot be lightly contemplated. Besides, in a situation in which industries have varying degrees of access to economies of scale, and face varying degrees of monopoly and divergence in conditions of external demand, there are no simple rules to operationalise equal incentive or neutral trade policies. While the case for an improved policy environment is pretty strong, as an aid to sensible policy planning it is necessary to identify factors other than import substitution *per se* which have hampered the growth of industry.

Available data show that the slowdown in India's industrial growth rate after the mid-1960s was to an extent the result of a cut back in investment which was in turn rooted in the difficulties of mobilising domestic savings on an adequate scale. As a result, capacity created in newly-established capital goods lay idle, thereby adding to costs of production. Moreover, since public investment in capital goods' industries ceased to expand until 1975, the resulting sluggishness of demand led to neglect of technological upgrading in several industries. It is well known that in an expanding economy, many industries update their technologies in the process of replacement of old equipment. This process receives a set-back if the rhythm of expansion is broken. This is precisely what happened in India during 1966–74. Thus, in part the rather poor performance of the Indian industrial sector during this period has to be attributed to factors which have

nothing to do with import substitution *per se*. With a more expansion-
ary stance of public investment policies, the over-all rate of industrial
growth rate might have been higher.

It is, however, correct to argue that heavy industry strategy demands a high degree of fiscal discipline and restraint on current
consumption which is not easy to enforce in democratic societies over
prolonged periods. Failure to enforce such discipline often leads to
inflation and to a balance of payments crisis, both of which have often
proved to be disruptive of the smooth implementation of development plans.

It is also clear that even when import substitution was associated
with high cost of production and persistent balance of payments
difficulties, some of these problems were due to lack of adequate
foresight and absence of careful planning of import substitution.
Failure to anticipate balance of payments difficulties often led to
indiscriminate imposition of import restrictions which encouraged
domestic production of even those items in which the country may
have had no long-term comparative advantage. Where such goods
entered as inputs into the production of other goods, the resulting
high cost of production constituted a major barrier to the growth of
exports of manufactures. Had there been careful planning of import
substitution, some of the observed pitfalls could have been avoided.
For example, it is well known that in several branches of capital
goods industries, the economies of scale are not of great significance
even in developed countries. Thus developing countries like India
which have low efficiency wages of skilled labour do possess the
potential to become competitive in some of these industries. Thus
their competitiveness can be substantially enhanced if these industries have access to critical raw materials and inputs at close to
international prices. This assumes that import substitution is carefully
planned, and the temptation to become self-sufficient in all inputs of
modern industry regardless of cost is resisted.

The Indian experience also suggests that the extent, duration and
form of protection and techniques of industrial regulation can have a
major effect on the inducement to reduce costs, upgrade technology
and the quality of products. Notwithstanding the conclusions of
modern neoclassical economics, protection is necessary in the initial
stages of industrialisation so as to overcome the entrepreneur's fear
of the unknown and uncertainty of the future. However, when
protection is available for an indefinite period, is not subject to a
periodic review, and competition in the domestic economy is also

weak, the incentive for efficiency may suffer. Where protection takes the form of import controls maintained indefinitely, accompanied by rationing of scarce imported raw materials on the basis of installed capacity, and by restrictions on the expansion of capacity of more efficient firms, the results will be differentiated product markets with each displaying the characteristics of a semi-monopolistic producer. By now, there is a fair amount of evidence that techniques of import control and industrial regulation adopted in India have weakened the pressure for reduction of costs.

For all these reasons, a reform of the industrial policy regulatory framework is high on the agenda of several developing countries. There is a growing realisation that modifications of past techniques of regulation could create an environment which is conducive to greater efficiency and cost reduction. And yet if the reform is not carefully planned, paying particular attention to problems of transition, it may turn out to be abortive. For example, notwithstanding the adverse effects of quotas, a wholesale replacement of import controls by tariff equivalents may not be a practical proposition in a world characterised by excess capacity and in which exporters operate on the basis of short-term marginal cost pricing. Moreover, if an economy is faced with strong inflationary pressures as well as a weak balance of payments, balance of payments considerations will themselves dictate a careful selective approach to import liberalisation. Indeed, import liberalisation is likely to run into serious economic and political difficulties if exports are not increasing fast enough and additional imports are seen as a substitute for domestic resources. Liberalisation of the import regime for input supplies can no doubt improve the competitiveness of export industries using these inputs. However, it is necessary to recognise that immediate costs of import liberalisation are clearly visible, while its beneficial effects can be felt only over a period of time and that, too, if the overall policy framework is favourable. If domestic industrial structure is not sufficiently competitive and there are barriers to expansion of more efficient firms and fiscal and monetary policies produce an explosive inflationary situation, the beneficial effects of import liberalisation in terms of increased exports or improved efficiency may well be rather limited. Some of the transitional problems, particularly the immediate balance of payments consequences of liberalisation are easier to deal with if adequate support is available in the form of international credit. However, the international credit mechanism contains strong political elements, and if donors' perceptions of what constitutes good performance and sensible policies are different from those of the recipient country, sustained international credit support cannot be relied upon to deal with various transitional problems. Thus a simple taxonomic approach to planning of economic policies which does not pay adequate attention to specific conditions and circumstances prevailing in each country is apt to be a misleading guide.

By now, there is ample evidence that in the initial stages of development, Indian planners considerably underestimated the scope for the expansion of exports of India's traditional manufactures like textiles and footwear. Excessive pessimism about export prospects led to these industries being denied opportunities for modernisation so as to compete effectively in international market. As a result, India was unable to benefit from the very substantial expansion in world trade in these products during the 1960s. More systematic attention to emerging export opportunities in the 1960s would have improved India's aggregate growth rate as well as industrial performance. The capital-output ratio would also have been lower and growth of employment faster. The balance of payments constraint would also have been less severe.

While formulating a plan, planners are no doubt required to take a view of export prospects. However, in over-centralised systems, attitudes often do not change fast enough in line with changes in objective conditions. There is thus a need to devise planning techniques and regulatory devices which have built-in flexibility to enable the economy to adjust to fast changing conditions in the world markets. In this context, it is of crucial importance to devise a macroeconomic policy framework which keeps the real effective exchange rate at a level which provides a sustained incentive for exploiting available export opportunities.

To turn to another theme, in the Indian literature there has been an intensive discussion of the relationship between agriculture and industry and several authors have made an attempt to trace the roots of India's slow industrial growth in the behaviour of India's agricultural economy. That in a country where the majority of the population depends for its livelihood on agriculture, sustained advance in agricultural incomes and productivity is crucial to the well-being of the masses, does not require any great elaboration. However, in an open economy with possibilities for both trade and import of capital, the linkages between agriculture and industry need not be very rigid.

The role of agriculture as a source of surplus for capital accumulation in early stages of development has often been emphasised in the literature on the subject. However, some recent studies of Japanese agriculture after the Meiji revolution show that the role of agriculture as a source of surplus was not as pronounced as is often believed. In any case, in countries like India, operating in the framework of a parliamentary democracy based on adult franchise, it is not easy to use the fiscal system to generate a surplus from agriculture for the development of industry. And in a world of increased mobility of international capital, there may be no particular necessity for agriculture to perform this role. Provided industrial projects are well designed and the balance of payment is so managed as to preserve the image of creditworthiness, several newly-industrialising countries should be able to tap the international capital markets for their industrial development. The possibilities in this direction have increased very substantially since the early 1970s, despite the severe overhang of the debt burden experienced by a number of middle-income countries in recent years. However, the potential of the international capital markets cannot be exploited on a large scale by developing countries if real rates of interest in these markets remain as high as they have been in the first half of the present decade.

As regards the role of agriculture as a source of demand for industrial products, the linkage gets weaker if industrial products can be exported. Certainly, countries like South Korea, Taiwan, Hong Kong and Singapore could have never industrialised if the sole source of demand came from their domestic agriculture. However, if the international trading environment becomes more protectionist, the role of domestic agriculture in generating demand for industrial products is bound to increase. Even then, there is likely to be substantial unsatisfied demand for expansion of industrial activity notably in the area of social overhead capital. Inadequate expansion of capacities in social overhead capital has to be explained more in terms of inadequate mobilisation of savings rather than a deficiency of domestic demand. For all these reasons, while recognising the importance of sustained growth of agriculture in the process of development, I am sceptical of those studies which postulate a rigid one to one relationship between agricultural growth and industrial expansion.

In the classical discussions of the relationship between agriculture and industry in the early nineteenth century, there was a great preoccupation with diminishing returns in agriculture setting a limit to the pace of industrial expansion via the terms of trade effect on the rate of industrial profits. With the rapid expansion of the production frontier in agriculture in the New World, the concern with diminishing returns in agriculture as setting a limit to the pace of industrial expansion disappeared. However, in a balance of payments constrained economy, a rise in relative price of agricultural commodities, particularly food, in relation to industrial commodities, can no doubt adversely affect the inducement to invest in industry. For this reason, technical progress in agriculture, with particular emphasis on land and capital saving innovations is of great importance for the success of the development process. However, with increased emphasis on purchased inputs for the modernisation of agriculture, the distinction between agriculture and industry ceases to be very significant. By the same logic, attempts to generate surplus from agriculture by manipulating the terms of trade may well turn out to be counter productive if in the process they affect the farmers' incentive to produce more. Remunerative farm prices, expansion of the banking facilities in rural areas and public policies (irrigation, extension, marketing support) designed to increase the return from investment in agriculture, are likely to be more successful in increasing the flow of rural savings than confiscatory taxation or manipulation of the terms of trade. At the same time it is necessary to recognise that if a sustained advance in agriculture is dependent on increased supply of such capital intensive inputs as irrigation and fertilisers, the difference in sectoral capital output ratios between agriculture and industry over time may not be as large as is sometimes assumed. Agriculture-led growth, even if a possibility, may not necessarily yield higher growth rates with given rates of investment and savings.

An important aspect of structural transformation in countries like India is that, while the share of primary sectors in national income has shown a perceptible fall, there has been no perceptible fall in the share of the working population dependent on agriculture and related activities. Contrary to earlier expectations, modern industry has failed to generate large-scale employment opportunities. This is partly a reflection of the high capital intensity of the process of industrialisation. Besides, the net addition to industrial employment has been affected because a part of additional factory employment may have been at the expense of employment in handicrafts and other traditional cottage industries. In agriculture itself, there is a pronounced tendency for a rise in the share of landless workers in the total working population. Up to a point, modernisation of agriculture through expansion of irrigation and multiple cropping can create new job opportunities in rural areas. However, at the same time one cannot lose sight of the fact that the new agricultural technologies, based on increasing application of new high-yielding varieties of seed, fertiliser and water, and which improve the profitability of capitalist farming, can unleash certain growth processes which, in the absence of corrective action on the part of the state, may lead to the impoverishment of small and marginal farmers. Thus, agricultural growth by itself is not likely to generate large-scale employment opportunities on a long-term sustainable basis, and conscious policies are needed to provide gainful employment to the landless and other new entrants to the labour force.

In this context, the growth of new employment opportunities in non-farm activities in rural areas assumes considerable importance. Well-designed programmes of rural development seeking to mobilise locally available resources can make a valuable contribution to the growth process by creating useful durable community assets which can lead to an improvement in the quality of rural life. Extension of electricity to rural areas could greatly improve both the economic viability of non-farm rural activities and the quality of rural life. However, we must resist the temptation of romantic illusions about the contribution of rural industrialisation to the solutions of basic economic problems of an over-populated country like India. For one thing, the pace of non-farm activities in rural areas will be greatly influenced by the trend of agricultural incomes and productivity. Secondly, in modern industrial processes, even where economies of scale are not of great significance, economies of agglomeration are often very important, and these place a premium on geographical concentration of industry and militate against wide-spread industrial dispersal. We may need to devise special employment programmes to deal with the transitional problems of absorbing surplus rural labour which cannot be employed productively elsewhere, but these must be seen as performing essentially a holding operation rather than being regarded as a lasting solution to the problems of unemployment and income generation.

This brings me back to the crucial role of a fast-expanding industrial economy for finding meaningful solutions to the problems of poverty and underemployment in an over-populated country such as India. Sustained growth of agricultural production and productivity is essential for an orderly management of the problems of transition, but industry has to perform the role of being the leading sector. Thus the founding fathers of the Indian planning process cannot be faulted for the essential correctness of their vision and perspective. Indeed, if one takes into account the employment characteristics of modern industry, the pace of industrial growth will need to be substantially accelerated if a significant impact is to be made on the occupational pattern. For example, one has to recognise that the difficult problems that often arise in managing a large labour force influence managements' decisions about the capital intensity of production processes both in developed and developing countries, and this is probably an irreversible trend. Besides, the growing concern with the quality of products also works in favour of more automatic production processes. Furthermore, due to the increasing saturation of market opportunities in developed countries for products such as textiles and footwear, the labour intensity of industrial exports from the developing countries in the next decade will most probably be lower than in the past. All these factors will have to be taken into account in industrial planning for the future.

The preceding argument also suggests that, at the international level, the maintenance of an open trading system which helps developing countries to expand the export of their manufactures can provide an important push to the process of structural change in the countries of the Third World. Despite problems of adjustments in selected sectors, the developing countries' over all share in the consumption of manufactures by the developed countries is still insignificant. It is thus to be sincerely hoped that the unemployment problems that have arisen in several developed countries will be resolved in a manner consistent with the preservation of a liberal trading environment. At this session of the World Economic Congress, there has been considerable discussion of agriculture and rural development, and it has also been suggested by some that in the changed environment for world trade, developing countries would do well to pay greater attention to their rural sector rather than rely on exports of manufactures. The case for paying more adequate attention to agriculture and rural development, both on grounds of equity and efficiency is no doubt very strong. But I do hope that this argument will not be used to condone the growth of discriminatory protectionism in developed countries aimed specifically at restricting the growth of manufactured exports from the Third World.

The arguments I have advanced earlier in this paper also suggest that the famous Kuznets' findings about shifts in the occupational pattern in the process of development in favour of industry may not apply with the same force in newly-developing countries. With the growing integration of national economies, services such as transport, communications and banking assume much greater importance than in a regime of enclave type development confined to specified coastal areas. With the increased importance of technology in economic processes, both in agriculture and industry, education, training and research and development expenditure also assume greater importance. One has also to reckon with the growing demand which inevitably arises in a democracy for expansion of social services like education, health and provision of other basic civic amenities. For all these reasons, the share of services may rise faster that that of secondary sectors. However, one must also recognise the limits to the sustainability of this growth process. In so far as the provision of additional services is the responsibility of the state, the contemplated expansion can be sustained only if the tax system and public enterprises are so managed as to finance both public investment and increased public consumption of social services. This also implies that the industrial sector should be charged primarily with the responsibility to generate adequate surpluses, and it should not be burdened with too many social obligations which erode its profitability.

Another important aspect of structural change to which I wish to draw attention is that in the prevailing world environment the process of structural change will demand much larger resources of capital than has been the case in the past. Even if the world trading environment remains favourable and developing countries pursue more export-oriented policies, the capital-output ratio is unlikely to be as favourable as in the past. For example, with the near saturation of market opportunities in more labour intensive products, the South Korean economy since the mid-1970s has experienced a sharp rise in capital-output ratio. Also, domestically, the inevitable growth of urbanisation and the increasing substitution of commercial energy for non-commercial energy will also lead to higher capital intensity. Even in agriculture, as I have argued earlier, increased emphasis on irrigation and fertilisers is likely to be associated with higher capital intensity than in the past. And if developing countries are to sustain reasonable growth rates, they will need to provide adequate institutional mechanisms to sustain the incentive for increased savings. In particular, conscious efforts will have to be made to resist aping the life styles of post-industrial societies, for this will pre-empt scarce national resources for low priority activities rather than being used for meeting the basic human needs of the people. Without extensive application of modern science and technology, developing countries are unlikely to break the vicious circle of low productivity, poverty and stagnation. However, unless application of modern technology in economic processes is combined with a Gandhian value system, the developing countries may not successfully complete the transition to a state of self-sustained growth.

The rising capital intensity of economic processes has also implications for the functioning of the international economic system. In so far as improved access to the markets of developed countries for labour intensive products can help to reduce the capital intensity of production, the commitment to an open trading system with a carefully designed safeguard mechanism could be of immense assistance to the Third World in its war against poverty and underdevelopment. The creation of a global economic environment which encourages increased flows of financial resources from developed to developing countries is also of great significance. The present set-up where the world's richest country, the USA, is sucking in a disproportionately large share of surplus savings of countries like Japan, is clearly far removed from the ideal we seek. Clearly, development cannot simply be imported, and the major responsibility for a successful transformation of their economies must rest with the developing countries themselves. However, in an increasingly interdependent world, one should not minimise the importance of an orderly and equitable management of global interdependence for banishing poverty, ignorance and disease from our planet. Thus the prospects for the domestic transformation of the economies of the Third World are linked to the prospects for restructuring of international economic relations, particularly on the willingness of the developed countries to undertake necessary supporting structural adjustments in their own economies.

Part II

The Historical Perspective

Introduction to Part II

Paolo Sylos-Labini
UNIVERSITÀ DEGLI STUDI DI ROMA

Of the six papers presented in this part of the volume, three are concerned with the history of economic thought, two with specific historical experiences (Spain and Italy) and one with a neglected aspect of the long-run evolution of both developed and developing countries, that is, the role of market and non-market activities.

The first point which emerged from the papers and from the discussion was concerned with the process of over-urbanisation and the growing unemployment in the cities. It appears that, to try and slow down such a process, the integration between agriculture and industry, bridging the territory between them, is to be systematically promoted. The basic question is whether such a development is economically viable, and whether it can take place at a sufficiently high rate.

To answer this question the history of economic thought and that of the experiences of specific countries now advanced can be of great help. Three centuries ago, in the times of William Petty, rather than the dichotomy between agriculture and industry we find a dichotomy between countryside and town; and whereas in the latter handicraft and commerce were the exclusive economic activities, in the countryside not only agricultural goods but also, in rudimentary forms, certain goods that we now call industrial were produced – textiles, shoes, furniture and the like. On the other hand, food was produced more for self-consumption than for the market, in a way similar to what is still now the case in many Third World countries. In advanced countries, when the factory system made its appearance, the cottage industry operating in rural areas entered a period of crisis and, through different stages, was supplanted by modern industries; these, in a sense, can be viewed as an outgrowth of agriculture, precisely as, in our time, an increasing number of services can be seen as an outgrowth of industry, both developments being the result of a historical process of division of labour.

For a long period in advanced countries mass production and

153

economies of scale were of increasing importance, and gave rise to a process of concentration of productive units, especially in industry and in certain services. Recently it seems that this process has slowed down, for a variety of reasons, although scale economies and large companies are declining in relative, not in absolute terms. Among the reasons of the new trend we find the new technologies, that are creating new space for small and vigorously dynamic firms. In general, technological innovations and productivity increases, rather than capital accumulation *per se*, are essential to economic development both for small and large firms. The new opportunities opened up to small firms as well as to the self-employed can make an increasing dispersal of industrial activities in rural areas convenient, thus slowing down the over-urbanisation process and allowing a considerable saving in the costs incident to that process (new houses and infrastructure, not to mention pollution and traffic problems). An increasing dispersal of industrial activities is in fact occurring in several advanced countries, such as Spain and Italy. The strategy to be pursued in a country like India to speed up this process must be very different; in fact, in India the cottage industry is still important, and the problem is to avoid its destruction and to facilitate its transformation and modernisation; at the same time, the problem is to help the development of modern and dynamic small firms, within and outside agriculture. In any case today small firms are completely different from those of the past; and agricultural development, that can be speeded up by technological innovations, especially those of biotechnology, meets with entirely different problems. Yet we have to consider not only technology, natural resources and human resources that are conditioned first of all by education, but also, and as a preliminary, the institutional factors, such as property relations and tenancy contracts. This lesson of the classical economists, especially of Adam Smith, is still valid, particularly in India.

The important aim is to try to reach a dynamic balance between agriculture and industry in general and, within each sector, between large and small firms. And although state intervention should not be pushed too far, it can be necessary for the instalment and the growth of large firms, as well as to promote the growth of small firms, not so much by supplying financial subsidies but, rather, by providing real services, such as specific infrastructures, marketing facilities, technical and managerial assistance. The work of early economists such as François Quesnay suggests that to rely heavily on protectionist strategies to speed up industrialisation can be a very wrong course of action, particularly if it is based on measures intended to push the price of food down artificially.

The fundamental question is how to profit from the lessons to be drawn from the experience of advanced countries when we deal with an entirely different context such as that of India.

9 William Petty and the Conceptual Framework for the Analysis of Economic Development

Alessandro Roncaglia[1]
UNIVERSITÀ DEGLI STUDI DI ROMA

1 INTRODUCTION

Economic analysis establishes relations connecting theoretical variables, corresponding to abstract concepts. These concepts constitute a simplified representation of the complex web of economic events and thus provide a systematic framework for economic analysis. However, after continued use economists tend to take these concepts for granted, as if they were not creations of the mind, but entities with an independent existence.

Abstract concepts useful at a specific stage of history, for the analysis of specific issues, may lose validity over time owing to changes in the economy and in the relevant issues. This is a vital aspect of economic research, and one which is very rarely gone into. The question must be examined in a historical perspective. This means not so much a historical account of past solutions, but an appraisal of the developments leading up to the current specification of the analytical issue.

In such a perspective, this paper discusses the historical and conceptual prehistory of the agriculture-industry dichotomy.

For economists, the balance to be struck between these two sectors may appear to present a perpetually recurring problem, and one which is at the heart of any analysis of economic development. It should therefore be stressed that the approach to this problem is now generally based on specific past developments in the division of labour and on corresponding developments in the conceptualisation of the economic process. While these developments took place over a

157

considerable period, this paper concentrates on William Petty's times (seventeenth century England) and on his contribution to the origins of classical political economy. In section 2 we will touch on a number of aspects of the pre-eighteenth century economic structure which still obscured the emerging agriculture-industry dichotomy, and in section 3 we will discuss the limited degree to which such a dichotomy was perceived by William Petty and a few of his contemporaries.

The use of this dichotomy in economic analysis presupposes not only a certain degree of economic development, but also the elaboration of a method and a conceptual framework concerning, e.g., the role of the state, the market and the division of labour. These factors thus correspond to the institutional basis of an economy in which agriculture and industry can be conceived as two distinct parts of the economy, and in which the balance between them is central for economic development. In our historical analysis, therefore, we will consider:

(i) Petty's method (political arithmetic, or political anatomy) (section 4);
(ii) his conceptualisation of prices (section 5);
(iii) the relationship between the notion of the economic system and the nation-state (section 6).

Then in section 7 we will examine Petty's analysis of the division of labour, and some specifications paving the way for the application of that concept to the industry-agriculture dichotomy. Finally, section 8 will list some questions raised by this foray into the history of economic thought and stress the specific historical nature of any economic problems, including those regarding the balance between agriculture and industry.

2 THE SLOW EMERGENCE OF THE AGRICULTURE-INDUSTRY DICHOTOMY

The representation of the economic system as a process centred on the dichotomy between agriculture and manufacture (or rather between the productive and the sterile sectors) is the work of the Physiocrats around the middle of the eighteenth century. Writing in the 1730s, Richard Cantillon (1964) foreshadowed this concept; but artisans were put on a par with merchants, and hence were treated as a secondary factor in a society clearly based on the peasant-landlord and town-countryside dichotomies.

Writing at an earlier date, William Petty (1623–87) did not even make any clear-cut subdivisions of the economy into sectors (as we will see in section 3). To understand this failure, we may recall Petty's own experience as a capitalist-landlord. Around 1670 Petty started a number of 'improvements' in his holdings (in County Kerry in Ireland) with the object of increasing the surplus obtained from them. Thus he established iron and copper works as well as fishing operations, all of which were designed to be vertically integrated, from the mine to the blast-furnace in the first case, and from the sewing of the finishing nets to the building and operation of the boats in the second case (Fitzmaurice, 1895, pp. 149–50).

This suggests that, in Petty's times, the development of the division of labour was not necessarily accompanied by the separation of commodity production into distinct sectors, each containing productive units distinct from those in other sectors. Various considerations help, together with the rudimentary inter-firm division of labour, in explaining this situation.

First, if the economy is regarded as being subdivided into sectors of activity, the implication is that a sufficient degree of integration of the economy has been achieved, while on the contrary, near self-sufficiency of small areas was the rule at Petty's time. Hill (1975, pp. 245–50) attributes mainly to high transportation costs the subdivision of England into 'self-contained economic regions', up to the 'canal era of the seventeenth-sixties'. Heckscher (1955, pp. 45–109) stresses that transportation costs were artificially increased by a large number of tolls. As a result, as Braudel (1981, p. 23) notes, 'around 1600, corn by land does not travel further than ten miles, generally no more than five; . . . wool and cloth no more than twenty to forty miles . . .' As a consequence, long-distance trade, including trade between different regions of the same country, were only in expensive products (Heckscher, 1955, p. 192), unless cheap water transport was available. In other words, the first steps in market-oriented production mainly covered luxury goods, and not the 'productive core' of the economy.

Secondly, the guild system (which in England was extended in 1563 to the whole nation by the Statute of Artificers) provided an institutional framework in which the interests of each 'trade' conflicted with those of the others, which made it difficult to recognise a clearly-defined category embracing only 'manufacturing'. Many historians (e.g., Hill, 1975, p. 249) point to the prevalence of trade over class interests right down to the end of the eighteenth century, e.g., in the clash between the wool and cotton trades.

Thirdly, the town-countryside dualism cannot be identified with the manufacturing-agriculture dichotomy. As Heckscher (1955, p. 204) stresses:

> spinning, weaving and dyeing were practised very extensively among the peasantry for their own requirements in all countries well into the 19th century, within the framework of a more or less closed household economy . . . Even that kind of industrial activity which was based on exchange was combined . . . with agriculture, and for obvious reasons . . . – plenty of spare time for the rural population during the winter months.

The clash between town and countryside, in this respect, was due rather to the fact that the guild system dominated town manufactures, while, on the whole, the primitive rural manufacturing activities escaped attempts to impose regulations, especially those on the labour process and those governing standards of quality. Thus, the cheaper and substandard goods produced in the countryside did not generally come into direct competition with town handicrafts; rather, a large portion of the rudimentary countryside handicrafts went to satisfy the needs of the immediate neighbourhood – so that the dichotomy between unregulated countryside handicrafts and guilds corresponds, at least in part, to the contrast between 'natural' and market-oriented activities, a distinction which was still very important at the time. (It will be recalled that this antithesis is used by Kula in 1970 as the basis for his model of the feudal economy, and by Lewis, 1954, in his model of developing economies).

Parallel to this, a fourth factor is the by no means clear-cut distinction between wage labour in unregulated manufacturing and independent peasant activity. Poor peasants, and especially their wives and children, were often forced to engage in by-earning in the clothing industry (cf. Heckscher, 1955, p. 204; Hill, 1975, p. 83). This pressure was obviously intensified by the wide seasonal variations in the demand for agricultural labour.

In short, it can be argued that in the situation in the seventeenth century, there were subdivisions of the economic system which were more important than the agriculture-industry dichotomy. These subdivisions range from territorial categories to the town-countryside dichotomy, the distinction between different guilds, the division between guild and non-guild activities and between 'natural' and market-oriented activities. These subdivisions were in fact much more generally utilised by writers on economic issues at the time than the agricultural-industry dichotomy.

3 'PETTY'S LAW' CANNOT BE ATTRIBUTED TO PETTY

Two notes of caution must be sounded at this point. First, we have suggested that the concept of industry and agriculture as two separate sectors presupposes a certain stage of economic development, and that such a stage was not fully reached at Petty's time. But the position is somewhat more complex. Some factors may be present in economic life without dominating it. Moreover, in conceptualising economic life, different economists may stress different aspects of it. Nobody could deny the existence, in Petty's days (or indeed much earlier), of the exchange between agricultural and manufactured products brought to the market by separate, independent producers. But, while economic historians are generally eager to go further and further back and discover instances of the organisational forms of modern economies, thus tending to superimpose on the past their conceptual categories, we should also be aware of the potential importance of more traditional forms of organisation: e.g., the largely self-sufficient, vertically integrated productive units, which marketed only their surplus product, in Petty's time. In these circumstances, the problem of the interrelations between autonomous sectors of commodity production was not so visible as it is now.

The second note of caution concerns the attitude of pre-eighteenth century writers. Of course they used terms such as husbandry (or agriculture) and manufacture (see, e.g., the passage in Petty quoted below in section 6). At the same time, we should recall that the term 'industry' usually meant production in general, or human productive capacity and effort; and the term 'trade', which was commonly used at the time in the titles of pamphlets on economic issues (the stream of *Discourses on Trade*) was currently meant to refer to the whole of market-oriented productive activities. But the terms husbandry and manufacture were not used to define the two sectors of commodity production which, together with the services sector, reflect the current three-way split of the economy.

To understand this, one has but to look at the early statistical examinations of the English economy (i.e., the various essays in political arithmetic), such as those by William Petty and his followers, King and Davenant. In fact, neither of these men, both writing in 1695, refers to manufactures as a specific category of economic activity (see Thirsk and Cooper, 1972, pp. 770ff).

As for William Petty, some misunderstandings may be due to the well-known law attributed to him by Colin Clark (1951, pp. 395–7). According to that economist, 'Petty's Law' concerns 'the movement of working population from agriculture to manufacture and from manufacture to commerce and services'. This 'brilliant and entirely correct generalization' is attributed to Petty on the basis of the following quote:

> There is much more to be gained by *Manufacture* than *Husbandry*; and by *Merchandise* than *Manufacture* . . . Now here we may take notice that, as Trades and Curious Arts increase, so the Trade of Husbandry will decrease, or else the wages of Husbandmen must rise and consequently the Rents of Lands must fall.

Clark does not give the reference for this passage, only noting that Petty was writing in 1691. But Petty died in fact in 1687. Fortunately the passage can be tracked down in *Political Arithmetick*, written around 1671–72 and published posthumously in 1691. However, the first and second parts of the passage come from two different sections of the work (Petty, 1963, pp. 256, 267), and cannot be combined into a statement on the evolution of the internal structure of the economy. For instance, 'Trade and Curious Arts' in the second passage cannot be considered as exactly equivalent to 'Manufacture' and 'Merchandise' in the first passage, which shows that such terms were far from constituting precisely defined analytical categories. In fact, like King and Davenant after him, Petty does not use consistent subdivisions of the economy into well-defined sectors.

An analogous conclusion can be reached by examining the economic pamphlets of the period. For instance, in the eight pamphlets published between 1621 and 1701 collected by McCulloch in 1856 in *Early English Tracts on Commerce* (including writings by Mun, Roberts, Fortrey, Petyt, North), the nearest thing to a subdivision of productive activity into sectors is the classification into 'naturall' and 'artificial' riches or wealth adopted, e.g., by Thomas Mun in the 1630s (McCulloch, 1952, pp. 191ff), and by Roberts in 1641 (McCulloch, 1952, pp. 60ff). However, this distinction, which also provides the conceptual foundation for Colbertism in seventeenth century France, can be considered as being more closely linked to the ancient concept condensed in the formula 'labour is the father and active principle of wealth, as lands are the mother' (Petty, 1963, p. 68) than with the modern agriculture-industry dichotomy. The two dichotomies have certain points in common. So much so that the first can be considered as an immediate forerunner of the second. But the two cannot be identified, especially as regards their analytical utilisation.

We are therefore justified in concluding that the use of terms such as husbandry and manufacture on the part of pre-eighteenth century economists does not imply a full recognition of the now current industry-agriculture antithesis.

4 POLITICAL ANATOMY AND THE ECONOMIC SYSTEM

The agriculture-industry dichotomy, then, was not a prominent characteristic of the economy in Petty's days, nor was it a clearly recognised analytical tool in his writings and in those of his contemporaries. But it is clearly a basic feature of our understanding of the economies in which we live. However, parallel to the economic developments which were then paving the way for this dichotomy, there were certain developments in economic thinking which constitute the prerequisites for the *analytical* use of the industry-agriculture dichotomy. Such prerequisites cover both the method of economic analysis and its conceptual framework. These prerequisites are often lost sight of in specific problems related to the agriculture-industry dichotomy, though – as we will see in section 8 – they may raise important questions. Because of their importance – both as regards method and conceptual framework – we will concentrate on Petty's contributions (drawing on my earlier research on his economics – Roncaglia, 1985).

The dominant economic issues in the sixteenth and early seventeenth century were usury, coinage as part of government financing policy, and state intervention in foreign trade. The 'just price' was still a live issue. The treatment of specific economic problems was not usually related to a full-fledged conception of the economy from which a reply to each specific problem could be derived. Rather, moral considerations provided the stuff of largely normative discourses on economic issues. Outstanding examples of such an approach can be found in the writings of Thomas Wilson (1963) and

Samuel Von Pufendorf (1934), originally published in 1572 and 1688 respectively.

From this point of view, Petty's writings represent a turning point parallel to the one taking place, round about the same time, in other fields of research as well. There are two bases on which Petty's methodology is built. The first is Bacon's inductive method, a fusion of empiricism and rationalism which superseded both the Renaissance tradition of pure empiricism (technicians and alchemists), and the syllogistic-deductive method of the Aristotelian tradition. The second factor is the stress on the measurement of quantities as the object of enquiry (Hobbes's *logica sive computatio*) reflecting the mechanical conception of man and of the world, put forward in particular by that philosopher. This second factor is decisive for the interpretation of Petty's 'Political Arithmetick' ('the course . . . to express my self in terms of Number, Weight and Measure', Petty, 1963, p. 244) as political economy, i.e., as an *interpretation* of economic life rather than as economic statistics, i.e., the simple recording of the most disparate aspects of economic life. The search for precise quantitative relationships between the phenomena under study reflects the idea (advanced by Hobbes in particular) that knowledge of the world requires the construction of arithmetic or geometric models. This idea in turn can be related to a kind of metaphysical view, according to which quantitative relations constitute the inner structure of the world: as Galileo said (in *Il Saggiatore*, 1623), 'this great book which lies open before our eyes – I mean the Universe – . . . is written in mathematical characters'.

Petty's method, Political Arithmetic, is meant to discover quantitative relations *written into* the economy. The economy is thus conceived as a machine, or more precisely, as a 'body Politick', with a traditional comparison with the human body (a comparison which goes back to Menenius Agrippa, but here we should recall that the human body is also conceived as endowed with a mathematical-geometrical structure). Hence Petty's favourite term for his method, Political Anatomy.

In order to understand the revolutionary impact on the birth of the new approach to the social sciences of the conception of the economy as a machine endowed with inner quantitative 'laws' and the role of the new developments in the sciences of nature, we must revert to the situation in the seventeenth century. 'Fires . . ., unstable prices, arbitrary taxation, famine, pestilence, sudden and early death' were not only the source of a 'profound emotional instability of our forefathers' (Hill, 1975, p. 110), they were also obstacles to the notion of 'regularities' embedded in social life. In the economic sphere, the search for riches was not channelled into production in a competitive environment, but into the battle to obtain royal favour or into outright plunder in foreign trade (buccaneering, the slave trade, or the wealth extracted from India). In Hill's words (1975, p. 188), 'in the heroic early days of predatory capitalism, there was a speculative windfall element in many forms of economic activity'. In such a situation, Gramsci's (1975, p. 1350) observation seems appropriate: 'there was a period in which "science" could not exist . . . because the preconditions which create those particular "regularities" or "automatisms" whose study provides the origin of scientific research were not present'. We can thus appreciate Petty's systematic and searching mind imposing on an unruly economic process the idea of a hidden quantitative structure – thus, in a sense, identifying the seeds of the future rather than the characteristics of his own time. This is apparent in Petty's development of the notion of the market and of natural price, which we will consider in the following section.

5 'POLITICAL' AND 'NATURAL' PRICES

A basic prerequisite for treating agriculture and industry as separate sectors is the development of market exchange, e.g., in the form of mediation between the different sectors. Market exchange, in turn, brings up the problem of prices.

In this respect too, Petty provides a basic contribution to the development of the conceptual framework without which any theoretical analysis of prices would be impossible. This aspect is generally ignored by economists, but it is a fundamental one. Indeed, theoretical concepts such as 'commodity' or 'market' or 'natural price', which are accepted as if they were inherent to economic analysis, are the result of a complex process of abstraction.

Each individual act of exchange concerns a specific individual object, exchanged at a specific time and place, at a specific price; but the myriad of individual objects and exchanges can be grouped into sets (such as the 'market for diamonds') because of the similarities between the particular objects collected in the category of 'diamonds', and because of the links among the various individual exchanges of particular diamonds. These links are generally provided by the fact that a specific group of traders is involved (e.g., jewellers) each of them keen on observing the behaviour of the other members of the group and ready to adjust his decisions accordingly. As Braudel (1981, p. 126) notes, markets are 'coherent commercial areas'. Petty provides a beautiful example of this kind of consideration in his *Dialogue of Diamonds* (in Petty, 1963, pp. 624–30), where an inexperienced buyer, unable to decide on whether to buy a specific diamond offered to him at a specific price, is referred by an expert to the 'price' prevailing in the 'market for diamonds'.

Once the concepts of market and commodity are arrived at, the next step is to formulate an abstract concept of price. Here Petty proposes a three-way split: the actual market price, determined by 'contingent' factors as well as 'permanent' ones; the 'political' price and the 'natural' price. These latter two categories are grouped together as the 'natural price' by later classical economists such as Smith and Ricardo. The difference which Petty establishes among them is linked with the difference between 'necessary' production costs, depending on the state of technical knowledge and on the subsistence costs for the workers, and 'political' costs, which also take into account social costs, such as hidden unemployment. Petty regards these costs as waste, since their existence implies that actual production is lower than the potential level.

The disappearance of the notion of 'political price' in the subsequent classical literature might be connected with the new role of competition among producers of the same commodity, which brings the price down to the level of 'necessary' costs (including the general profit rate) and drives out producers unable (or unwilling) to stay within the cost limits set by the prevailing technology. But in cases where the technology available to private producers incorporates 'social' costs, Petty's distinction would still be useful. And it was certainly important in a period in which feudal traditions (and especially the guild system) constituted a very powerful barrier to competition.

We need not consider here Petty's theory of value, but would recall that it can be interpreted as a theory relating prices to physical costs of production. Once again, such a theory does not take into account productive interrelations, which lead into a circularity problem. Such a problem has only recently been solved, on classical lines, by Piero Sraffa (1960).

Hence, as far as the issue of exchange ratios between different sectors of the economy is concerned, Petty's contribution lies once again in his pioneering work on the conceptual framework which, with slight modifications, is still used as the (often unconscious) basis for analysis. However, Petty offers very little in terms of analytical models, owing to the absence of two key elements: the notion of productive interrelations between sectors, and the role of competition connecting the determination of product prices in the different sectors through the tendency of profits to settle at a uniform rate throughout the economic system. But clearly the analytical recognition of these two elements required a parallel growth in their role in economic reality.

6   THE NOTION OF THE ECONOMIC SYSTEM AND THE NATION-STATE

The systemic nature of Petty's economic enquiry is not to be found in a fully-fledged analytical model of productive interrelations, but emerges clearly in his conceptual framework. In this respect, stress must be laid on Petty's choice of the 'body politick' as the object of inquiry.

The 'body politick' (which coincides with the economic system) is identified with the nation-state. This means that, out of the complex network of social interdependencies (economic and political), certain relations are singled out as being of the greatest importance: those among the citizens of a state, and those between the sovereign and his subjects. This represents a doubly significant decision about the level of aggregation. A lower level of aggregation is rejected because the relations among the citizens of a single state, and between the sovereign and his subjects, are considered as fundamental as regards, for example, the relations between the inhabitants of a village or between a justice of the peace (or any other local government official) and those under his jurisdiction. A higher level of aggregation is rejected because the system of international relations among citizens of the various states is regarded as being subordinate to the interrelations among the states themselves.

The parallel between the economic system and the human body – between political anatomy and human anatomy – is also utilised by Petty to express his ideas on wealth and money. He shifts away from the traditional parallel between money and blood (which expressed the concern of sixteenth and seventeenth century economic writers for precious metals, considered the foundations of national wealth), and compares money to 'the Fat of the Body-politick, whereof too much doth as often hinder its Agility, as too little makes it sick', while 'the blood and nutritive juices of the Body Politick' are 'the product of Husbandry and Manufacture' (Petty, 1963, pp. 28, 112).

According to Petty (1963, p. 113), scarcity of money need not be tackled by favouring the influx of precious metals into the country: 'Nor were it hard to substitute in the place of Money (were a competency of it wanting) what should be equivalent onto it'. His favourite proposal in this respect is the creation of a land bank. Petty (1977, p. 47) stresses that, 'if men were excellently Versed in accompts, Money were not necessary at all and many places as Barbados etc have made shift without it and so they do in Banks'.

With reference to the identification of the 'body politick' with the nation-state, it should be recalled that, shortly before Petty wrote, Machiavelli had advanced a unified conception of the nation-state, giving particular attention to the problem of the political unification of the city and the countryside. In a sense, it can also be said that the limits of Petty's notion of the economic system parallel the limits of Machiavelli's concept of the nation-state. Gramsci (1971, p. 43) notes that 'Machiavelli was only able to express his programme and his tendency to relate city to countryside in military terms'. Something similar can be said for Petty: he perceives that the network of economic relations is subordinate to a unique political authority, but seems unaware of the 'input-output' interrelations connecting the various productive activities, none of which could survive without the others. Machiavelli does not realise the interrelationship between city and countryside, nor Petty those between agriculture and industry, *from the point of view of production*. Both Machiavelli and Petty situate in the political superstructure the relationships that link city and countryside, and in general the various parts of the economic system. It is precisely the ability to go beyond this and to discover the technological relations of production that link the various sectors of the economy that constitutes the major contribution of the Physiocrats to the development of economic science. This analytical step is a necessary one for the specification in modern terms of the problem of the balance between agriculture and industry. This problem thus assumes its full significance only after a long process of economic reflection, which proceeded hand in hand with certain transformations in economic reality. In this perspective, the division of labour is of central importance.

7   THE DIVISION OF LABOUR

In explaining the wealth of a nation, Petty attributes a key role to technological and organisational factors such as land improvements (drainage, irrigation, etc.) and investments in infrastructure (roads and navigable canals), or the development of the financial structure (the creation of land banks) and the legal framework providing a firm basis for exchanges of property (the creation of a land register). A very important role is also attributed to people and their productivity. This, in turn, is linked to the division of labour, which we will consider in this section.

The division of labour is, as Schumpeter (1967, p. 56) says, an 'eternal commonplace of economics'. Plato's *Republic*, or the Latin proverb 'nec sutor ultra crepidam' (let the cobbler stick to his last), testifies to the early consciousness of the fact that the technical division of labour provides the basis for a hierarchical social structure. Petty's examples (the fabrication of clothes and watches: see Petty 1963, pp. 260–1, 473) highlight the division of tasks among the different labourers within the same productive activity, and also stress the importance of the technical progress embodied in specialised implements of production (e.g., 'those who command the Trade of Shipping, can build . . . a particular sort of Vessel for each particular Trade', Petty, 1963, pp. 260–1). However, Petty never makes it clear whether the technical division of labour is associated with the rise of specialised independent units of production at each stage of the labour process.

In fact, this point has been a source of confusion even in recent times. For instance, Smith's causal link between the increasing size of the market and the development of the division of labour has been taken to imply (e.g., by Stigler, 1951, or Arrow, 1979, p. 156) an increase in the size of individual firms or industries, so that the system-level relationship between economic growth and technical progress has been arbitrarily reduced to the concept of increasing returns to scale for the individual firm or industry. In order to clarify this point, let us try to classify the different aspects of the division of labour.

The most common distinction contrasts the *social* division of labour (i.e., the differentiation of jobs within society) with the *manufacturing* division of labour (i.e., the subdivision of a specific production process into separate stages). These two categories may or may not overlap. Thus, the same job may be present in different

firms and different sectors: e.g., administrative employees are required by a chemical firm just as they are by a mechanical firm. But,
more to our point, there are different aspects in the manufacturing
division of labour: it can take place *within* the firm, but it may also
involve the partition of the productive process into different parts,
each of which is carried on by a separate firm (vertical disintegration). We noted above Petty's own experience in the management of
his Irish holdings (or in his activities for the survey of Irish lands,
where he employed more than a thousand people in different tasks:
see Fitzmaurice, 1895, pp. 49–55). These cases show that the technical and social division of labour can appear *within* a large productive
unit, a sort of vertically integrated subsystem of the economy. At the
limit, only final consumption goods might be exchanged on the
market, avoiding any market exchange of means of production
among different sectors of the economy – which today represents the
majority of market exchanges.

We can thus distinguish *intra-firm* and *inter-firm* varieties of the
manufacturing division of labour; and we may proceed, in the latter
case, to a further subdivision into *intra-industry* and *inter-industry*
varieties of the division of labour, according to whether the different
firms originating in the partition of a production process remain
within the boundaries of the original industry or can be classified as
belonging to other sectors of activity.

In the latter case (which is the key one for the rise of the
agriculture-industry dichotomy), a moment's reflection will show that
the evolution of the inter-industry division of labour is not unequi-
vocally related to purely technical changes in the processes of production. In this context, political and social elements, and factors
pertaining to the stage of development reached by the economic
system in general are the important ones. Furthermore, it should be
recognised that the boundaries separating different industries are not
basically inherent in the real world, but are drawn by the observer,
who picks out the distinguishing characteristics used in classifying
each productive unit in a specific sector of activity. Thus, e.g., a
geographical aspect (town-based manufacturing versus countryside-
based agriculture) may be combined with other aspects pertaining to
the organisation of production, to the role of natural forces such as
the cycle of the seasons, to differences in market forms (competitive
agriculture versus oligopolistic industry). But, once this is recognised, it should also be recognised that the different distinguishing
characteristics may acquire or lose importance over time, so that

even such an apparently clear-cut dichotomy as the one between industry and agriculture may change its meaning over time.

8 CONCLUDING REMARKS

The discussion of the preceding sections can be used to raise questions concerning the historical and conceptual bases of various aspects of the industry-agriculture dichotomy. Let us consider some of these questions:

(i) (From section 2) While modern economic historians generally utilise the agriculture-industry dichotomy in analysing seventeenth century reality, we have seen that the historical conditions for the full validity of such a dichotomy were not present at the time. Similarly, are we sure that concepts flowing from the analysis of developed economies retain their validity, and indeed the same meaning, when applied to developing countries?

(ii) (From section 3) In discussing 'Petty's Law' we noted the difficulty of understanding economists brought up in conditions different from ours. When this happens, should we try to superimpose 'modern' analytical categories on 'lagging' realities, or should we rather try to understand the reasons why economists reared in these conditions tend to use different analytical categories, or to attribute (often only slightly) different meanings to our 'traditional' concepts and analytical tools?

(iii) (From section 4) If we reject the idea of 'mathematical laws written into the Universe' (and into the economy), what meaning should we attribute to 'economic laws'? (e.g., how can we interpret empirical regularities such as Engel's law, which are so useful in 'explaining' movements over time of the relative shares of agricultural and industrial products in final consumption?)

(iv) (From section 5) Do relative prices (e.g., of agricultural versus manufactured products) only express 'necessary' production costs, or are they also affected by social elements such as those considered by Petty in his 'political price'?

(v) (From section 6) Petty's concept of the economic system corresponds to the nation-state, i.e., to the political form of organisation which had asserted itself not much before Petty's time.

With the growing interdependence, both economic and political, among different countries in the contemporary world, can we still interpret the economic system as coinciding with the nation-state? or should we identify the economic system with the whole world, or with a block of countries such as the industrialised, developing and planned ones? or can we consider the situation as one of transition, and each time choose the interpretation best suited to the problem under consideration?

(vi) (From section 7) Since the institutional environment can be modified, what is its significance for the functioning of the economic system? e.g., how do the legal environment (such as anti-monopoly legislation), the greater or lesser certainty of property (such as can be ensured by an efficiently functioning land and property register), and institutional developments in the financial sector, affect the possibility of a smooth market solution to the problem of the balance between agriculture and industry?

(vii) (From section 7) We noted that the subdivision of the economic system into sectors is drawn by the observer, who chooses the distinguishing characteristics of the different sectors (as is also shown by the possibility of different levels of aggregation). Depending on the specific problem under consideration, different characteristics may turn out to be more or less important; the direct reference to traditional classifications by sector (such as the agriculture-industry dichotomy) may sometimes hide the vital characteristic, and the elements of the problem turn out to be specified only indirectly. As we have seen above, these factors cast doubt on the validity of the agriculture-industry dichotomy in analysing the seventeenth century conditions in which Petty lived. Similar difficulties arise when we consider the agriculture-industry dichotomy with reference to a developing country. For instance, are we tackling the social problem of the relationship between the 'traditional' and the 'modern' sectors of the economy, or the relationships between city and countryside, or the problem of the productive interrelationships between the two sectors (e.g., the need for food and basic raw materials on the part of the industrial sectors, and the need for fertilisers, tools and machinery on the part of the agricultural sector) or, as is generally the case, a mixture of all these problems together? In fact, we may find it useful to distinguish the three problems, though obviously related (so much so that we may also speak of three different aspects of a single problem), precisely because this may allow us to use different specifications of the agriculture-industry dichotomy for each problem, the specification which best fits the nature of the problem under consideration.

These are but a few examples of the questions arising from our discussion of the historical and conceptual-methodological preconditions of the agriculture-industry dichotomy. Of course, such questions – and similar ones – may emerge directly from the analysis of contemporary reality. But clearly they are most likely to be raised in a systematic way in a historical perspective.

Note

1. Thanks are due to M. Corsi, P. Groenewegen, P. Savona, M. Tonveronachi and especially P. Sylos-Labini for helpful suggestions and comments.

References

Arrow, K. J. (1979) 'The Division of Labor in the Economy, the Polity, and Society', in G. P. O'Driscoll (ed.) *Adam Smith and Modern Political Economy* (Iowa State University Press) pp. 153–64.

Braudel, F. (1981) *I giochi dello scambio* (Torino: Einaudi; original French edn, 1979).

Cantillon, R. (1964) *Essay sur la nature du commerce en général* (first published posthumously in 1755), ed. H. Higgs (New York: A. M. Kelley; reprint of the 1931 edn).

Clark, C. (1951) *The Conditions of Economic Progress, 2nd edn (London: Macmillan)*.

Fitzmaurice, E. (1895) *The Life of Sir William Petty* (London: Murray).

Gramsci, A. (1975) *Quaderni del carcere*, ed. V. Gerratana (Torino: Einaudi) (partially translated as *Prison Note-books*, ed. Q. Hoare and G. Nowell Smith, London: Lawrence & Wishart, 1971).

Heckscher, E. F. (1955) *Mercantilism*, 2 vols, 2nd edn., ed. E. F. Soderlund (London: Allen & Unwin).

Hill, C. (1975) *Reformation to Industrial Revolution* (Harmondsworth: Penguin Books).

Kula, W. (1970) *Teoria economica del sistema feudale* (Torino: Einaudi; original Polish edn, 1962).

Lewis, W. A. (1954) 'Economic Development with Unlimited Supplies of Labour', *Manchester School*, pp. 139–91.

McCulloch, J. R. (ed.) (1952) *Early English Tracts on Commerce* (Cambridge: Economic History Society; reprint of the 1856 edn).

Petty, W. (1963) *Economic Writings of Sir William Petty*, 2 vols, ed. C. Hull (New York: A.M. Kelley; reprint of the 1899 edn).

Petty, W. (1977) 'A Dialogue on Political Arithmetick', in S. Matsukawa, 'Sir William Petty: An Unpublished Manuscript', *Hitotsubashi Journal of Economics*, vol. 17, no. 2, pp. 33–50.

Pufendorf, S. Von (1934) *De Jure Naturae et Gentium libri octo* (1688), transl. by C. and W. Oldfather, in *The Classics of International Law* (Oxford: Clarendon Press).

Roncaglia, A. (1985) *Petty: The Origins of Political Economy* (New York: Sharpe).

Schumpeter, J. (1967) *History of Economic Analysis*, 6th edn (London: Allen & Unwin).

Sraffa, P. (1960) *Production of Commodities by Means of Commodities* (Cambridge: Cambridge University Press).

Stigler, G. J. (1951) 'The Division of Labor is Limited by the Extent of the Market', *Journal of Political Economy*, vol. 59, no. 3, pp. 185–93.

Thirsk, J. and Cooper, J. P. (eds) (1972) *17th Century Economic Documents* (Oxford: Clarendon Press).

Wilson, T. (1963) *A Discourse upon Usury* (1572), ed. R. H. Tawney (New York: A. M. Kelley; reprint of the 1925 edn).

10 The Role of Industry In Economic Development: The Contrasting Theories of François Quesnay and Adam Smith

Walter Eltis
NATIONAL ECONOMIC DEVELOPMENT OFFICE
AND EXETER COLLEGE, OXFORD

The benefits from industrialisation as seen by the great French Physiocrats and Adam Smith were immensely different. François Quesnay argued from 1759 onwards that the industrial sector of the economy was 'sterile', and that state support for industrialisation in France in the seventeenth century had reduced population, cut living standards and undermined government finances. Adam Smith insisted just seventeen years later, in *The Wealth of Nations* (1776), that the benefits from the division of labour which could only be enjoyed in industry had already raised the standard of living of a British labourer above that of an African King (pp. 23–4).

Quesnay and Smith both used rigorously formulated economic argument to arrive at these radically different results. What led Quesnay to his conclusion, which astonished his contemporaries no less than subsequent generations of economists, was a belief that industry as constituted in France in the seventeenth and eighteenth centuries could make no kind of net contribution to the nation's tax revenues. Its 'net product' (*produit net*), or taxable capacity, or economic surplus, was zero, which meant that at best, if its support cost the rest of society nothing, it could make no contribution to the military and welfare needs of the state. In less favourable circumstances where industry actually needed to be subsidised or protected, such diversions of real resources would impoverish the primary producing sector which provided the surpluses on which French

175

governments relied. Smith, too, believed that agriculture had the potential to provide a vastly greater economic surplus than industry, but in his judgement the surplus industry offered was not zero. In addition, industry could be expected to provide external benefits of great importance to the whole economy through the productivity advances associated with the division of labour, though according to Smith, these would be maximised if industrial development was left to market forces.

Virtually all subsequent economists have preferred Smith's analysis to Quesnay's, but there is an important line of argument in Quesnay which several developing countries have overlooked to their cost. This is the proposition that industry fails to provide a taxable surplus comparable to that offered by agriculture. In twentieth century Argentina the agricultural surplus is equivalent to 80 per cent of output, and the state has prevented significant agricultural growth by diverting a high fraction of this surplus to the support of industries which cannot compete internationally (Cavallo and Mundlak, 1982). In Pakistan the value-added of various industries, measured at world prices, has recently been shown to be negative (Little, Scitovsky and Scott, 1970, pp. 58, 64, 113). Such industries cannot be net contributors to the nation's tax revenues. Instead, as in seventeenth and eighteenth century France, they are net absorbers of revenues, and via protection, net inflators of agricultural costs. So such government support for industry may well damage the surpluses primary producers generate, and therefore reduce the size of the sectors of the economy which have a true net capacity to support government expenditure, and to finance economic growth. If the extraction of real resources from a primary surplus-generating sector, and their dissipation in an industrial surplus-absorbing sector, can occur as readily in twentieth century Argentina and Pakistan as in eighteenth century France, it is unfortunate for such countries that Quesnay's detailed theoretical and practical accounts of this line of argument are so largely neglected today.

In this paper the essence of Quesnay's and Smith's arguments will be set out at the start, and it will be suggested that there are important elements of truth in both. Twentieth century economies may therefore find that they are applying industry-boosting arguments which derive from propositions Smith established in conditions where Quesnay's reasoning is more appropriate.

1 FRANÇOIS QUESNAY ON THE RELATIONSHIP BETWEEN AGRICULTURE AND INDUSTRY IN ECONOMIC DEVELOPMENT

In Quesnay's analysis primary production offers an economic surplus (*produit net*) over wage, raw material and capital costs which ranges up to 100 per cent of these.[1] He contrasts three agricultural techniques of production of which the most capital intensive (*la grande culture*) yields a surplus to landowners and the state equal to approximately 50 per cent of output. With the more modestly capital intensive intermediate technology, *la petite culture*, the *produit net* is between 30 per cent and 40 per cent of annual agricultural advances and perhaps 25 per cent of agricultural production, and in the most labour intensive conditions where peasants use only spades and hoes, the land yields no surplus over their own meagre subsistence. *La grande culture* which offers a surplus of 50 per cent of output to landlords or the state involves heavy investments by farmers themselves, while with *la petite culture* which yields around 25 per cent of output, farmers invest modestly or else use landlords' capital and divide the harvest equally with them. The establishment of the high-surplus-yielding *la grande culture* requires a wealthy entrepreneurial class willing to invest in a capital intensive and highly efficient agriculture, with firm expectations that landlords and the state will allow them to enjoy the high profits that efficient farming can be expected to yield. These high farmers' profits are part of the 50 per cent of agricultural costs and not the 50 per cent of pure surplus or *produit net* that accrues to landlords and the state.

In industry, in contrast, there is no taxable surplus, and in conditions of perfect competition (*concurrence libre*), prices cover no more than wage and raw material costs. But the assumed wages of master craftsmen and the owners of manufacturing businesses are set very high in relation to average living standards to enable their incomes to include an element of normal profit to cover risk, trouble and a reasonable return on their capital.[2] Quesnay, and Turgot after him, took it for granted that the element of extra income of industrial proprietors was not a taxable surplus, for they would gradually cease to manufacture if this element in their rewards was removed.

It is an inevitable consequence of these assumptions of Quesnay's that the financial needs of the state can be met only from the economy's primary producing sector, because only this yields taxable surpluses. But it was none the less a notable fact which all, including

Quesnay, recognised that French industrialists and the merchant class that traded their goods often made vast fortunes. His insistence that industry and commerce could not support the needs of the state, or finance economic growth, and that their production was *sterile*, therefore bewildered his contemporaries. These also noticed that manufacturing and commercial states like Venice and Holland had accumulated wealth and power, so how could it possibly be argued that agriculture provided the ultimate source of all wealth and of all net government revenues?

It has always been a mark of the greatest economic thinkers that they can dispute the underlying explanation of facts that are self-evident to the untutored, and Quesnay insisted that taxable industrial and commercial profits could arise only where businesses had managed to achieve elements of monopoly power.[3] This had arisen in Quesnay's Europe in a variety of ways. States frequently granted monopoly privileges to political supporters, or else they sold future monopoly rights for current cash, or they allowed corporations with monopoly power to emerge by protecting their own countries' industries. Such policies were prevalent throughout Europe and they had allowed extremely profitable corporations to emerge. And it was also true that industrial innovators could sell at monopoly prices, but these would disappear as soon as others learned to make the same new products. In addition, France's great jewellers and furniture makers of the *ancien régime* had temporary monopoly-rights over their distinguished products which allowed them to sell at home and overseas at very high prices which yielded financial surpluses.

Quesnay insisted that any taxable industrial and commercial profits which arose in these ways could only result from such elements of monopoly power, which had the unfortunate effect of diverting a fraction of the true surpluses generated in the primary sector to wealthy industrial and commercial proprietors.

The agricultural surplus is the excess of agricultural output over the costs farmers must meet, and anything which reduces their expenses will increase the surplus as Quesnay explains in the 'Dialogue on the Work of Artisans' (1766d):

> we have to divide the reproduction generated by the cultivator into two portions, namely, the portion which provides for his own subsistence, and the portion which is in excess of this subsistence. Whence it follows that if it is possible, without detrimentally affecting the total reproduction, to cut down on the first portion,

the second will be correspondingly increased. For example, if we assume that the reproduction is 20, the cultivator's expenses 10, and the surplus 10, then if the expenses can be cut down to 8 the surplus will be 12. (p. 227[M])

The purchase of industrial goods required for the subsistence of labourers is a cost to agriculture. Quesnay explains in the same article how tailors make clothing so that 'the husbandman is not obliged to leave his plough in order to work at making his clothing' and this saving of the husbandman's time increases 'his productive labour' and therefore the rate of surplus in agriculture (p. 226[M]).

Increasing the cost of manufactures as a result of protection or monopoly privileges, which permit the generation of industrial profits, will therefore reduce the rate of surplus in agriculture. Part of the agricultural surplus is in effect diverted to monopolist merchants or industrial producers.

The restrictions on competition which make this state of affairs possible divert part of the agricultural surplus to industry or commerce, but the state cannot tax these *de facto* monopoly profits in the same way as the revenue from the agricultural surplus, for according to Quesnay in the 'Dialogue on Commerce' (1766b) commercial traders:

> know how to keep their profits and protect them from taxation; thus their wealth like the traders themselves has no country; it is unknown, mobile, and dispersed throughout all the countries in which they have dealings, and their true wealth is so confused with debts, active and passive, that it is impossible to evaluate it or assess it for proportional taxation. If their merchandise is taxed, the taxes will fall equally on domestic and foreign merchants and both will ensure through their sales and their purchases that the taxes fall on the nation.... (p. 851 [E])

Thus commercial capital is controlled by multinationals (to use a twentieth century label) which are in effect untaxable, and it makes no difference whether these enterprises are nominally domestic or foreign.

Profits of French companies are sometimes made at the expense of foreign countries, but foreign companies will equally gain at the expense of France, as Quesnay explains in the 'Dialogue on Commerce' (1766b):

Merchants transport and re-transport, and profit turn by turn in every country . . . Commercial costs are always paid at the expense of producers, who would benefit from the full price that purchasers pay if it were not for the expenses of intermediaries . . . These costs, it is true, may increase the wealth of the traders who profit from them, but not at all those of the nations which mutually contribute them. Since, once again, the traders do not allow nations to share in their wealth, but they themselves share in the wealth of nations. (pp. 835–6 [E])

If governments cannot obtain tax revenues from industrial and commercial producers, how are the great city states financed? Quesnay argued in the 'Dialogue on Commerce' (1766b) that the 'nations involved in maritime commerce may have a large number of wealthy merchants, but the State is always poor' (p. 829 [E]). Holland is an apparent exception, but Quesnay insists that the Dutch Republic is not merely commercial, 'It is also necessary to envisage it as proprietor of a territory which produces much: of colonies whose produce is extremely profitable to it, and of seas where it obtains a large product through fishing' (p. 852 [E]).

If the state cannot tax industrial and commercial profits, it can at any rate borrow from wealthy producers and traders, but this has obvious disadvantages as Quesnay makes clear in the 'Dialogue on Commerce' (1766b):

to lend is not to give, and it does not even contribute to the needs of the State, and to borrow is no proof of wealth and power in a State . . . If you say that it is at least a resource for a nation to have the power to borrow, you should also perceive that this ruinous resource is hardly to the advantage of the nation which provokes the usury of the lender. (p. 826 [E])

Since the industrial and commercial fortunes which arise from monopoly power, and accrue at the expense of the agricultural surplus, are difficult to tax and dangerous to borrow, there is an overwhelming case for removing the privileges, and import and export restrictions, which allowed them to emerge. It is argued powerfully in the 'Dialogue on the work of Artisans' (1766d) that a nation's overwhelming interest is always:

to extend commercial competition as far as possible . . . It is only by means of absolute liberty of commerce that the number of domestic and foreign merchants can be multiplied, monopoly be made to disappear, and burdensome costs reduced, nations be assured the highest possible prices in their sales, and the lowest possible prices in their purchases, and thus procure for themselves the most extensive and advantageous commerce they can hope for. (p. 858 [E])

This will have the added advantage of encouraging the growth of agriculture, for:

the highest price in the sale of your products, and the lowest possible price in the purchase of foreign produce will procure the greatest possible growth for your agriculture, which will then furnish you with the only true and solid means to increase your commerce, your wealth and the enjoyment you derive from it. (p. 842 [E])

Once the ideal state of perfect competition in industry and commerce is actually attained, the calculations set out in the *Tableau Économique* (1758–9) show the precise relationship between the output and the rate of return achieved in the surplus-generating and state-financing primary producing sector, and the consequent demand for the products of the industrial and commercial sector that this idealised economy will actually be able to sustain.

The question of the size of the economy's industrial and commercial sector in relation to the agricultural can be examined in two stages. The first and simplest is to examine the relative size of the two sectors in static conditions, and this is found by examining their relative size when the *Tableau Économique* is in stationary state equilibrium. Using the results of the static *Tableau* as a starting point, the dynamic conditions which will produce industrial growth or decline can then be derived.

Industry and commerce will provide employment for a considerable fraction of the population. The effective demand for their produce derives from landlords and the government who are assumed to spend half their incomes on the products of industry and commerce, and farmers who are also assumed to spend half their incomes in the industrial and commercial sector. Quesnay shows that when the full interrelationships of the *Tableau Économique* are set out and analysed, the aggregate demand for domestically produced industrial and commercial production will total $\frac{1}{2}(A + R)$, where A is farmers' total incomes (which also equal total agricultural costs or advances) and R is the agricultural surplus or *produit net*.[4]

If agricultural advances, A, yield a return of 100 per cent as in *la grande culture*, R the *produit net* will actually equal A, so that $\frac{1}{2}(A + R)$, the aggregate demand for the output of domestic industry and commerce will actually equal A. If the level of agricultural technology is merely that of *la petite culture* where agricultural advances yield no more than 30 to 40 per cent, the total *produit net* or aggregate rents will be perhaps one-third of agricultural advances, R will equal no more than $\frac{1}{3}A$ and the aggregate demand for home-produced manufactures, $\frac{1}{2}(A + R)$ will total $\frac{2}{3}A$. Hence the demand for manufactures will approximately equal annual agricultural advances with *la grande culture* but be only two-thirds of these with *la petite culture*.

The level of industrial and commercial employment will therefore depend upon both the level of agricultural investment, and the capital intensity of agricultural technology, which determine the rate of surplus in agriculture. That is a summary of Quesnay's static analysis, which explains the size of the industrial and commercial sector in a stationary state. In the formula where industrial production is $\frac{1}{2}(A + R)$, anything which raises A, the level of agricultural advances, and R the agricultural surplus or *produit net*, must raise demand for the output of the industrial and commercial sector.

The stationary state equilibrium set out in the static *Tableau* may be disturbed in a number of ways to produce economic growth or decline.

A possibility which concerned Quesnay was that the effective demand of landlords and workers might shift away from agriculture towards industrial products. An extraordinary result he arrived at which has no parallel in modern economics is that if a population wishes to purchase more industrial production, in his words, if it acquires a greater taste for *luxe de la décoration*, then the level of industrial production and employment will not increase: *it will actually decline*. This astonishing result follows directly from his assumptions.

Starting from an initial stationary state, if demand shifts away from agriculture and towards industry and commerce, these will receive extra cash flows (as calculated in two series of disequilibrium *Tableaux* which he published[5]) while agricultural producers will receive smaller cash flows than in the previous year. Because the agriculturalists suffer a financial shortfall, the advances or investment for the following year's production that they can afford will be reduced. The industrialists in contrast will receive an initial financial boost because demand shifts in their favour, and they will invest more in order to produce more in the following year. In consequence, in the second year, agricultural output (which is twice advances) will be lower, while industrial production will be higher than before. But only agriculture yields a *produit net*, so if the land yields 100 per cent as with *la grande culture*, each 100 livre fall in agricultural advances will also produce a 100 livre fall in the following year's agricultural surplus. If the landlords accept an immediate and parallel reduction in rents, farmers will achieve a new static equilibrium in which they invest less and produce less (to match the now reduced demand for food) and landlords will receive less rent. But the new situation is not a potential equilibrium redistribution of resources because Quesnay assumes that where the agricultural surplus falls, landlords are at first willing to reduce rents by only half the fall in the agricultural surplus which no one predicted when rent contracts were initially arrived at. Tenant farmers themselves therefore have to meet the other half of the financial loss consequent upon a lower *produit net* until leases come up for renegotiation, perhaps nine years later. This financial loss to tenant farmers will cause them to invest still less in the following year which will reduce the agricultural surplus yet again, but the rents they will have to pay will again be reduced by less than the fall in the *produit net*, so they will be forced to cut their advances still further, and each time they reduce their advances, production will fall in parallel and squeeze rents and farm profits that much more. So agriculture will slide downwards indefinitely, falling production levels continually reducing the *produit net*, and contractual rents falling more slowly than the *produit net*, with the result that farmers are perpetually short of cash and are therefore obliged to sell off more and more of their advances instead of being able to invest them in the land to generate future harvests.

The domestic demand for industrial production derives quite largely from landlords spending a fraction of their rents on the products of industry, and farmers spending a fraction of their wages on the industrial side of the *Tableau*. If both these classes are becoming poorer each year, their demand for industrial production will all the time fall. The industrial producers gain in the initial year in which the nation's tastes first move in their favour, and the extra cash flows they then receive enable them to invest and produce more in the second year, but after this, falling demand from agricultural producers and landlords will gradually reduce the domestic market for industrial production. This will be higher than it was originally for perhaps four years, but after that it will gradually decline in parallel with the falling trend in agricultural incomes.

Quesnay explains, correspondingly, that if the nation's tastes switch towards agriculture, industry and commerce will lose out for a few years but the growing agricultural sector will generate extra demand for industrial products which will steadily raise the demand for manufactures from then on. Within a few years the extra markets for manufactures from A and R which are both growing will more than make good the initial loss.

The formula for the growth (or decline) of agricultural production (δg_a) consequent upon a deviation in the propensity to consume the products of agriculture of δC_a from the steady state propensity (normally 0.5) can be shown to be (see Eltis, 1984, p. 47):

$$\delta g_a = \tfrac{1}{2}\delta C_a - \tfrac{2}{3}\,\delta C_a^2$$

Then if C_a rises from 0.5 to 0.6 (so that $\delta C_a = 0.1$), agricultural output (and therefore the effective demand generated from agricultural incomes) will grow at approximately 4.3 per cent per annum. If the propensity to consume food falls from 0.5 to 0.4, agricultural production will decline at an annual rate of approximately 5.67 per cent. When the propensity to consume food first declines from 0.5 to 0.4, the demand for manufactures rises by one-fifth (i.e., by 20 per cent) because the propensity to consume manufactured goods increases from 0.5 to 0.6. If agricultural output and hence the effective demand for manufactures then declines at a rate of 5.67 per cent, it will fall below its initial level after four further years, despite the 20 per cent increase at the start.

The logic behind this process is that agriculture generates a *produit net* while industry does not. Every 100 livres of demand that shifts the pattern of production away from industry and towards agriculture therefore generates *an external benefit* of 100 livres to the landlords (or the state, where rents are taxed). Similarly, an increase in the demand and supply of manufactures, and a corresponding reduction in the output of food, has a negative external impact on rents. The lower level of rents then adversely influences the effective demand for manufactures so that industrial producers lose on balance as soon as this unfavourable *external* effect on the demand for their produce outweighs the initial favourable effect.

The *dynamic* effect in the above processes is due to a lag between the generation of a higher or lower *produit net* and the market fixing of the rents farmers are actually obliged to pay. Where the *produit net* falls, farmers are squeezed because their contractual rents are still based on the formerly higher *produit net*, so output slides downwards. Where the *produit net* rises so that farmers benefit, output will rise from year to year until market determined rents in the end catch up with the rising agricultural surplus. Then, as the agricultural surplus and agricultural advances rise or fall, so will the demand for the products of industry and commerce which is always $\frac{1}{2}(A+R)$. Anything at all which produces an unpredicted rise or fall in the agricultural surplus will have these dynamic effects which strongly influence the long-term growth of both agriculture and industry.

Quesnay's own examples focus on the benefits from the establishment of free trade which raises the agricultural surplus and sets off a dynamic expansion of the economy[6] and the damaging effects on both agriculture and industry of a reduction in the agricultural surplus as a result of the adoption of protectionist policies misguidedly intended to foster industrial expansion. Quesnay's criticisms are especially levelled at the pro-industrial policies of Louis XIV's great Finance Minister, Colbert, and in his (1767) 'Maximes Générales du Gouvernement Économique d'un Royaume Agricole', he outlines the disastrous effects of Colbert's efforts to foster industrialisation, which actually resemble those that many countries have adopted in the twentieth century:

It will never be forgotten that a minister of the last century, dazzled by the trade of the Dutch and the glitter of luxury manufactures, brought his country to such a state of frenzy that no one talked about anything but trade and money, without reflecting on the true employment of money or on a country's true trade.

This minister, whose good intentions were so worthy of esteem but who was too much a prisoner of his ideas, tried to bring about the generation of wealth from the work of men's hands, to the detriment of the very source of wealth, and put the whole economic constitution of an agricultural nation out of gear. External trade in corn was stopped in order to bring about a low cost of living for the manufacturer; and the sale of corn inside the kingdom was subjected to an arbitrary system of regulation which cut off trade between provinces. The protectors of industry, the justices in the towns, in order to procure corn at a low price, ruined their towns and provinces through poor calculation by causing a gradual decline in the cultivation of their land. Everything tended to bring about the destruction of the revenue of landed property, manufactures, trade, and industry, which, in an agricultural nation, can be maintained only through the produce of the soil. For it is this produce which provides trade with a surplus for export, and which pays revenue to the proprietors and wages to the men engaged in remunerative activities . . .

Luxury in the way of ornamentation [*luxe de la décoration*] was encouraged, and made very rapid progress. The administration of the provinces, harassed by the needs of the state, no longer offered any security in the countryside for the steady employment of the wealth necessary for the annual reproduction of wealth, which caused a large part of the land to be reduced to small scale cultivation [*la petite culture*], to be left fallow, and to become valueless. The revenue of the proprietors of landed property was uselessly sacrificed to a mercantile trade which could make no contribution to taxes. It became vitually impossible for agriculture to provide for them, depressed and overburdened as it was; their coverage was extended more and more to include men, food, and trade in raw produce; they were increased through the expenses of collection and through the destructive plundering of the reproduction; and a system of finance grew up around them which enriched the capital with the spoils of the provinces. Traffic in money lent out at interest created a very important kind of revenue based on money and drawn from money, which from the point of view of the nation was only an imaginary product, eluding taxation and undermining the state. This revenue based on money, and the appearance of opulence, maintained by the splendour of ruinous luxury, imposed upon the vulgar, and reduced further and further the reproduction of real wealth and the money stock of the nation. Unhappily, alas, the causes of this general disorder remained unknown for too long a time. (pp. 245–6[M])

That passage underlines France's various seventeenth century errors in the manner priority was given to industrial development. The attempt to achieve a low cost of living for industrial producers by forcing agriculturalists to sell in the home market reduced agriculture's *produit net*, and therefore its output and the economy's rate of growth. The towns themselves were ruined by the destruction of agriculture in the surrounding countryside. The encouragement of luxury consumption added to the deterioration of agricultural markets. The impoverishment of the agricultural producers reduced the level of agricultural technique from *la grande culture* which yielded a *produit net* equivalent to half of output to *la petite culture* which yielded no more than 25 per cent. The tax-contributing agricultural sector was allowed to decline in relation to the industrial and mercantile sector which yielded no tax revenues, and tax collectors became increasingly desperate to obtain revenues so that methods of collection became increasingly supply-destructive. In the same 'General Maxims', Quesnay quotes Boisguilbert's (1707) calculations to suggest:

> the revenue from landed property, which was formerly 700 millions (1400 millions in terms of our money today) diminished by one-half between 1660 and 1699. He notes that it is not to the level of taxes but to the injurious form of assessment and the disorder which it brought about that this huge decline must be attributed . . . The assessment became so irregular that under Louis. XIV it rose to more than 750 millions but yielded to the royal treasury only 250 millions. . . . (p. 262[M])

The increasing disorder in the nation's finances led to the creation of yet larger untaxable financial fortunes, and raised interest rates, and these higher interest rates then added to the adverse effects on the surplus-producing agricultural sector.

Quesnay's analysis led him towards very simple policy principles which he summarised in the 'Dialogue on Commerce':

> Consumers multiply wherever subsistence expands; but it is only free competition with foreign buyers which can ensure the best possible price, and it is only a high price that can procure and sustain the opulence and the population of a kingdom through success in agriculture. That is the alpha and omega of economic science. (p. 824[E])

2   HOW ADAM SMITH'S ANALYSIS OF THE RELATIONSHIP BETWEEN AGRICULTURE AND INDUSTRY IN ECONOMIC DEVELOPMENT DIFFERED FROM QUESNAY'S

Smith's account of the potential benefits from industrialisation departs sharply from Quesnay's, but before attention is focused on

the differences, it is important to emphasise the common ground
between them. Smith spent ten months in Paris in 1765–66 where he
discussed economic issues extensively with several of the leading
Physiocrats, and in particular with Quesnay himself. The lectures he
gave in Glasgow before 1765 include no hint of the close interconnec-
tion between capital accumulation and growth which was to play so
fundamental a role in *The Wealth of Nations*. It has been inferred that
he owed his grasp of this to the thorough grounding in Quesnaysian
economics he acquired in 1765–66. The editors of the Glasgow
edition of *The Wealth of Nations* have commented that 'the model [of
Physiocracy] which Smith expounds [in Book IV, Chapter 9] is rather
more elaborate than that offered by Quesnay' (pp. 672–3), which
underlines how much he learned during this Paris visit.

The first fundamental issue where Smith's analysis follows Quesnay's is his agreement with the proposition that agriculture offers a
far larger taxable and investable surplus than industry:

> The labourers and labouring cattle, therefore, employed in agricul-
> ture, not only occasion like the workmen in manufactures, the
> reproduction of a value equal to their own consumption, or to the
> capital which employs them, together with its owner's profits; but
> of a much greater value. Over and above the capital of the farmer
> and all its profits, they regularly occasion the reproduction of the
> rent of the landlord. (pp. 363–4).

Smith thus agrees with Quesnay and the Physiocrats that extra
agricultural demand and production provide the *external benefit* that
unlike industrial production they raise aggregate rents. Because
agricultural production adds to rents while industrial production does
not, increments to agricultural production will have more potential to
finance the needs of the state than equal increments to industrial
production. The Ricardian theory of rent, originated by Malthus,
West and Ricardo in 1815, insisted that this line of argument of
Quesnay's and Smith's was incorrect. If, as the Ricardian theory
insisted, marginal land yields no rent, a *marginal increment* to agricultural production will add no more to aggregate output than the
increase in wages and profits that it generates, and precisely the same
is true of manufacturing. Ricardo therefore insisted that there is no
reason to suppose that expanding agriculture will generate more
'revenue' [profits plus rents in his analysis] than an equal expansion of

industry.[7] On this issue, Smith's position was identical to Quesnay's, and the Ricardians found them equally in error.

There is a further vital issue on which Smith and Quesnay were in complete agreement. Both wholly supported free trade and the maximisation of international competition, and they saw the benefits from these in very similar terms. Smith's position is better known than Quesnay's, and a very well-known passage from *The Wealth of Nations* in juxtaposition to a similar passage from Quesnay's 'Dialogue on the Work of Artisans' will underline the similarity of their reasoning. First Smith:

> every system which endeavours, either, by extraordinary encouragements, to draw towards a particular species of industry a greater share of the capital of the society than would naturally go to it; or, by extraordinary restraints, to force from a particular species of industry some share of the capital which would otherwise be employed in it, is in reality subversive of the great purpose which it means to promote. It retards, instead of accelerating, the progress of the society towards real wealth and greatness; and diminishes, instead of increasing, the real value of the annual produce of its land and labour.
>
> All systems either of preference or of restraint, therefore, being thus completely taken away, the obvious and simple system of natural liberty establishes itself of its own accord. Every man, as long as he does not violate the laws of justice, is left perfectly free to pursue his own interest his own way, and to bring both his industry and capital into competition with those of any other man, or order of men. (p. 687)

And now Quesnay:

> You will come round again to the necessity of accepting the greatest possible freedom of competition in all branches of trade, in order to cut down as far as possible on the burdensome costs involved in them. As soon as you have calculated the effects of this general freedom prescribed by natural right, by virtue of which *each person should have the legal power to render his situation as good as he possibly can, without infringing upon the rights of others*, it will become self-evident to you that it is an essential condition of the growth of public and private wealth. (p. 229[M])

Despite this identity of argument on the desirability of a system of natural liberty in industry and commerce, where all should be equally free to buy in the cheapest market and sell in the dearest; and also their agreement that agricultural expansion offers the largest potential economic surplus, Smith believed that there were significant errors in Quesnay's analysis. But the extent of their agreement should not be underrated. Smith said that Quesnay's system, 'with all its imperfections is, perhaps, the nearest approximation to the truth that has yet been published upon the subject of political economy' (p. 678).

The first important difference between Smith and Quesnay is that Smith believed industrial profits include an element of economic surplus in the sense that industrial capitalists can save and invest from their profits, with the result that they have the potential to add to the growth of the economy:

> The increase in the quantity of useful labour actually employed within any society, must depend altogether upon the increase of the capital which employs it; and the increase of that capital again must be exactly equal to the amount of the savings from the revenue, either of the particular persons who manage and direct the employment of that capital, or of some other persons who lend it to them. If merchants, artificers and manufacturers are, as this system [Quesnay's] seems to suppose, naturally more inclined to parsimony and saving than proprietors and cultivators, they are, so far, more likely to augment the quantity of useful labour employed within their society, and consequently to increase its real revenue, the annual produce of its land and labour. (p. 677)

It was extremely prescient of Smith to appreciate that merchants and manufacturers have the power (and the inclination) to save some of the ordinary or 'normal' profits which accrue to them in conditions of perfect competition. That merchants and manufacturers have the power to raise the rate of growth through their saving does not necessarily signify that they will generate a taxable surplus. A sufficient profit to leave something over for potential saving may be a necessary condition for the investment of private capital in industry and commerce, so profits sufficient to enable individuals to save may be part of the supply price of manufactures. But it does not follow that any part of these profits will necessarily be available to the state, for a lower net of tax return could discourage the supply of industrial capital. Smith does not actually discuss Quesnay's proposition that industry and commerce fail to generate a taxable surplus, but the history of the next century underlines that the industrial surplus soon became large enough to generate substantial tax revenues in addition to private saving. By the time the first volume of Karl Marx's *Capital* (1867) was published, industrial and commercial profits amounted to 30 per cent of Britain's gross domestic product, and agricultural rents plus the profits generated in agriculture amounted to no more than 13 per cent (Matthews, Feinstein and Odling-Smee (1982) p. 164). So within a century, Britain's industrial and commercial surpluses were to become vastly larger than the agricultural. Smith's analysis was compatible with this development, but not Quesnay's.

Smith's main objection to Quesnay's argument is of course its neglect of the enormous advantages a society can obtain from the division of labour which can be taken far further in industry than in agriculture, for 'the labour of artificers and manufacturers . . . is capable of being more subdivided, and the labour of each workman reduced to a greater simplicity of operation, than that of farmers and country labourers' (p. 676). Because of these potential advantages:

A small quantity of manufactured produce purchases a great quantity of rude produce. A trading and manufacturing country, therefore, naturally purchases with a small part of its manufactured produce a great part of the rude produce of other countries; while, on the contrary, a country without trade and manufactures is generally obliged to purchase, at the expence of a great part of its rude produce, a very small part of the manufactured produce of other countries. (p. 677)

So Smith argues that a country which successfully develops its industry can attain far more favourable terms of trade between agricultural produce and manufactures than one that is still without a substantial industrial sector. Smith formulated the benefits from the division of labour in industry so that each expansion in industrial employment leads to more extensive subdivisions of employment, and hence to the achievement of higher productivity through the invention of superior machinery to exploit the opportunities this offers:

What takes place among the labourers in a particular work-house, takes place, for the same reason, among those of a great society. The greater their number, the more they naturally divide themselves into different classes and subdivisions of employment. More heads are occupied in inventing the most proper machinery for executing the work of each, and it is, therefore, more likely to be invented. (p. 104)

This proposition was present in lectures Smith gave in Glasgow just before and immediately after his Paris visit, where different students have recorded his words as, 'Twenty millions of people perhaps in a great society, working as it were to one anothers hands, from the nature of the division of labour before explained would produce a thousand times more goods than another society consisting only of two or three millions', and 'For twenty millions in a society, in the same manner as a company of manufacturers, will produce a hundred times more goods to be exchanged than a poorer and less numerous one of 2 mill'.[8] As industrial employment grows and the division of labour is extended, industrial productivity will continually increase, so the quantity of production of each industrial worker will all the time rise. If the relative price of manufactures does not fall entirely in line with this continuing increase in industrial productivity, the amount of corn the product of a manufacturing worker can be traded for will all the time rise. Thus if manufacturing productivity grows at a rate of 2 per cent a year, and the relative prices of manufactures fall only 1 per cent per annum, while agricultural productivity and the price of corn are constant, the output of a manufacturing worker will be tradable for 1 per cent more corn in each successive year. Hence the basis for Smith's statement that '[A trading and manufacturing country] exports what can subsist and accommodate but a very few, and imports the subsistence and accommodation of a great number' (p. 677).

The country that succeeds in expanding its manufacturing employment sufficiently to achieve the highest productivity levels, and the greatest terms of trade benefits, implicitly faces only modest competition from other manufacturing countries, so it will be able to reduce the relative prices of its manufactures less than the annual advance in its relative productivity. In Smith's argument, other countries will only achieve matching industrial productivity if they can attain comparable employment and production levels, so those who first attain high industrial production and efficiency will enjoy advantages which will not be readily competed away in the manner Quesnay assumed throughout his analysis of the tendency of competition to eliminate industrial profits.

The logic of Smith's argument indicates that a country with inferior industrial output and productivity might be able to compete with its more efficient competitors if it could pass through an initial loss-making phase as it expands its industrial production to their levels. Its companies could only survive these losses if, during the interval in which they were still inefficient owing to an inadequate scale of production, they were protected from the competition of overseas industries which had already attained high output and productivity. Smith discussed this case for infant industry protection which followed so directly from the logic of his argument:

> By means of such regulations, indeed, a particular manufacture may sometimes be acquired sooner than it could have been otherwise, and after a certain time may be made at home as cheap or cheaper than in the foreign country. But though the industry of the society may be thus carried with advantage into a particular channel sooner than it could have been otherwise, it will by no means follow that the sum total, either of its industry, or of its revenue, can ever be augmented by any such regulation. The industry of the society can augment only in proportion as its capital augments, and its capital can augment only in proportion to what can be gradually saved out of its revenue. But the immediate effect of every such regulation is to diminish its revenue, and what diminishes its revenue, is certainly not very likely to augment its capital faster than it would have augmented of its own accord, had both capital and industry been left to find out their natural employments.
>
> Though for want of such regulations the society should never acquire the proposed manufacture, it would not, upon that account, necessarily be the poorer in any one period of its duration. In every period of its duration its whole capital and industry might still have been employed, though upon different objects, in the manner that was most advantageous at the time. In every period its revenue might have been the greatest which its capital could afford, and both capital and revenue might have been augmented with the greatest possible rapidity. (p. 458)

In Smith's argument an extensive scale of production and a large capital stock are both necessary if high levels of industrial efficiency and employment are to be attained. Infant industry protection can create a large captive home market, but by reducing the economy's overall net revenue, or *produit net* as Quesnay described it, protection actually reduces the economy's capacity to expand the capital stock and therefore to take advantage of its new found opportunities for industrial growth.

So while Smith saw far greater benefits from the growth of manufacturing industry than Quesnay, he entirely agreed that the state should not interfere with market forces to further industrial growth. The very different analyses of Smith and Quesnay therefore indicate an identical policy stance.

3 CONCLUSION

Since the Second World War, Hong Kong, Taiwan, South Korea and Singapore have followed policies extremely close to those that Smith and Quesnay advocated,[9] while the countries of the Indian subcontinent have preferred to pursue Colbertian policies involving massive tariff protection, industrial subsidies, agricultural price controls, and the diversion of agricultural surpluses in order to seek to build up industry.

The theory of infant industry protection and of the potential external benefits from industrial development have advanced greatly since 1776, but the eighteenth century propositions of Smith and Quesnay that these policies will not actually assist long-term industrial development pose questions which twentieth century economists cannot safely lose sight of.

The first questions are raised by the line of argument which is most powerfully present in Quesnay's work. This focuses attention on the taxable surplus or *produit net* that industry and agriculture generate. Quesnay was of course wrong to suppose that only agriculture generates a *produit net*, but the question still needs to be asked of countries which have devoted vast real resources to industrial growth: Is industry a net generator of funds capable of supporting government defence and welfare spending, or is it actually a net absorber of such funds? Is industry capable of supporting social welfare, or is it a part of the welfare system that the sectors which are truly surplus-generating are required to finance?[10]

A second vital question is raised most sharply by Smith's analysis: Have pro-industrial policies actually raised or, alternatively, have they perhaps reduced, the long-term rate of capital accumulation? If they transitorily reduce the gross national product because they force the substitution of low (or even negative) value-added production (when measured at world market prices) for production which offers a higher value-added, then the probability is that there will be less saving and capital accumulation from this lower real national income. If saving and capital accumulation are diminished in the short term, does the evidence indicate that long-term capital accumulation is truly raised as the advocates of twentieth century Colbertian policies invariably suppose?

It certainly appears that the questions raised by the eighteenth century analyses of François Quesnay and Adam Smith may still be pertinent to the development policies of several countries in the Third World.

Notes

1. Quesnay's account of the techniques of production available to agriculture are summarised in Eltis (1984) pp. 4–11.
2. The evidence of the higher incomes of industrial entrepreneurs is set out in chapter 7 of Quesnay *et al.* (1763) and summarised in Eltis (1984), p. 12–13.
3. Quesnay discusses the relationship between industrial and commercial profits, the degree of competition and the national interest in three important articles: 'Répétition de la Question Proposée dans la "Gazette du Commerce" au Sujet du Bénéfice que la Fabrique des Bas de Soie Établie à Nîmes Produit à la France' (1766a), and the two dialogues between Monsieur H. (Quesnay pretending to be an intelligent critic of Physiocracy) and Monsieur N. (Quesnay the Physiocrat), 'Du Commerce' (1766b) and 'Sur les Travaux des Artisans' (1766d). In the passages from these articles that follow, [M] after a page reference signifies that a translation is by Ronald Meek, and [E] that the responsibility for a translation is mine.
4. It is stated twice in *Philosophie Rurale* (Quesnay *et al.*, 1763) that the annual advances of the industrial and commercial sector will be half its output (vol. 1, pp. 124, 328: the formula is explained in Eltis (1984) pp. 27–9, 37–8).
5. See *Philosophie Rurale*, vol. III, pp. 33–53, and *l'Ami des Hommes* (Quesnay *et al.* 1756–60) vol. VI, pp. 192–202.
6. Examples are set out in Quesnay's (1766c) '(Premier) Problème Économique' and in *Philosophie Rurale*, vol. II, pp. 354–78, and restated in Eltis (1984) pp. 57–61.
7. His objections are developed in Ricardo (1817) chapter 26.
8. These are reprinted in *Lectures on Jurisprudence* (1762–3, 1766) pp. 392, 512.
9. See, for instance, Chen (1979).
10. It is shown in Eltis (1979) that even in a country with industries as advanced as Britain's, the nationalised industries were for many years

part of the welfare state, which the rest of the economy had to finance from its surpluses, instead of generating real resources to provide the wherewithal to finance social welfare.

References

Boisguilbert, P. de (1707) *Le Détail de la France* (Paris); reprinted in *Pierre de Boisguilbert ou la Naissance de l'Économie Politique*, 2 vols (Paris: Institut National d'Études Démographiques).

Cavallo, D. and Mundlak, Y. (1982) *Agriculture and Economic Growth in an Open Economy: The Case of Argentina* (Washington: International Food Policy Research Institute).

Chen, E. K. Y. (1979) *Hyper-Growth in Asian Economies: A Comparative Study of Hong Kong, Japan, Korea, Singapore and Taiwan* (London: Macmillan).

Eltis, W. (1979) 'The True Deficits of the Public Corporations', *Lloyds Bank Review* (January).

Eltis, W. (1984) *The Classical Theory of Economic Growth* (London: Macmillan).

Little, I., Scitovsky, T. and Scott, M. (1970) *Industry and Trade in Some Developing Countries* (Oxford: University Press for OECD).

Malthus, T. R. (1815) *An Inquiry into the Nature and Progress of Rent* (London).

Marx K. (1867–83) *Capital*, 3 vols; reprinted (Moscow: Progress Publishers for Lawrence & Wishart).

Matthews, R. C. O., Feinstein, C. H. and Odling-Smee, J. C. (1982) *British Economic Growth, 1856–1973* (Oxford University Press).

Meek, R. (1962) *The Economics of Physiocracy* (London: Allen & Unwin).

Quesnay, F. (1758–9) *Tableau Économique*, three edns; republished and translated in Kuczynski, M. and Meek, R. L. (eds) (1972) *Quesnay's Tableau Économique* (London: Macmillan).

Quesnay, F. (1766a) 'Répétition de la Question Proposée dans la "Gazette du Commerce" au Sujet du Bénéfice que la Fabrique des Bas de Soie Établie à Nîmes Produit à la France'; reprinted in L. Salleron (ed.) *François Quesnay et la Physiocratie* (1958), 2 vols (Paris: Institut National d'Études Démographiques) [Abbreviated below as INED].

Quesnay, F. (1766b) 'Dialogue entre M. H. et M. N. "Du Commerce"'; reprinted in INED.

Quesnay, F. (1766c) '(Premier) Problème Économique'; reprinted in INED.

Quesnay, F. (1766d) 'Second Dialogue sur les Travaux des Artisans'; reprinted and translated in Meek (1962).

Quesnay, F. (1767a) *Physiocratie, ou Constitution Naturelle du Gouvernement le Plus Advantageux au Genre Humain*, 2 vols, Paris.

Quesnay, F. (1767b) 'Maximes Générales du Gouvernement d'un Royaume Agricole'; reprinted and translated in Meek (1962).

Quesnay, F. with Victor de Riqueti, Marquis de Mirabeau (1756–60) *L'Ami des Hommes*, 6 vols; reprinted (1972) (Scientia Verlag Aalen).

Quesnay, F. with Victor de Riqueti, Marquis de Mirabeau (1763) *Philosophie Rurale*, 3 vols; reprinted (1972) (Scientia Verklag Aalen).

Ricardo D. (1815) 'An Essay on the Influence of a Low Price of Corn on the Profits of Stock' in Sraffa, P. (ed.) (1951) *Works and Correspondence of David Ricardo*, vol. IV (Cambridge: Cambridge University Press).

Ricardo, D. (1817) *On the Principles of Political Economy and Taxation* in Sraffa, P. (ed.) (1951) *Works and Correspondence of David Ricardo*, vol. I (Cambridge: Cambridge University Press).

Smith, A. (1776) *An Inquiry into the Nature and Causes of the Wealth of Nations*, 2 vols. (London); republished Campbell, R. H., Skinner, A. S. and Todd, W. B. (eds) (1976) 2 vols, as vol II of *The Glasgow Edition of the Works and Correspondence of Adam Smith* (Oxford: Oxford University Press).

Smith, A. *Lectures on Jurisprudence*, delivered in 1762–3 and 1766 in Meek, R. L., Raphael, D. D., and Stein, P. G. (eds) (1978), V of *The Glasgow Edition of the Works and Correspondence of Adam Smith* (Oxford: Oxford University Press).

Turgot, A. R. J. (1770) *Réflexions sur la Formation et la Distribution des Richesses* (Paris).

West, E. (1815) *Essay on the Application of Capital to Land* (London).

11 The Analytics of the Agriculture-Industry Relation

Krishna Bharadwaj
JAWAHARLAL NEHRU UNIVERSITY, INDIA

1 INTRODUCTION

The agriculture-industry relation has featured prominently in economic theory since its early beginnings in classical political economy, and similar themes have re-emerged in the context of attempts by developing economies to accelerate the pace of accumulation and industrialisation. Our purpose here is to outline some of these seminal analytical issues with a view to bringing out the theoretical perceptions and approaches that informed them at each stage.

In the following I have attempted to draw a contrast between two alternative theoretical approaches. First, I note how the analytics of the agriculture-industry relation took shape within the theoretical approach and framework of classical political economy and, in particular, how the structure of production and exchange relations in a predominantly agrarian society on the threshold of capitalist development, influenced the framework and approach of the progenitors, Petty and the Physiocrats. It was thence carried forward into the 'era of manufacture' by Smith and Ricardo, to be reconstructed by Marx, advancing it critically in novel directions. Some important primitives in the approach continued, despite the fact that the changes in historical conditions and analytical developments radically transformed the focus and conclusions of these political economists. In fact, it is the flexibility and versatility that the basic theoretical framework demonstrated which is of interest to us when theorising about the processes of accumulation in the developing economies of today. With a shift of paradigm to the neoclassical theory connoting a radically different approach to the analysis of production and exchange relations, and a different theoretical structure and explanation of prices and quantities, the agriculture-industry related issues in the process of accumulation assumed a different form and perspective.

The beginnings of 'scientific political economy' and the first attempts to generate a framework to analyse interrelations within the conception of 'an economic system' are discernible in the works of Petty, and even more clearly so, in those of the Physiocrats.[1] With settled agricultural communities, increasing commercialisation of economic activities through trade, the emergence of towns and cities as well as administrative and political structures to 'manage' public policies, the notion of a web of interdependent economic activities, forming a system, took shape. While their theoretical perception and mode of reasoning was heavily influenced, on the one hand, by the predominance and centrality of agriculture as a source of sustenance and as a mainspring of all economic activities and, on the other, by the nascent but advancing capitalist relations, the Physiocrats initiated certain basic ideas and concepts which were to be amended, reconstituted and extended in the later political economy. Writing in a different setting of England where capitalist relations were advancing at a rapid pace, in agriculture and in industry, Adam Smith (1776) was to conceptualise the regime of competitive capitalism, providing the appropriate new categories and concepts. Thus the stage was set for a political economy whose analytical advance reflected the dynamics of the process of capitalist development from a predominantly agrarian, feudal economy breaking out of its shell into capitalism.

The changing 'agriculture-industry' relations reflected changes in the extant historical conditions, the pace and character of the process of capitalist development, and assumed different forms of new problematics at every stage of development. The 'agriculture-industry' dichotomy itself emerges with different contours, with different degrees of clarity, depending upon the extent of specialisation and division of labour, and the character of institutions of property. In Petty's time when different sorts of activities were carried on within the same enterprise, neither social nor intra-enterprise division of labour had progressed much so that the producers, mostly in possession of their own means of production, employing also family labour, catered to a variety of their own needs, the distinction between 'agriculture' and 'industry' did not emerge sharply. It was in the works of the Physiocrats that such a sectoral separation emerged significantly, although 'industry' was perceived more as an appendage to agriculture, and constituted predominantly artisan households.

With the growth of surplus, increasing specialisation and division of labour and advancing capitalist relations in agriculture as well as in manufactures, the sectoral distinction sharpened (see Roncaglia's essay in this volume). The nature of interlinkages between 'industry' and 'agriculture' also vary with accumulation and the growth of capitalist relations. The interlinkages between industry and agriculture grow through the progress of technology (through agriculture using more and a greater variety of industrial inputs and the emergence, on the other hand, of a variety of agro-based industrial activities). With increasing commercialisation, new products appear and production is diversified in inputs as well as outputs. Thus the separation between the two sectors, their contours and their interrelations are all importantly related to the pace and character of the accumulation process and the changing property relations.

In the following we shall trace how the political economy framework adapted itself flexibly to incorporate the varying institutional conditions within which operate the processes of generation, appropriation, distribution and utilisation of 'surplus'. We shall contrast this approach with the neoclassical paradigm which focuses on relative-price-guided-allocation of scarce resources by atomistic 'agents' acting on competitive markets.

2   THE POLITICAL ECONOMY FRAMEWORK

2.1   The Analytical Framework of Classical Political Economy

A certain methodological approach shared by the classical writers was the belief that a particular social formation could be abstracted on the basis of observations and viewed as a system governed by certain objective rules, or 'systematic tendencies'. The 'Tableau Economique' of Quesnay and his followers was an attempt to analyse the interconnections within the economy through tracing the circulation of commodities. The table was designed to give quantitative relationships as would be observed to prevail in a 'natural' or 'average' state of the economy. A methodological distinction between the 'stable or permanent' and 'temporary or accidental' forces was made so that a 'natural' or 'central' position could be conceptualised. The role of theory and analysis was to discover the conditions of reproduction of such a state of production, exchange and distributive relations, and analyse the forces of change, described often as 'tendencies' and 'countertendencies', operating on the system.

The central concept was that of 'net product' or 'surplus' defined as the difference between 'gross produce' and 'productive consumption', the latter constituting material requisites of production and of sustenance of labour employed in production. The characterisation of the economic system stipulates the mode of generation and appropriation of surplus and the rules of distributing the surplus among the sharers. Each mode is conceptualised as possessing certain property and production relations which defines the relevant classes. Given the classes of surplus-sharers and the rules by which the distribution is governed (e.g., uniform rate of profit under competitive capitalism), the exchange values of products would be such as to satisfy the rules of surplus distribution while adequate also to replace the value of the means of production used up in the process. In other words, natural (exchange) values are the ones that are compatible with the social reproduction of the relations in the economy. At different stages of capitalist development the theorists adopted a different sectorisation, gave a different content and scope to concepts like 'net product', 'productive consumption', considered different mechanisms of surplus appropriation as well as different rules of surplus distribution among the classes, characteristic of that state of the economy. Determinants of social output, consumption, methods of production and wage were discussed in mutual interaction outside the core of price-determination[2] – prices mainly being seen as providing consistent terms and levels of exchange to make reproduction viable. A foundation for this broad approach was provided in a primitive, bare, but essential form, in the agriculture-centred model of the economy by the Physiocrats. Supplemented by the independent contributions of Adam Smith, commensurate with the task of analysing a rapidly industrialising, nascent capitalist economy, the foundations of future analysis in political economy were laid.

2.2 The Predominance of Agriculture: The Physiocrats

In the Physiocrats we see a first analytical conception of an economy constituting interdependent sectoral relations. A division between agriculture and the manufactures is maintained and the diverse character of production relations in agriculture (with strong feudal vestiges of servitude and land relations of various kinds), different from those in the manufactures (mainly constituting self-employed artisans and craftsmen), is explicitly acknowledged. In conformity with the prevalent conditions, the latter appear as a mere appendage of agriculture. Agriculture dominates as a major producer, as providing a critically essential component of subsistence and as a major activity where surplus is generated and appropriated by the powerful landed proprietors. The Physiocrats were prompted to conceive of agriculture as the only productive sector (meaning generating 'nett produit') and rent as the only form that surplus assumed. The nature of the material activity in agriculture where 'productive consumption' (seed + 'food' for workers) constituted largely the self-same commodity (particularly since very little capital entered agricultural production) sharpened the conceptualisation of 'surplus product' which assumed a 'tangible' form. Analysis of utilisation of 'surplus' and its distribution apparently seemed possible in material terms. (At least, the Physiocrats did not enter into the valuation questions which plagued the later theorists, particularly with regard to the explanation of distribution.) Discussions on pricing mainly pertained to a desirable 'fair price' for agricultural produce that would make better technology in production viable, and is the one to be advocated in opposition to the restrictive mercantilist policies and fiscal imposts that had hindered productive agriculture.

A discussion of the size of net product turned their attention to the determinants of social consumption levels ('effectual demand'), the technology in use and to the level of wage. Since the artisan (manufacture) sector was believed not to produce any surplus (and hence called 'sterile'), the demand for the products of artisans emanated mainly from the rental revenues of the proprietors. Social demand (effectual demand) thus consisted of the consumption of the proprietors, the subsistence of the workers in the agricultural and manufacturing sector, and the intermediate needs of circulating capital. Cantillon, in particular, was to theorise about the employment and output effects of landlord's consumption and the historical growth of commodities and skills as well as of commerce, leading to the growth of towns and cities. Custom, habit, availability of commodities, class composition and income distribution influenced the level and composition of social demand: a sharp distinction was made between the productive consumption of producers ('necessaries and conveniencies') and the consumption of the landed proprietors.

The level and utilisation of the agricultural surpluses thus determined the level of economic activity. Noticing the seasonal cycles of production in agriculture, the Physiocrats adopted an 'annual' cycle of production and treated capital as 'advances' of the surpluses made by proprietors to productive workers at the beginning of the cycle. They also considered wage as 'given' at a certain subsistence level. Even though they thus had the notions of 'capital' and of a given 'wage', they did not however develop the full complement of a capitalist mode – a task which Adam Smith was so admirably to perform.

The level of agricultural surplus also determined the sustainable level of population which adapted itself to the social demand through migration, through skills selection, and through natural population growth. Boisguilbert and Turgot were particularly concerned with the interaction among the levels of surplus, employment demand, the population changes and the level of wage. Turgot in one of his remarkable passages writes (1844, p. 437):

> The exchange value of food products, rents, the level of wages and the population are phenomena mutually interconnected and interdependent. The balance among them is established in accordance with a peculiar natural proportion and the proportion is constantly maintained if trade and competition are completely free.

The interaction was visualised as follows: A higher wage (above the natural) increases costs of production, reduces net product, decreases rents. On the other hand, a reduction below the proper level reduces efficiency of labour and hence the level of surplus. This, however, reduces their consumption demand, leading eventually to a fall in prices of the produce. A high wage may encourage growth of population or lead to immigration and then, competition among the labourers would tend to lower wages again. Thus, for the continued and harmonious economic reproduction, wages and rents must bear a natural proportion.

Although crude and elementary, the Physiocratic analysis provided the first macro-modelling of an economy where the interrelations between the level of agricultural surplus, the level of effectual demand, the technology and the wage level were attempted, with the agricultural sector providing the core.

2.3 The Era of Manufacture: Smith and Ricardo

With the advancement of capitalist relations in agriculture and industry, the relation between agriculture and industry itself transformed radically and the contents concepts of such as 'net product','capital', 'real wage' altered. Adam Smith recognised that industry contributes also to 'net product'. The specialisation and division of labour differentiated industries, as well as intensified links between industry and agriculture. With it the simplistic homogeneity of aggregates such as 'productive consumption' or 'subsistence' (which was earlier identified with 'food') disappeared. Alongside technological differentiation, however, the rule of competition was active which, with its postulated mobility of labour and capital, exerted a homogenesing influence. With generalised commodity production, the rule of competition extended across industries and sectors. In the competitive capitalist mode, Smith identified the tripartite division of classes with their corresponding revenues (rents, profits and wages) and the competitive tendency towards the uniformity of the rate of profit and wage set the norms for exchange values and distribution of the surplus. Nevertheless, in Smith's surplus-based approach to analysis, agriculture retained its particular significance as an important provider of 'subsistence', 'food' being the major component of wage goods. The remarkable feature of political economy was their analysis of social consumption in terms of 'wage goods', 'landlords' consumption', 'capitalists' consumption' so that consumption was linked directly with the processes of generation, appropriation and distribution of the surplus which were themselves analysed in terms of the 'classes'. Wage goods occupied a special place in their analysis as they defined the conditions of reproduction of 'labour' and labour itself constituted a 'material necessity' of production. Adam Smith was to open his *Wealth of Nations* (in 'Introduction and Plan of the Work', p. viii) with the significant statement:

> The annual labour of every nation is the fund which originally supplies it with all the necessaries and conveniencies of life which it annually consumes, and which consists always either in the immediate produce of that labour, or in what is purchased with that produce from other nations.

Adam Smith considered a historically natural gradation of commodities wherein the 'subsistence' (or, 'food') was considered 'in the nature of things' as 'prior to conveniency and luxury'. The progression of commodities was not only a historical evolution of the needs of the society but he clearly perceived, in this evolution, the central, facilitating role of agricultural surpluses for accumulation. 'The number of workmen increases with the increasing quantity of food, or with the growing improvement and cultivation of the lands'. In contrast, however, to the Physiocrats, who similarly saw the potentiality of inducing employment growth through food surpluses, Adam Smith recognised the ability of industry also to contribute productively to surplus,[3] and given his observation that a greater degree of division of labour and technical change was possible in the industry, such contributions to surplus would be accelerated:

> As the nature of their business admits of the utmost division of labour, the quantity of materials which they [workmen] can work up increases in a much greater proportion than their numbers. Hence arises a demand for every sort of materials which human invention can employ, either usefully or ornamentally.

It was thus that the world of commodities grew in number, in quality and variety, widening the domain of effectual demand, reflecting the increasing productivity of labour. This relation between agriculture and industry was viewed by Smith in terms of the symbiotic relation between 'country' and 'town', where the country supplies towns with the necessary subsistence and the materials of manufactures. The town repays this supply by sending back a part of the manufactured produce for the inhabitants of the country. Smith attributed a priority to 'subsistence' in this case: 'It is the surplus produce of the country only, or what is over and above the maintenance of the cultivators that constitutes the subsistence of the town which therefore increases only with the increase of surplus produce'. Agricultural surpluses thus were seen as a necessary, prior condition for industrial expansion.

Further, the availability of 'food' also determined sustainable levels of population and hence the potential work force: 'Countries are populous, not in proportion to their number of people whom their produce can clothe and lodge but in proportion to that of those whom it can feed'.

In terms of the price and distributive relations, too, the role of agriculture was seen as significant. A much-debated question in classical political economy since Adam Smith was the influence of 'corn price' on the prices of other commodities, and the influence a rising corn price could have on the rate of wages and of profits. Smith held that a rise in the price of corn would be followed by a rise in all other prices: in the absence of a rigorous theory of relative prices, Smith held that a corn price rise, via its influence on money wage (given the 'real wage') would tend to move all prices upwards. Such a conjecture was implicitly supported by Smith's analysis of the 'components of price' wherein natural price was seen as an adding up of the costs of material inputs, wages, profits and rents as payments for labour, capital and land used up in production. Smith discussed also the separate determinants of wages, profits and rents and treated them as if each was determined independently of the other. Such an 'adding up view' of prices was to mislead Smith in not seeing the 'inner connection' among the distributive shares – an issue at the centre of Ricardo's analysis of distribution.

Smith also tended to argue that food was the original source of rent:

> Human food seems to be the only produce of land which always and necessarily affords some rent to the landlord. Food is not only the original source of rent, but every other part of the produce of land which afterwards affords rents, derives that part of its value from the improvements of the power of labour in producing food by means of the improvement and cultivation of land.

Smith did not have a consistent explanation of rent, and would seem to suggest here as if rents were an additional surplus on land (see note 3, p. 215). Moreover, the fact that in the production of food, rents could be seen as a part of surplus product in the material form appears to have induced attributing to it a determining role.[4]

While the interlinkages between agriculture and industry were seen to grow in mutual interdependence and capitalist relations to advance rapidly in industry, Smith as well as Turgot (the 'last' of the Physiocrats) were much concerned with the distinctive and changing institutional forms in agricultural property relations. Land being a non-reproducible asset and property rights having a long social and juridical history, rents were seen as arising from monopoly rights as well as bargaining – although necessarily unequal – between land-owners and tenants, while the force of competition also gave rise to differential rents. The various systems of tenancy and farming were discussed with regard to their effect on exploitation, appropriation and distribution of surplus and their effect on productivity of land. While competition was interpreted as implying free mobility of capital and of labour, the mode of extraction of surplus in agriculture was recognised to be different from that in industry. Smith also recognised that the division of labour – which is a source of gains in productivity – has more limited application in agriculture than in industry, and therefore the industrial productivity advances more rapidly. On the other hand, with limited land, extended cultivation was threatened with diminishing returns as better soils were exhausted or as cultivation intensified. The tendency was therefore for corn prices to rise, and being a prime subsistence good, its price had important effects on wages and distribution.

Ricardo's paramount interest was in the question of distribution, particularly the explanation of the rate of profit. In the *'Essay on Profits'* (1815), and earlier in his letters, he maintained that the general rate of profit was determined by the farmer's rate of profit. In agriculture, Ricardo maintained, extended cultivation, while increasing rents, would tend to diminish the rate of profit, given the wage. The rational foundation of the farmer's profit principle advanced by Ricardo, appears (see Sraffa, 1951) to be as follows: In a situation where wages consist of only corn and so corn is the entire capital, the rate of profit in agriculture would seem to be determined as a material rate of produce, and the general rate of profit, under competition, would need to conform to this corn rate of profit. While evidently the 'model' was very restricted and Ricardo, immediately after the publication of the 'Essay' was to attempt to generalise his theory of determination of profit, it served a major analytical purpose, of bringing out clearly the structure of Ricardo's surplus-based explanation of profit: that, profits depended upon wages alone, and given the methods of production, the rate of profit was inversely related to the wage (or, share of wages in net product).

The *'Essay on Profits'* played an important role in the Corn Law controversy: Ricardo's argument was against restrictions on corn imports, as any such restriction would imply compensatory increases in domestic production to meet social demand, necessitating moving on to inferior lands and consequently effecting the higher value of corn (i.e., labour embodied per unit of corn). In terms of the distributive consequences, such an extension of cultivation would favour the landlords and would be against the rest. (Even if real wages were maintained, profits would diminish and affect the future employment prospects of the workers.) In 'Principles' where Ricardo moved on to consider wage as consisting of commodities apart from corn, the 'farmer's profit principle' disappeared. However, since 'food' constituted a major part of wage, the consequences of productivity changes in agriculture and long-term changes in the price of corn did affect the process of accumulation, through possible effects on wages; and the state of agriculture continued to be significant for the determination of the general rate of profit.

Ricardo drew the consequences of competitive capitalism much more rigorously than Smith. He challenged Smith's proposition that all prices move sympathetically with the corn price and tried rigorously to derive the relative price movements on the premise of a uniform rate of profit and wages. He understood, none the less, the importance of food (i.e., significance of changes in its price as well as the productivity changes in that sector), it being a major component of natural wage.

Ricardo made an important distinction between 'market wage' and 'natural' wage, the former referring to the actual wage governed by the temporary supply and demand conditions, while the natural wage was dependent upon custom, habits, etc. i.e., upon the notion of what constituted a conventional wage (not to be taken as *fixed* or *invariant*), and defined as 'that price which is necessary to enable the labourers, one with another, to subsist and perpetuate their race without increase or diminition' ('Principles', p. 98). He analysed the effects of accumulation on wages under various conditions: the customary real wage or the 'natural wage' was not related functionally to labour productivity and would be taken as 'given' by 'custom, habit or convention'. The wages (or, to be precise, 'the value of wages'), which, given the methods of production, constrain the rate of profit, may or may not rise with accumulation, depending upon the consequences accumulation has on 'the difficulty of producing the quantity of capital'. (The latter was proxied by 'food and necessities'.) Thus natural wage will rise if the 'difficulty of production' (measured in terms of labour embodied) of 'food and necessities' increases. The importance of 'agriculture' lay thus in determining the 'value of wages', which in turn constrained the rate of profits, given the methods of production. The price of food therefore was a crucial variable influencing the pace and the process of accumulation.

Historically the agricultural surpluses were seen at first as the only source of investible resources (as in the Physiocrats), and remained an important part of the society's surplus, playing a crucial generic role in Smith's analysis. With the share of industrial surpluses increasing (along with the expansion of volume and composition of industrial net product), the quantitative dominance of agricultural surpluses (as well as of rents and the power of the rentier class) receded. However, as a crucial provider of wage goods, 'agriculture' retained its significant role in influencing the shape and pace of the process of accumulation.

2.4 Capital–Labour Relations: Marx

Ricardo, although theorising in terms of a competitive capitalist economy, tended initially to highlight the conflict between landlords and the rest – the historic conjuncture of the Corn Law controversy brought this conflict into sharp focus. It was, however, the wage-profit relation (and, particularly the explanation of profit as a 'leavening of wages') that was the continuing thread running through his theoretical investigations. On the eve of his premature death, the mounting labour unrest compelled attention of analysts on the capital–labour relation. The major reconstruction of political economy occurred in the hands of Marx, who focused attention on the capitalist system, with generalised commodity production wherein surplus took the form of surplus value and was realised as profits in circulation. The capital–labour relation occupied the centre of the stage; the forces of capitalist development and of industrialisation had vitality enough to subsume agriculture within its sway and agriculture was progressively rendered 'a branch of industry'. Profits dominate and mould the accumulation process and pure rents, quantum-wise, recede, reflecting an eventual subordination of the landed aristocracy and rentiers.

Marx, however, continued with the basic structure of value and distribution: wages too, in Marx, were determined historically by a complex of factors, mainly influencing the capitalist's strategies of control over the labour process such as the historically-evolved notion of subsistence, the bargaining strength of the workers, the nature of the available technology, the state of the reserve army of labour and the capitalist perceptions of prospects of accumulation. The source of profit was traced by Marx to surplus value and the strategy of the capitalist was seen as directed to extract the maximum surplus value through manipulating the difference between labour productivity and the 'necessary wage'. The general rate of profit was therefore dependent on the value of wages or the conditions of reproduction of labour, and hence, the conditions of production or availability of wage goods played an important part in shaping the progress of profits and accumulation. Hence the production conditions and relations in agriculture appeared importantly relevant for the process of accumulation. Thus it was that Marx regarded that technological progress in wage goods production, or such other factors, cheapening the value of wages (or 'necessary labour') allow larger exploitation of surplus. Bortkiewicz (1906–07), using the Marxian scheme, was to establish that the rate of profit is determined in the wage-goods sector alone (see also Garegnani, 1970).

Marx, as did Smith and Ricardo, also treated mobility of capital and labour as the prime characteristics of competition. That agriculture may, however, have very diverse land relations with feudal vestiges which persist, although drastically reformed and reshaped by the force of capitalist competition, was recognised also by Marx. Land being a non-reproducible, and hence a scarce, asset (scarce in the absolute sense, for the society) gives rise to monopoly ownership and hence to ground rents, apart from the 'differential rents' that could arise even under the full sway of competition. Thus the transformation of agrarian conditions – the transition from feudalism to capitalism – becomes in Marx, an important part of the analysis of capitalist accumulation.

It was the experience of England, the first country to advance on this path, that influenced Marx's analysis. He saw the formation of wage-labour in the historical process of primitive accumulation whereby the producer, divorced from the means of production and labour, rendered free in a double sense ('freed of feudal bondages and freed of means of sustenance and production), becomes a seller of labour power, a 'commodity' like others. The starting point of the development was the change in the form of feudal servitude, a transition from feudal to capitalist exploitation. 'The expropriation of the agricultural producer, of the peasant from the soil is the basis of the whole process'. He nevertheless acknowledged that 'the history of this expropriation, in different countries, assumes different aspects, and runs through its various phases in different orders of succession and at different periods'.

Marx himself focused upon the 'classic case' of England (*Capital*, vol. I, p. 716). His discussions of this transition are by now well known. He believed that the capitalist relations would ultimately engulf agriculture as well as industry with a concentration of property in land, the proletarianisation of peasants, large productivity gains of capitalist agriculture, displacement of working capital and labour previously engaged in small-holdings and artisan manufactures. The process, on the one hand afforded supply of wage-labour to industry, while capitalist agriculture grew in its symbiotic relation with industry, creating demand mutually for each other's products, and hence the home market. The transition marked the resolute advance of capitalist forces, and although the primitive accumulation, the expropriation and expulsion of the agricultural population was marked at times by 'reckless terrorism', it 'conquered the field for capitalistic agriculture, made the soil part and parcel of capital, and created for the town industries the necessary supply of a "free" and outlawed proletariat' (p. 733).

The theme of the transition from feudalism to capitalism – the differences in patterns, pace and character of this transition, or even the 'possibility', 'desirability' or the 'inevitability' – have been issues that have been revived and debated in the context of the developing economies of today. What needs noting is that the historical character of the *process* of capitalist development of an economy does generate specificities in the production and exchange relations of the economy. Marx himself analysed more fully and comprehensively the (competitive) capitalist mode where labour power had already become a commodity, and the exchanges conformed to the competitive capitalist rules (of equivalent exchanges). In dealing with the process of capitalist development, Marx underlined the important structural changes in agriculture that were symbiotically related to the advance of industry. The path of capitalist development and industrialisation as well as its pace and structure have been influenced by, and influencing, the institutional changes in agriculture and thus the theme of this transition has been revived with some force in the recent debates on developing economies.

3 THE NEOCLASSICAL PARADIGM

In contrast to the historical and the accumulation-centred perspective that informed the analysis of agriculture-industry relations in political economy, a change-over to the neoclassical paradigm engendered a different focus and perspective. The economy was now analysed in terms of decisions of individual agents (producers and consumers) with given endowment of resources and in pursuit of the objective of maximisation of returns to their resources, given the feasible options of allocating these (i.e., producers maximise profits, given the technological possibilities, and consumers maximise satisfaction, given their preferences). The economic problem is seen essentially as one of efficient allocation of the given resources. Under the assumption of competition each individual is presumed to have uniform, free access to markets and given the relative prices, parametrically, each seeks to achieve the optimum combination of quantities out of the feasible ones, substituting the relatively cheaper for the dearer commodities. While individuals respond to relative price variations through adjusting quantities demanded and supplied, the relative prices themselves are expected to move in a way to lead to the clearance of markets so as to wipe out excess demands or supplies that may be eventuated by aggregating individual demand and supplies for a commodity. Under certain conditions imposed on the feasible sets of technology, preferences and additional assumptions like ruling out of 'externalities', the substitution principle is presumed to be sufficiently active and to be appropriate, in magnitude and in direction, to generate price and quantity responses so as to clear markets in equilibrium. Thus, in equilibrium, the entire set of relative prices, including commodity and factor prices, all quantities (level and composition of demand, of output and factor utilisation) are determined simultaneously through the same scheme of determination based on the equilibrating forces of supply and demand.

In such a model the relative prices play the central role of determining quantities of demand, output and distribution. The relative prices are also summary indicators of relative resource scarcity since the prices, *given the resources*, act as signals for allocating the resources to optimise the objectives of the individual agents.

In such a world, a symmetry is implicitly postulated among all 'factors' who have co-ordinated status in production. The peculiarity of land which was noted by the classicals, as a non-reproducible factor and hence 'scarce' in the absolute sense, leading to the distinctiveness of rents as a revenue share out of the surplus product, disappeared. In fact, the case of the intensive margin (additional 'dose of capital and labour' applied to a fixed quantity of land) is, in theory, generalised to a case of varying factor-proportions through factor-substitution so that the principle of diminishing marginal returns on land as explaining rents is now extended to all other factors, and a relation postulated in all cases between the factory-intensity and its return (e.g., the inverse relation between capital-intensity and the rate of profit). This indeed is taken as the basis for generating a well-behaved demand function for the factor, whether capital, land or labour. In the classical theory, on the other hand, not only wages, profits and rents were explained on different grounds but they were also differently positioned with respect to the process of surplus generation and appropriation. Consequently, for example, a tax on wages and a tax on rents had qualitatively different consequences on the system; the former affected the rate of profit while the latter not.

With the explanation of demand now in terms of individuals' optimal choice of the consumption basket, given his budget constraint and preferences and at parametrically given prices, the dichotomy (or, the qualitative distinctions) in the world of commodities, such as 'wage goods' and 'luxury goods', loses its analytical significance. The commodities may be differentiated according to their price and/or income elasticities. (It is to be noted again, that it is the relation between consumption and income – e.g., Engel expenditure curves or, the relation as in the Keynesian aggregate consumption function – that has found a more useful application.) the peculiarity of the classical division of commodities into 'wage goods', 'capitalist consumption', 'rentier's consumption' was that these categories are integrally linked to the process of accumulation and therefore play an important analytical role in the dynamics of accumulation.

A symmetry among all 'agents', their process of decision-making and basis of choice, is postulated under the assumption that markets are competitive with free and equal access for all.

In a conception of a fully competitive capitalist economy that so establishes a symmetry among all factors, among products and agents, the distinction between agriculture and industry recedes in theory. The agricultural farm as a micro-unit of production is, for all purposes, considered on a par with an industrial firm, as one among the producing agents; just as consumption of labourers is treated as any other individual consumer's choice of commodities, subject to his budgetary constraint and the given preferences. The typical problems thus analysed relate to the efficiency of resource allocation by individual producers, or to the choice of methods of production by individual producers, given the input and output prices, or to the analysis of price-formation in commodity and factor markets in terms of supply and demand, aggregated from responses of individual producers and consumers.

4 CONCLUSION

To sum up: given the conceptualisation in political economy of the economy as a circular process, and their focus on discovering conditions of its reproduction, their concepts and categories as well as the structure of their theory were devised to aid the analysis of generation, appropriation, distribution and utilisation of surplus. They were thus geared to the problems of resource creation and resource mobilisation as much as to resource allocation. Illustrative of these are the categories of 'class', 'productive consumption', 'absolute value', 'productive and unproductive labour', 'wage goods and luxury goods' as well as territorial divisions like 'town' and 'country' or sectoral divisions such as 'productive and sterile' or 'basic and non-basic' (see Sraffa, 1961). Their concern was with discovering the 'laws of motion', or 'tendencies and counter-tendencies' that shape the dynamics of this process, generating conflicts and contradictions as well as forcing sustaining and stimulating growth. In particular, they recognised the varying nature of the agriculture-industry relation and the specific character conditions of production (e.g., the consequence of 'non-reproducibility' of land) and of production relations (the diversity of production and exchange systems) in agriculture. The status of 'agriculture' even in a fully developed competitive regime, remained distinctive because of the institutional variations which were themselves influenced by, and shaping, in turn, the process of industrialisation. Agrarian conditions were important as they affected the supply (the availability as well as the terms on which supplied) of one of the main constituents of 'wage goods'. That apart, they also influenced the supply of 'wage labour' to industry and were important in the formation of a home market, wherein agriculture was related symbiotically with industry.

In contrast, the neoclassical paradigm, conceptualising the economic process as a one-way-avenue (starting with given resources and moving on to the 'maximum satisfaction' of individuals) essentially focuses upon the resource allocational issues. For the relative prices to play their market-clearing role, while acting as efficient allocators, it is theoretically necessary to restrict the feasible sets of technology and preferences and place appropriate restrictions on the choice-domain of individuals and their interaction. ('No externalities' assumption, for example). The structure of the theory thus renders the resource allocational task 'static' and 'micro-based' so that the ideal conditions for its operationality remain the domain of the competitive individual, optimising within the restricted field of 'change' and 'choice'. Typically, the individual producer's problems, such as the choice of the optimum methods of production, could be usefully treated within this framework.

However, the typical problems of agriculture- industry relation, as seen above, arise in the context of the process of accumulation; the relation itself evolves with the pace of capitalist development. It is not surprising, therefore, that in the analysis of developing economies, where the concern is predominantly with resource mobilisation and creation apart from resource allocation, the political economy viewpoint has been revived with some force. In the course of applying the strict supply-and-demand based logic of market operations, in their case, any number of 'conundrums', 'paradoxes' and 'imperfections' have surfaced in explaining the supply-and-demand responses, 'the choice of techniques' and 'factor-utilisation', at the micro-level as well as at the level of the economy. Moreover, direct observation has brought to light the different kinds of exchange involvements of different classes of producers and the diverse exchange systems that get formed on the 'market' so that the 'market' itself can no more be characterised as a universal and uniform and static category, leave alone as a 'competitive' one. (see Bharadwaj, 1985a). One of the main tasks of research in their case in constructing, on the basis of sound and careful observation, a framework that can take into account the institutional variations in production and exchange relations that influence and are influenced by the process of accumulation.

Notes

1. See Petty (1691), Cantillon (1755), Quesnay (1763), and Turgot (1844). An exhaustive review of the works of Physiocracy is to be found in Meek (1962). An excellent assessment of the Physiocratic contributions to analysis is in Marx (1862–63).
2. See, for the notion of a 'core', Garegnani (1984). This separation of domains of determination of relative prices and quantities does not rule out the influence of prices on quantities (Bharadwaj, 1985b).
3. At times Smith appeared to echo the Physiocratic view, conceding that agriculture produces an additional surplus in the form of rents. While recognising, for example, that all the 'four different ways of employing capital' (procuring raw produce, manufacturing, transport and trade) are 'all necessary', he argues (p. 345):

    Capital employed in agriculture not only puts into motion a greater quantity of productive labour than any equal capital employed in manufactures but in proportion to the quantity of productive labour which it employs, it adds a much greater value to the annual produce of the land and labour of the country.
4. This has some resemblance to Ricardo's early theory of profits where he

maintained, as evidenced from his correspondence, that the farmer's rate of profit determines the general rate of profit. (see Sraffa's (1951) introduction to Ricardo's 'An Essay on the Influence of Low Price of Corn on the Profits of Stock', *Works and Correspondence of David Ricardo*, vol. IV.)

References

Bharadwaj, K. (1976) *Classical Political Economy and Rise to Dominance of Supply and Demand Theories* 2nd edn (1986) (Calcutta: Orient Longmans).

Bharadwaj, K. (1978) 'Towards a Macroeconomic Framework for a Developing Economy', Manchester School.

Bharadwaj, K. (1985a) 'A View of Commercialization in Indian Agriculture and the Development of Capitalism', *Journal of Peasant Studies*, (July).

Bharadwaj, K. (1985b) 'Sraffa's Return to Classical Theory: Change and Equilibrium, Political Economy', *Studies in the Surplus Approach*, vol. 2, no. 2.

Bortkiewicz, L. von (1906–07) Wertrechnung und Preisrechnung im Marxian System: Archiv für Sozialwissenschaft und Sozialpolitik, transl. *International Economic Papers*, no. 2 (1952).

Cantillon, Richard (1755) *Essay on the Nature of Commerce*.

Garegnani, P. (1970) 'Heterogeneous Capital, the Production Function and the Theory of Distribution', *Review of Economic Studies*, vol. 37, pp. 407–36.

Garegnani, P. (1984) 'Value and Distribution in the Classical Economists and Marx', *Oxford Economic Papers*, vol. 36.

Marx, K (1867) *Capital*, vol. I (London), vol. II (1855), and vol. III (1894), Engels (ed.) (London).

Marx, K. (1862–63), *Theories of Surplus Value*, vols I–III, (Progress Publishers).

Meek, R. L. (1962) *The Economics of Physiocracy* (London: Allen and Unwin).

Petty, Sir William (1691) *Political Anatomy of Ireland*, in Hull (ed) *Economic Writings* (London).

Quesnay, F. (1758) 'Le Tableu Economique' in Oncken (ed.) *Oeuvres Economiques et Philosophiques de F. Quesnay* (Paris, 1888).

Ricardo, David (1815), 'An Essay on the Influence of Low Price of Corn on the Profits of Stock', *Works*, vol. IV, in P. Sraffa (ed.) (1951).

Ricardo, David (1817) 'On the Principles of Political Economy and Taxation', *Works*, vol. I, P. Sraffa (ed.) (1951).

Smith, Adam (1776), *An Inquiry into the Nature and Causes of the Wealth of Nations* 2 vols (London). Republished Campbell, R. H., Skinner, A. S., and Todd, W. B., (eds) (1976) 2 vols, as II of *The Glasgow Edition of the Works and Correspondence of Adam Smith* (Oxford: Oxford University Press).

Sraffa, P. (1951), 'Introduction to Principles of Political Economy,' vol. I of

Works and Correspondence of David Ricardo Sraffa, P. with Dobb, M. H. (eds) (Cambridge University Press).
Sraffa, P. (1961), *Production of Commodities by Means of Commodities* (Cambridge: Cambridge University Press).
Turgot, A. (1844) *Turgot on Progress, Sociology and Economics* edited by Meek, R. L. (Cambridge: Cambridge University Press).

12 Market, Non-market, Quasi-market and the 'Real' Economy

Ignacy Sachs
ECOLE DES HAUTES ETUDES EN SCIENCES
SOCIALES, PARIS, AND THE UNITED
NATIONS UNIVERSITY

1 ON RURAL INDUSTRIALISATION AND NON-MARKET ACTIVITIES

Complementarities and trade-offs between agriculture and industry are usually examined within the context of a commoditised economy and of a division of labour between the countryside and the city, the former being responsible for the production of foodstuffs and other agricultural produce, the latter for turning out industrial goods.

Both these assumptions need to be somewhat qualified. On the one hand, *rural industrialisation* constitutes the backbone of the official Chinese strategy aimed at withdrawing before the end of this century about 200 million labourers from agriculture. Rural industries, enabling large numbers of rural people to engage in industrial production without leaving the countryside, are rooted in the tradition of supplementing agriculture with handicraft. The objective now is to disseminate as many modern plants as possible in small towns and in the countryside, and to employ as workers members of peasant families, commuting to the factory for the day, but still living in their villages. Labour force is thus shifted to industry without assuming the responsibility for feeding it out of the marketed food surplus, and without having to cope with the prohibitive social cost of providing the residential urban infrastructure. Efforts are made to employ as industrial workers one member from each peasant family to ensure a more adequate distribution of income (industrial wages being higher than the monetary income of farm-hands). Each family is thus expected to become an agro-industrial household, the basic cell of

218

the modernised economy and of the society. 'A household is the production unit, consumption unit and a living unit combined in one. Household management, at present, is both a key yardstick for measuring the social division of labour, while at the same time conditioning its development' (Fei Hsiao Tung *et al.*, 1986, p. 180).

Clearly in this case the dichotomy *rural-agricultural/urban-industrial* is blurred. So is the borderline between the *commoditised* and the *subsistence* economy. It is true that the scope and the efficiency of rural industrialisation are being questioned by many Chinese economists who believe in the virtues of a more classical industrialisation path, linked with unavoidable, even though costly, urbanisation processes; planning efforts should aim at strengthening medium-sized towns rather than allowing further concentration in very large cities.[1]

The emerging rural-urban configuration in China, based on a massive application of 'intermediate technologies' and on local sources of accumulation, may prefigure a pattern of industrialisation that will be adopted by many other developing countries. But a broader issue ought to be raised in this connection. Recent progress in electronics, communication, biotechnologies, etc., renders obsolete our concepts of economies of concentration, as well as of economies of scale. Decentralisation and even 'ruralisation' of *modern* secondary and tertiary activities becomes feasible and, therefore the trend toward urbanisation and metropolisation, which has marked so deeply the twentieth century, may perhaps be reversed in the future.[2] To quote only one example, agricultural refineries, blending traditional and advanced knowledge-based technologies, may generate a wide spectrum of competitive industrial products derived from agricultural biomass.[3]

For the sake of completeness, let us mention, furthermore, that *urban agriculture* is a reality in many countries, both in the North and in the South. Some urban dwellers grow food inside the cities as part of survival strategies and responses to the crisis; others do it for their pleasure or out of philosophical convictions. Whatever the motive, urban agriculture is on the increase.[4]

On the other hand, *non-market* economic activities are by no means restricted to tribal and primitive peasant economies where they play a predominant or, at least, important role in both producing consumer goods and services, as well as in undertaking non-monetary investment. In the industrialised countries about half of the total working time of the society goes to daily *household* chores, not speaking of an embryonic *social sector* where people indulge in collective, voluntary production of services and goods. Above all, the citizens of welfare states are still entitled, in spite of the regressive trends now operating under the influence of conservative neo-liberal ideologies, to a fair amount of public goods and services freely distributed.

The ways in which the market and the non-market economic activities combine are quite complex. They constitute the fabric of the 'real' economy. The non-market economic activities should not be viewed as a residual category doomed to disappear with the technical progress, sweeping away the underdevelopment understood as a *co-existence of asynchronisms*. Quite to the contrary, their share, in terms of time allocation, may increase *pari passu* with the reduction of the working-time against wage, as a matter of a deliberate choice on the part of people (I shall return to this question later on). The market/non-market dichotomy offers, therefore, a useful starting point to move in the direction of a development theory not exclusively predicated on the categories of the market economy and on the monetary metrics.

2 NON-MARKET VERSUS MARKET BEHAVIOUR

Ever since Adam Smith, conventional economic history associates the division of labour with market development and accordingly views the *degree of commoditisation* as an indicator of economic progress.

Yet, specialisation, which depends on the concentration of demand, is already present in non-market economies of both types: the *customary economy* with its complete 'belowness' and the *command economy* with its complete 'aboveness', as well as in the mixed types that come between, such as feudalism or classical bureaucracies. Hicks, from whom these definitions are borrowed, describes the Revenue Economy as one

> in which a 'surplus' of food and other necessaries is extracted from cultivators, and used to provide sustenance for the public servants . . . It is a genuine form of economic organization, which is to be contrasted with the market form; it is the principal background against which the evolution of the market is to be studied. It precedes the market, but it has of course survived the market. (Hicks, 1969, pp. 23–4)

The extraction of the 'surplus' imposes on the producers an effort going beyond the satisfaction of their direct needs, in other words an *alienated work*, in which people produce for other people without exchange or reciprocity. Such a situation presupposes already the existence of a power. As Clastres put it, the political relation of power precedes and establishes the economic relation of exploitation, the power comes before the work; the emergence of the state constitutes the bench-mark between the savage and the civilised. By contrast, the *subsistence economy* is a 'refusal of useless surplus', the will to tune productive activity to the satisfaction of needs and nothing else. (Clastres, 1974).

Under these circumstances, the degree of commoditisation of an economy does not tell us much *per se* about the well-being of the people. The access to the market creates opportunities for an expanded production and for beneficial exchanges: it stimulates the technical progress. But the market also acts as a powerful mechanism of exploitation, benefiting the strong at the expense of the weak.

Nor is it possible to present the evolution of the economy as a linear process of commoditisation, culminating in a post-industrial, entirely commoditised, service society. The urban poor in Asian cities have been buying their food from street vendors since long before the appearance of fast-food chains in the industrialised countries, while well-off American families discover the delights of cooking at home and of growing their own produce. Partial 'decommoditisation' of services is one of the choices open to the future societies, ever less absorbed by work to produce the necessaries.

Subsistence economy in its pure form seldom exists. But the majority of mankind, constituted by the peasantry, still operates mixed forms of *subsistence-cum-market* economy. At the same time the majority of the urban poor lives in self-built homes. Self-help construction employs mainly the unpaid labour of the family and friends, while only resorting to the services of skilled artisans for some specialised services; building materials are usually purchased on the market, at least in part. Once more we are in presence of a mix of *non-market-cum-market* form of an important economic activity. Even middle-class people often use their spare time, and all sorts of 'do-it-yourself' kits, to repair, expand or beautify their homes instead of contracting the services of a firm. Whether they act in this way for economic reasons or out of a more complex cultural motivation need not be discussed at this stage.

In the passage referred to above, Hicks considers that the experience of market forces has transformed the Revenue Economy, i.e., by 'offering it opportunities for economic calculation, which in the primitive Revenue Economy must have been almost wholly lacking'. Is economic rationality exclusively predicated on the exchange value, as implied in the above statement?

Such a reductionist view is contradicted by the growing body of literature on peasant economies pioneered by the writings of Chayanov. In his important study of the Polish feudal economy, Kula has shown that economic choices were made without passing through a monetary common denominator so, to say, by reasoning directly on use values and by considering different options for the allocation of the work-time available within the peasant family. There was indeed little use for money, and for thinking in monetary terms in an economy based on the interplay between market-oriented (but subsistence self-sufficient) manors, and predominantly subsistence-oriented peasant farms, compelled to supply the manor with unpaid labour (corvée) and spending whatever little money was earned on liquor and beer produced in exclusivity by the manor (Kula, 1980, 1983).

Furthermore, production and consumption within the peasant family, as well as work and non-work activities, were tightly interwoven. Economy was still embedded in social relations, to use Polanyi's (1957) terms, autonomous activities were preferred to heteronomous work,[6] the political and institutional economy could not be separated from the moral economy. This is, as a matter of fact, a situation still prevailing today in many configurations based on the mixed market/non-market form. A recent study found that there is a significant territorial segmentation of the labour market in some clusters of villages in West Bengal: labourers often do not go to work in adjacent villages where the wage rate may be higher, or do go to work to villages where the wage is lower. Patron-client relationships between employers and employees based on considerations of trust, credit, familiarity and dependability may thus constrain the development of an open, competitive labour market over contiguous villages. According to the authors of the study, 'these relationships, viewed in a long-run perspective, are not necessarily economically irrational and may even be regarded as a rational response to imperfect information on worker characteristics, costs of enforcement of contracts with unfamiliar people, and the general absence of credit and insurance markets' (Bardhan and Rudra, 1986).

At any rate, economic analysis should not eliminate from its field a whole series of non-rational behaviour patterns. Nor should it seal itself off from any substantive evidence by transforming its assumptions and concepts into postulates. The distinction between economic and non-economic factors is meaningless. In Myrdal's words 'from a scientific point of view, the only demarcation that is logically tenable when building our models is between relevant and less relevant factors' (Myrdal, 1975, p. 89).

In order to capture the relevant qualitative information on the working of the market/non-market mixed forms, an institutional and anthropological analysis is called for along a line somewhat parallel to the one followed by Herbert Simon in his study of decision-making in business organisations (Simon, 1979).[7]

3 THE REAL ECONOMY

The 'real' economy can be seen as a lattice of segmented yet interconnected labour and product markets and non-markets (see Figure 12.1). The two basic labour-product configurations are: the commoditised economy and the non-market household economy (arrows 1a and 2a).

Now, side by side with the organised sector of the commoditised economy, operated by enterprises – large and small, public and private[8] – complying with all the legal, fiscal and administrative regulations of the labour and product markets, there exist several 'informal' markets (arrow 1b) which can be classified according to their degree of illegality, ranging down to the crime syndicates. A neighbouring segment of the labour market, usually included in the definition of the informal sector, is the group of self-employed (arrow 4); strictly speaking the latter are not on the labour market, however, the produce of their work comes to the product market.

The 'informal' sector is often referred to as 'hidden' or 'invisible'[9]. A better term would be 'statistically unrecorded', as most of the activities in the market segments encompassed by these names are conducted in the open. Anyhow, neither the dichotomy 'formal/ informal' nor the 'open/hidden' one offer a suitable framework to describe the lattice of the real economy. Moreover, they lend themselves to statistical manipulations, as both the 'informal' and 'hidden' sectors are in reality residual categories. By definition, they comprise everything that has not been specifically recorded as belonging to the narrowly defined organised sector of the commoditised economy. By postulating that all those who do not find a regular job in the

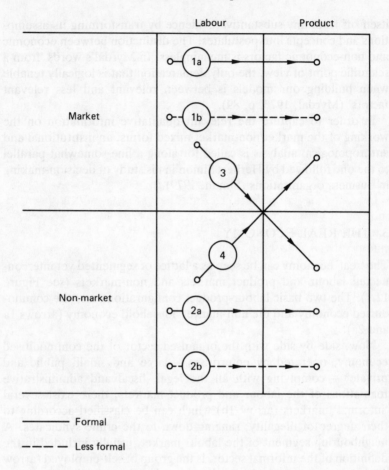

Figure 12.1 Classification of sectors of the real economy according to whether labour and product pass through markets formally or informally

1a	Commoditised sector (wage labour, product sold on the market)
1b	Informal markets
2a	Household sector (labour and product don't pass through the market)
2b	Social sector (collective non-market production) and quasi-markets
3	Public sector (wage labour, product distributed freely)
4	Petty commodity economy (self-employed producers, marketed product)

organised sector are absorbed by the informal economy, it becomes possible to assume away the problems of unemployment and under-employment, as well as to play down the disruptive social consequences of the emergence in the industrialised countries of a *'two-gear' economy* with a highly performing and competitive sector open to a minority, and a residual one for the rest of the population.[10]

By contrast with the commoditised economy, the household activities are situated both outside the labour and the product markets (arrow 2a), although the household consumption consists obviously of a bundle of goods and services purchased on the market and self-produced.

In addition, the non-market segment of the economy comprises in addition the social sector (arrow 2b) consisting of all collective activities organised outside the market by neighbourhood and community groups, citizen associations and, in some cases, co-operatives. Their common trait is that they are founded, just like the household sector, on the principle of the *reciprocity*, i.e., the donation of an unpaid productive activity, deemed of social interest and matched by free consumption of goods and services collectively produced (Kolm, 1984).

James Robertson speaks in this connection of 'the progressive localisation of the welfare state', consisting of the collective self-provision of a growing range of goods and services, previously provided by the public sector, and which offer a potential scope for community contracting (Robertson, 1986).[11]

A natural extension of the social sector are the *quasi-markets*, i.e., local exchange arrangements functioning without money.

For sake of completeness, we ought to mention the public sector (arrow 3) providing free goods and services, produced by public servants who earn wages just like the workers of the commoditised sector.

4 CHOICE IN ALLOCATION OF TIME

The lattice of the real economy provides a suitable framework to address the question of choice configurations open to individuals, households or extended families with respect to the allocation of their time and incomes and the resulting consumption and life-style patterns. In other words, anthropological economics should unfold into a generalised consumption theory, in which consumption is simultaneously described in terms of bundles of goods and services purchased on the markets and/or self-produced, as well as in terms of patterns of time-use.

Two equally reductionist temptations must be avoided: putting a price tag to time, and reasoning exclusively in terms of time allocation.

We shall use, however, the latter as an entry point.

Four choice configurations are theoretically open to, whatever the case, the individual, the household or the extended family (see Figure 12.2):

- allocation of time for economic and non-economic activities;
- apportionment of time of economic activities between market and the non-market;
- apportionment of time devoted to market activities between the formal and the informal markets;
- apportionment of time outside the market between the household and the social sectors.

In practice these choices are constrained by institutional, cultural and conjectural factors. But the range of choice configurations broadens *pari passu* with the increases in the overall productivity of the economic system and the reduction of work time required to produce the necessities of life.

Now, the time spent on market-oriented activities generates a flow of income, whose alternative uses are consumption, investment in consumer durables, savings, or taxes. The purchase of 'durables' is in reality an investment in household producer goods rather than a consumption expenditure. Investment in housing is an example.

In so far as the productive capacity of the household depends, at least in part, on such previous investment, the household sector in our modern economies becomes increasingly 'colonised' by the commoditised sector.

The consumption structure is conditioned by the choices made both with respect to time and income allocation. It consists of goods and services purchased through the market, self-produced and freely distributed by the government which finances them out of taxes (see the bottom right hand side of Figure 12.2 called the 'Structure of everyday life').[12]

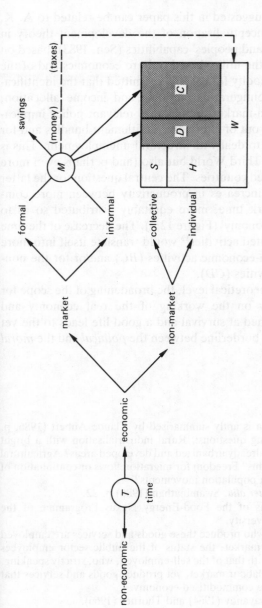

Figure 12.2 Structure of everyday life: time allocation and consumption patterns

Key to 'Box' diagram showing goods and services consumed

C – consumer goods and services purchased through the market

D – durable consumer goods purchased through the market

W – public goods and services distributed outside the market

H – household goods and services produced and obtained outside the market

S – social sector goods and services produced and obtained outside the market

5 CONCLUSION

The type of analysis suggested in this paper can be related to A. K. Sen's important reconceptualisation of the development theory in terms of entitlements and peoples' capabilities (Sen, 1983), based on the rejection both of the utility-based welfare economics and of the fetishism of the commodity forms. It is submitted that the identification of the choice configurations in time and income allocation, relative to market/non-market options, has relevant policy implications for the mapping out of alternative entitlement bundles and for the design of policies to deal with structural unemployment. This is true, not only for the Third World but also (and perhaps even more so) for the industrialised countries. The central question for the latter is the sharing of the increases in productivity between more commodities and less work time, more equitably distributed so as to avoid the 'two-gear economy' (Figure 12.3). The decrease of the time spent on market-oriented activities[13] would translate itself into more time available for non-economic activities (*BC*) and/or for the non-market economic activities (*CD*).

Finally, at a more theoretical level, the broadening of the scope for a substantive enquiry on the working of the real economy and peoples' strategies aimed at survival and a good life leads to the yet insufficiently explored borderline between the *political* and the *moral* economy.

Notes

1. The debate in China is aptly summarised by Claude Aubert (1986, p. 747), in the following questions: 'Rural industrialisation with a bright future or limited to already urbanized and developed areas? Agricultural exodus or rural exodus? Freedom for migration flows or continuation of controls imposed on population movements?'
2. On this point see *inter alia*, Swaminathan (1986) p. 22.
3. See the publications of the Food-Energy Nexus Programme of the United Nations University.
4. Even though those who produce these goods and services are employed through the labour market, the status of the public sector employees may be contrasted with that of the self-employed, who, strictly speaking, operate outside the labour market, yet produce goods and services that circulate through the commoditised economy.
5. See Kerblay and Chayanov (1964) and Thorner (1966).
6. 'Better one's own duty, (even) imperfect, than another's duty well performed' Bhagavad Gita (Quoted by Marglin, 1986.)

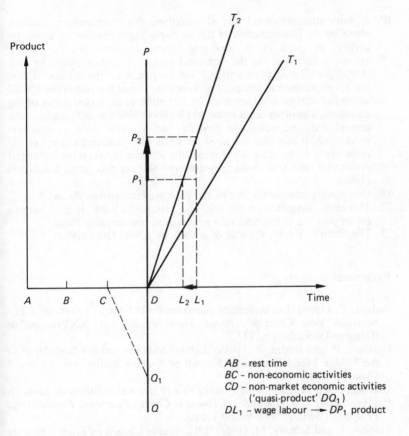

Figure 12.3 The sharing of increased productivity

7. Cf. 'The principal source of empirical data about organizational decision-making has been straightforward "anthropological" field study, eliciting descriptions of decision-making procedures and observing the course of specific decision-making episodes' Simon (1979) p. 501. For a more detailed justification of the need for an 'anthropological economics' see Sachs (1984).
8. Even co-operative enterprises should be included here rather than put in the social economy, defined as operating outside the market. Rigorously speaking, there is a market component and a social economy component in the activities of the co-operatives.
9. The Italians speak of 'economia sommersa' which corresponds to our arrows 1b and 4. For a review of all these concepts and of the literature see Gaudin and Schiray (1984).

10. A more straightforward way of describing this phenomenon, brought about by the dissemination of labour-displacing technologies, would be perhaps to speak of the emerging 'apartheid economy'. As for the extensive literature on the 'informal sector', it is permeated by two sharply conflicting perspectives. One sees in it all the virtues of free market economy and functioning; hence the recent interest of the US aid and other international agencies for this hitherto neglected sector of the economy. The other tends to neglect its very existence and considers the mutual aid and solidarity practices among the poor as counter-productive. It sees that the need for wholesale structural change of the economy is to be achieved through the alliance between the industrial proletariat and the working peasantry. See on this point Kalpagam (1986).
11. Community contracting is a mixed case between arrows 2b and 3.
12. This term, suggested by the title of F. Braudel's book, is used here to encompass the entire field of a generalised consumption theory.
13. The 'Path to Eden', the title of a book by André Gorz (1983).

References

Aubert, C. (1986) 'Les Réformes Agricoles ou la Genèse Incertaine d'une Nouvelle Voie Chinoise', *Revue Tiers Monde*, vol. XXVII, no.108 (October–December) p. 747.

Bardhan, P. and Rudra, A. (1986) 'Labour Mobility and the Boundaries of the Village Moral Economy', *Journal of Peasant Studies*, vol. 13, no. 3 (April) p. 114.

Clastres, P. (1974) *La Société contre l'Etat* (Paris: Les Editions de Minuit).

Fei Hsiao Tung *et al.* (1986) *Small Towns in China – Functions, Problems and Prospects* (Beijing: New World Press).

Gaudin, J. and Schiray, M. (1984) 'L'Economie Cachée en France: Etat du Débat et Bilan de Travaux', *Revue Economique*, Paris, vol. 35 (July).

Gorz, A. (1983) *Les Chemins du Paradis: l'Agonie du Capital* (Paris: Galilée).

Hicks, J. (1969) *A Theory of Economic History* (Oxford: Clarendon Press).

Kalpagam, U. (1986) 'Organizing Women in Informal Sector', *Mainstream*, vol. XXV, no. 15 (December).

Kapp, K. W. (1961) *Toward a Science of Man in Society* (The Hague: Martinius Nijhoff).

Kerblay, B. and Chayanov, A. V. (1964) 'Un Carrefour dans l'Evolution de la Pensée Agraire en Russie de 1908 á 1930', *Cahiers du Monde Russe et Soviétique*, no. 4, pp. 411–60.

Kolm, S.-C. (1984) *La Bonne Economie – La Réciprocité Générale* (Paris: Presses Universitaires de France).

Kula, W. (1980) 'Money and the Serfs in Eighteenth Century Poland', in Hobsbawm, E. J. *et al* (eds) *Peasants in History* (New Delhi: Oxford University Press) pp. 30–41.

Kula, W. (1983) 'Teoria Ekonomiczna Ustroju Feudalnego', 2nd edn ('Ksiazka i Wiedza') (Warsaw).
Marglin, S. A. (1986) 'What do Bosses do again? An Essay on the Moral Economy of Work' (Helsinki: WIDER/UNU) mimeo.
Myrdal, G. (1975) *Against the Stream – Critical Essays on Economics* (New York: Vintage Books).
Polanyi, K. (1944) 1957 *The Great Transformation* (Boston: Beacon Press).
Robertson, J. (1986) 'The Economics of Local Recovery', (London: TOES) mimeo.
Sachs, I. (1984) *Développer les Champs de Planification* (Paris: Université Coopérative Internationale).
Sen, A. K. (1983) 'Goods and People', in Urquidi, V. L. (ed.) *Structural Change, Economic Interdependence and World Development*, vol. 1 *Basic Issues* (London: Macmillan, 1987), pp. 153–78.
Simon, H. A. (1979) 'Rational Decision-Making in Business Organizations', *American Economic Review* vol. 69, no. 4 (September).
Swaminathan, M. S. (1986) 'Sustainable Nutrition Security for Africa: Lessons from India,' The Hunger Project Paper, no. 5 (October) p. 22.
Thorner, D. (1966) 'Une Théorie Néo-populiste de l'Economie paysanne: l'Ecole de A. V. Chayanov', *Annales: Economies, Sociétés, Civilisations*, no. 6, pp. 1232–44.

13 Small-scale Industry in Rural Areas: The Spanish Experience since the Beginning of this Century

Antonio Vásquez-Barquero
UNIVERSIDAD AUTONOMA DE MADRID, AND
INSTITUTO DEL TERRITORIO Y URBANISMO,
MOPU, MADRID

1 INTRODUCTION

Economic growth and structural change in Spain have so far been analysed mainly through the traditional growth concentration/diffusion model. Economic development would have, according to this model, taken the form of urban-based industrial growth, led by big enterprises. Rural areas would have taken part in the industrialisation process only because of industrial diffusion from metropolitan areas.

This paper, however, presents a different approach to Spanish economic growth. The process of industrialisation in Spain started before its industrial revolution, and local industrialisation is one of the features of the formation and development of its production system. The industrial concentration process took place when industrial production had begun in small rural centres and manufacturing activities were diffused in rural areas.

Local development processes have been made possible thanks to a set of economic, institutional and sociocultural factors that stimulated local communities to solve their own problems. When the industrial revolution was completed, and modern economic growth achieved, two paths of growth stand out: One, the urban-industrial concentration/diffusion model; the other, the decentralised rural industrialisation model.

The aim of this paper is to show that local industrialisation is a real and viable development strategy, which can inspire industrial and regional policies. After defining local industrialisation as an alternative growth pattern, and pointing out that industrialisation in rural areas has been, in fact, a hidden development strategy of the Spanish economy, we discuss how present technological change creates the conditions that favour the use of this development strategy. The paper finishes with a few remarks on the general characteristics of a strategy for local development.

2 LOCAL INDUSTRIALISATION, A STRATEGY FOR ECONOMIC DEVELOPMENT

During the 1960s and 1970s, polarised growth and diffusion of development 'from above' constituted the predominant theoretic paradigm on which the growth strategies were based (Robert, 1982). Growth was made possible through the expansion of (large) industrial firms, focused in (large) cities, given that the technological innovations (within the production methods, energy and communications) allowed for external and scale economies.

Industrial diffusion begins when the rise in the price of the labour force and other 'inputs' distort the firms' costs structure, the agglomeration diseconomies increase, and the information and communication economies reduce costs' spatial differences. The firms react, and alter their location strategy seeking new areas where the factor prices are lower, and where locational advantages exist that will permit them to continue to compete within the markets, maintain the profit rate, and continue the capital accumulation process.

The concentration/diffusion growth model has been amply theorised, and development 'from above' has become for decades the main spatial strategy, both in advanced and developing countries (Gore, 1984). Since the late 1960s, changes in demand, the continuous increase in costs, and the growing presence of newly-industrialised countries (NICs) in international markets, alter, to a large degree, this pattern. The introduction of new technologies and the changes in the firms' organisation transform the production processes, modify the plants optimum size, reduce industrial employment, and change the firms strategies and their location pattern. As a result, the spatial movements of the productive factors (capital and labour, above all) are reduced and the traditional mechanisms of diffusion are weakened. It is then that criticism of the development 'from above' model grows.

It has often been said that the traditional concentration/diffusion model tends to generate important disfunctions in backward regions (Stöhr, 1985). On the one hand, it alters the functioning of the labour markets, introducing a spatial dualism that stands out between developed and underdeveloped areas; besides this, it generates territorial exchange of products and factors, which reduces the development potential of the less developed regions; and lastly, it is accompanied by cultural and institutional transformations, with a relatively high valuation of urban industrial growth. The strengthening of the spatial hierarchy encourages a regional growth differentiation, which leads to poor development of rural areas, and in general, of peripheral regions (Guindani and Bassand, 1982).

The decline in the level of acceptance of the paradigm of the development 'from above' has recently activated research that has contributed to the construction of the not very well-defined paradigm of development 'from below'. The attempts at defining local development and its theoretical links with regional development (Friedmann and Weaver, 1979; Sachs, 1980; Stöhr, 1981, 1985), and the interpretation of case studies on local industrialisation (Fuà, 1983; Vásquez-Barquero, 1983) have permitted the (ambiguous) conceptualisation of the endogenous development strategy (with important nuances, according to each author) and the use of an ever more precise terminology (endogenous potential, self-reliant or autonomous development, endogenous development).

One can find a particular productive system, labour market, entrepreneurial capacity, natural resource, political and social structure, culture and tradition within any territorial community. These resources are its endogenous development potential.

At a specific historical moment, a territorial group, of its own initiative, can find new ideas and projects that will allow them to use their resources and find solutions to their problems. In a mixed market economy, the emergence of local entrepreneurship is a necessary condition for a path leading to autonomous development that starts or continues in a new direction. The capacity to lead its own development process along with the mobilisation of the available resources on the area, of its endogenous potential, leads to a form of development called endogenous development.

These concepts (endogenous potential, autonomous development, endogenous development) may be seen from any territorial scale.

Nevertheless, when a community assumes its own impulse from its endogenous potential with a decided effort to exclude that foreign (inter-territorial) presence, that goes against local development, the outcome is a development 'from below' strategy (Stöhr, 1981, 1985).

But, how to specify local development strategy? A number of proposals have been formulated in recent years, among which we will mention the following: Johnson's strategy of market towns and rural growth centres; Rondinelli and Rudle's strategy of integrated regional development; Sach's ecodevelopment strategy; Stöhr and Tödtling's strategy of selective spatial closure; Friedmann and Douglass's strategy of agropolitan development (Gore, 1984).

My purpose here is not to summarise each of these proposals. I wish only to point out that the majority of them advocate an alternative development strategy capable of overcoming the failure of the accelerated and polarised industrialisation strategy. As Stöhr and Taylor (1981) say, 'development from below strategies are basic-needs oriented, labour-intensive, small-scale, regional resource-based, often rural-centred and argue for the use of appropriate technology'.

It may prove interesting to comment, in passing, on the agropolitan develoment strategy of Friedmann and Douglass (1978) for its representativeness. Friedmann and Douglass advocate a development strategy for the Asiatic countries that will integrate rural with urban development, the country with the city. To do this they find it necessary to create local economies, with their own local market, parallel to that of the export economy, and internationally competitive. The objective of the local economies is the satisfaction of the local communities' basic needs through self-centred development and the promotion of its own capabilities. Among their proposals, the following stand out:

- The creation of agropolitan districts, around towns of between ten and twenty-five thousand inhabitants. Investment efforts should promote social facilities, infrastructures, agricultural improvements and labour intensive light industries.
- Devolution of power to the local governments and change within the public financial system, so that each district has sufficient autonomy, and the necessary resources in order to undertake its own development.
- Agricultural reform that will guarantee a control of the wealth on behalf of the members of each local community. Agriculture should be regarded as the propulsive sector of the economy.

- A commitment by the central government to support the development projects with financial, material and technical resources; to assure inter-territorial equity in the allocation of resources and to maintain the macro-economic balance that will allow the system to work.

Although proposals such as these are attractive alternatives to the traditional policies of diffusion, they have serious limitations that obey the weakness of the analysis under which they have been outlined, and they are highly utopian. It's not only that the concept of agropolitan development is rather ambiguous and that the implementation of this strategy is always left undefined; the problem is mainly that this kind of proposal is hardly workable.

One wonders how developing countries can finance this type of programme, which needs large investments in infrastructure, and in basic and intermediary industries without increasing foreign dependence? How can local economies function with a market isolated from the rest of the country's economy, which is considered to be integrated within the international economic system? How are the objectives of equity and improvement in the standard of living going to be achieved? In any case, this kind of strategy is not a viable proposal, given that it is likely that its implementation would give rise to a network of small rural communities, with low development levels (Gore, 1984).

In my opinion, the endogenous local development strategy is viable when it tries to foment an increase in the standard of living, without trying to isolate the local communities from the context defined by the national economic system. The effort should be focused towards progressive change in the productive system of each local community, on the basis of their own capacities, of their endogenous potential, following a local industrialisation pattern such as the one that is actually in use in some recently industrialised countries like Spain.

In this context, we can be more precise about the concept of local development strategy: local development is a process of economic growth and structural change that results in an improvement of local population standards of living (Coffey and Polese, 1985). At least two dimensions can be identified: one, economic, in which local entrepreneurs use their capacity for organising local resources with a sufficient productivity level as to be competitive in the markets; another, sociocultural, in which local values and institutions serve as the basis for the development process.

Local development strategy should consider a third dimension (Stöhr, 1985), the political-administrative dimension, in which territorial policies permit the creation of a local economic climate, protect it from external interference and favour and protect the development of local potential.

3 LOCAL INDUSTRIALISATION IN SPAIN, A STIMULATING EXPERIENCE

Stöhr and others have felt the scepticism of the professional and international institutions when putting forth local development strategy. Nevertheless, recent research (Vásquez-Barquero, 1983; ITUR, 1986) shows that local industrialisation and development is a reality in recently industrialised countries like Spain.

Local development experiences are vastly different from each other, which is why it is difficult to give a definition that represents the variety of cases. When we speak of local development in Spain, however, we refer to sets of entrepreneurial experiences in industrial activities. They have developed by using the local (mainly human and financial) resources, and in any case without the direct intervention of the administration. They are located in small rural centres scattered throughout the territory. Small-scale rural firms produce mainly for a market located outside the local community boundaries.

In order to know more about local industrialisation in Spain the Institute for Territory and Urbanism (Instituto del Territorio y Urbanismo – ITUR, 1986) has just finished research which permits to a certain extent the quantification of the phenomenon, and more precise definition. The objective was to make a map showing which are the endogenous development areas and the specific weight of the local industry. The research was established starting from a set of quantitative and qualitative variables and indicators, to permit the quantification of the process that has been previously identified through pilot studies (Vásquez-Barquero, 1983). Use was made not only of the available local statistical information, but also local experts helped to identify the local industrial experiences.

The first conclusion of this study is that local industrialisation is a phenomenon extended throughout Spain (Figure 13.1). It affects sociopolitical, in which local values and interest serve as the basis for the development process.

Local development strategy should consider a third dimension (Stohr, 1985), the political dimension. This dimension, which complements endogenous creation of (idealistic) endogenous protect it from external interference and bypass and protect the development potential.

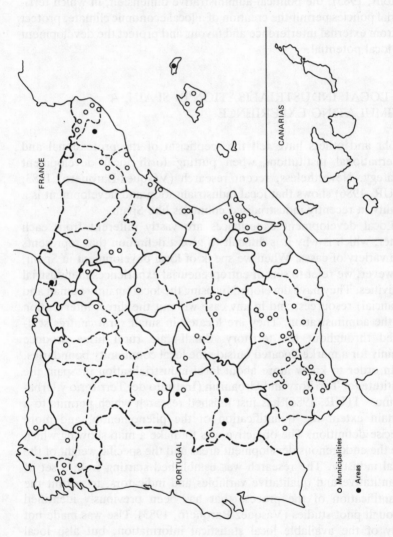

Figure 13.1 Location of the endogenous industrialisation areas and

eighty-three different zones in the peninsula and islands which conform quite closely to the above definition of local industrialisation. Industrial employment in these areas represents at least 10 per cent of the active population in Spanish industry. The population affected by local industrialisation is around 6 per cent of the total population. This is significant, particularly if we keep in mind that the criteria used in the research were very restrictive.

Only municipalities with more than 1000 inhabitants were studied, with the exception of those included within a distance of 70 km of Madrid and Barcelona, and of 25 km of those cities with more than 100 000 inhabitants. This is too strong a restriction, given that, even in some of the Spanish metropolitan areas, local endogenous industrialisation processes have been historically identified. On the other hand, only centres with industrial employment of over 10 per cent of total employment, and with a minimum of 0.5 kW per inhabitant of power capacity installed in a municipality were considered, which excludes certain transitory local development processes.

By typifying the local development areas with respect to criteria such as the provincial industrialisation level, the relation to the agricultural sector and the productive specialisation, certain common features arise (Table 13.1). Large parts of the local development areas are located in provinces with low and medium levels of industrialisation (this result has been partially influenced by the restrictive methodological criteria used in the research), areas specialised in one industrial activity are more frequent and the dependence on agricultural resources is limited at present (2 per cent of the cases).

On the basis of this research it has been possible to draw a map of the endogenous industry that shows significant territorial diffusion. Although a relative concentration of local industry exists in the Mediterranian coast (Gerona, Alicante and Murcia represent the higher levels of endogenous employment), the Basque country (mainly Guipúzcoa) and the Ebro Valley axis (Navarra, Rioja and Tarragona), important experiences exist in the inland areas (such as Albacete, or Toledo), in Galicia (Pontevedra), and there are numerous cases in Andalucia (see Figure 13.2 for the identification of regions and provinces).

On the other hand, local endogenous industrialisation is one of the basic supports of the industrial system of important areas of intermediate industrialisation (Alicante, Gerona, Castellón, Baleares, Navarra, Rioja) and of weak industrialisation (Jaen, Albacete, Murcia, Burgos, Toledo, Badajoz, Ciudad Real and Córdoba), which gives it

Table 13.1 Classification of local development areas

	Level of provincial industrialisation					
	High		Medium		Low	
Dependence on local agricultural inputs	Dependent	Non-dependent	Dependent	Non-dependent	Dependent	Non-dependent
Strong industrial specialisation	Ribera del Ebro Tortosa-Amposta La Selva		Santoña-Laredo Molina de Segura Ejea de los Caballeros Quintanar de la Sierra El Barco-Ponferrada Ría de Arosa Mollerusa	Medina Campocuellar Pedreguer-Gata Ontinyent Elda-Petrel Crevillent Illueca-Brea Arnedo	Morón S. Vicente de Alcántara Valle del Jerte Vega Alta Vega Baja Benaoján-Montejaque Olula-Macael	Alcázar de S. Juan Socuéllamos-Almansa Menorca Linares-La Carolina Alcalá de Real Navalmoral de la Mata Ribadavia
Industrial diversification (Areas)		Alto Deya Olot Ripoll Plana de Vic Banyoles El Vendrell La Bisbal		Alcoy Vinaroc-Benicarló Onda-Alcora Xàtiva		
Strong industrial specialisation	La Seu d'Urgell		Guissona Nájera Aguilar de Campóo			Gilena Purullena Huétor-Tajar Alcaudete

241

Municipalities		
Industrial diversification	La Estrada	Sarria
	Vall d'Uxó	Manacor
	Xixona	Bailén
	Ibi	Ubeda
	Yecla	Mancha Real
		P. Genil
		Béjar
		La Rambla
		Priego
		Ubrique
		Chiclana
		Estepa
		Castilleja
		Inca
		Llucmajor
	Sigüenza	Campillos
	Sonseca	Andújar
	Aranda de Duero	Lucena
	Lalin	
	Valverde del Camino	
	Talavera de la Reina	
	Tárrega	
	Calatayud	
	Padrón	

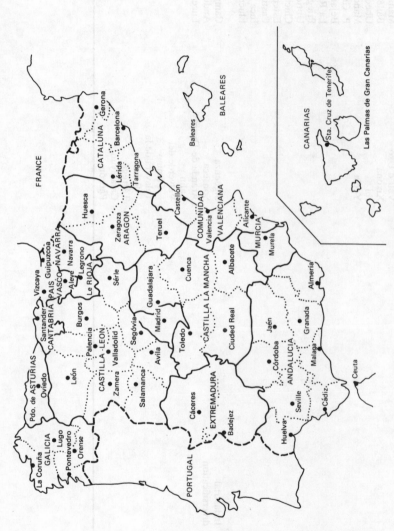

Figure 13.2 Regional and provincial divisions of Spain

a strategic role in the productive structure (Table 13.2 and Figure 13.3).

Besides this, the research has shown that local enterprises produce a wide range of mature industrial goods from food products, textiles, furniture, shoes and ceramics to machine tools, equipment and plastics. Local industrialisation is based on small and medium-sized production units, with an important contribution made by family-run and co-operative enterprises.

The number of local firms in any one area or municipality varies. A high concentration of firms has been found in some cases: more than one hundred firms in the Alto Deva, Olot and Ribera del Ebro, and more than two hundred in towns like Ubrique or Yecla. The local firms' average size is above that of the national average (fourteen workers per firm, according to the 1978 Census) as shown in the cases of Arnedo, Béjar, Santoña and Sonseca (local firms' average size between 24 and 45 workers by firm). But in the case of Mahón, Ubrique or Yecla, the local firms average size is under the national average.

How did local industrialisation begin? Which are the factors that have favoured local development? Local industrialisation is a process, whose birth, development and maturity is based on a combination of causes that go from necessity (case of the Vinalapó Valley in Alicante, where during the mid-nineteenth century *phylloxera* destroyed the vineyards, the main productive activity of this area), to the availability of natural resources (case of Olula-Macael with marble) and/or good locations (case of Aranda de Duero, traditional market centre in Castilla). As previously mentioned, all of these processes have started spontaneously without public intervention, and contain both an economic and sociocultural dimension.

The local industrialisation process begins with the transformation of the traditional productive system. The existence of a certain entrepreneurial capacity, an abundant and cheap labour force, a consolidated social structure, a practical knowledge of products and markets, the availability of some savings coming from the entrepreneurs' previous activity (agricultural and/or commercial), and, in certain cases, a good location, allows the industrialisation process to start, and so, satisfy a need for change that was felt at the local level. Occasionally the process has been favourably influenced by the fact that local resources were highly valued within the markets (Vásquez-Barquero, 1983).

Table 13.2 Local endogenous employment in provincial industrial employment

Per cent of local endogenous employment in industrial employment	Provinces with more than 100 000 industrial employees	Provinces with between 100 000 and 75 000 industrial employees	Provinces with between 75 000 and 50 000 industrial employees	Provinces with between 50 000 and 25 000 industrial employees	Provinces with less than 25 000 industrial employees
More than 25%	Alicante Murcia	Gerona Castellón	Baleares	Jaén	Albacete
Between 25% and 15%		Navarra		Burgos Rioja Toledo Badajoz C. Real Córdoba	Lugo Orense León Palencia Salamanca Segovia Soria Almería Cáceres Zamora Avila Huesca Teruel Guadalajara Cuenca Huelva
Between 15% and 5%	Guipúzcoa Zaragoza	Coruña Pontevedra	Cantabria Tarragona Valladolid Cádiz	Lérida	
Less than 5%	Madrid Vizcaya Barcelona Valencia Sevilla	Asturias	Alava Málaga	Granada	

Source: ITUR, 1986.

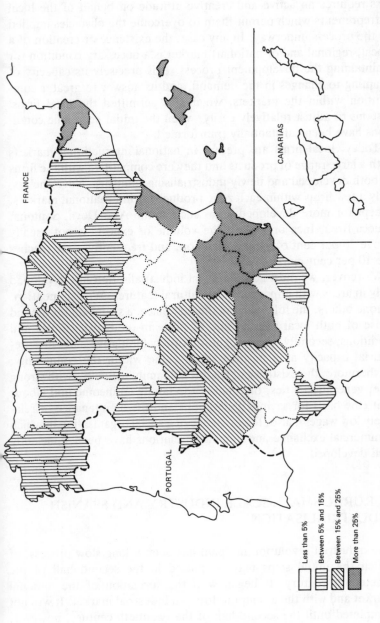

Figure 13.3 Local endogenous employment in provincial industrial employment.

Source: ITUR, 1986.

The birth and continuity of the endogenous industrialisation process requires an active and creative attitude on behalf of the local entrepreneurs which permit them to overcome the obstacles implied by the process underway. In any case, the existence or creation of a (local, regional and/or national) market is a necessary condition for maintaining the development process. It is precisely its capacity of adapting to changes in the demand, and its answer to greater competition within the markets, which has permitted the local firms' systems to adjust relatively easily, when the initial economic conditions have been substantially transformed.

Today, local firms are present in national/international markets with a large range of products and they are competitive with the firms of both developed and newly-industrialising countries. Nevertheless, only a few firms within each zone produce for international markets, except for more developed areas such as the Alto Deva, Santoña, Illueca-Brea, Inca or Elche. The volume of exports is not usually above 20 per cent of local production, and frequently, only reaches the 10 per cent mark.

Moreover, we must add that local industrialisation has developed only in areas with important sociocultural features. We can mention, among others, the following: in the first place, a strong and profound sense of both local identity and of pride in their own culture and traditions; secondly, the recognition of local initiative and entrepreneurial capacity as a positive social value within the community; furthermore, the existence of traditional family structures with strong inter-generational ties, that makes the family an income and labour unit (the basis for savings generations and the maintenance of relatively low wages); also, the existence of a social organisation in which commercial exchange and monetary relations have been sufficiently well developed.

4 RURAL SMALL-SCALE INDUSTRY AND SPANISH INDUSTRIALISATION

The industrial revolution in Spain has been a long slow process, of which the initial steps may be placed in the second half of the nineteenth century. It began with the formation of the national market and with the attempt to form an industrial market. It was not completed until the second half of the twentieth century, however, when strong economic growth rates and structural changes were produced, favoured by the interaction between endogenous and exogenous forces in the process of capital accumulation (Fuà, 1980).

The role played by local industry within the industrialisation process in Spain has not yet been studied sufficiently, due no doubt to the negative effect of the modernisation theory on the studies of economic history in general (Mendels, 1984), and the predominance of quantitative aspects in the definitions of industrialisation (Crouzet, 1975). Despite this, an attempt can be made to relate small-scale industry in rural areas to the Spanish industrialisation process.

Spanish industrialisation began before the diffusion of the factory system in the Spanish economy, under the cloak of diffuse industry in rural areas. Carande (1977) pointed out that already in sixteenth century Castilla, manufacturing activity was spread out into the countryside. The transformation of rural industry in a process of local industrialisation was the next step, when in the late nineteenth century machinery was introduced in the Spanish productive system. The failure of the industrial revolution, however, at the beginning of the twentieth century, permitted local industrialisation to consolidate itself, and so become one of the pillars of the Spanish industrial system.

From Rural Industry to Local Industrialisation

During the nineteenth century, the formation of the national market in Spain took place with the loss of the colonies and the construction of the radial system of railroads (initiated in 1847) and roads. The basis for the iron and steel industry were laid down (at the end of the century in the Basque country) as well as for the transformation industry, though the most dynamic sector was that of textiles, mainly in Cataluña (Tortellá Casares, 1975 and Nadal, 1973).

Though the process of industrialisation took on a strong impetus in Spain during the 1870s (industrial jump), the industrial sector was of little importance at the end of the period. Following the Census in 1900, 68 per cent of the active population was employed in the agricultural sector, while 16 per cent was in the industrial sector. Nevertheless, small-scale industry and decentralised industry in rural areas was very important during this period.

Before the industrial revolution took place in Spain, an important part of the rural population worked in the production of metallurgical products, textiles, or leather transformations, using manual production methods for their later sale in non-local markets. In these cases, the work in rural manufacturing was frequently on a part-time basis with agriculture. The Spanish experience adjusts quite well to what has been termed by Mendels and others as proto-industrialisation.

Many local industries in Spain have emerged as rural industrial activities, even though the origins of local industrialisation go back only to the previous century. Thus, of the twenty-one cases studied in the ITUR report (1986), fourteen began their industrialisation process before the twentieth century. We can mention, among others, the following examples: the elaboration of chocolate pastries in Aguilar de Campóo, begun at the end of the nineteenth century; steel weapon production in the Alto Deva since the mid nineteenth century; the creation of the first textile factory in Béjar in 1784 (Jewish handicraft); gold and silver work in Mahon during the first half of the nineteenth century; leather transformation started in Ubrique during the early nineteenth century.

During the nineteenth century, a large part of Spanish rural industry adjusted to the putting out system, as is shown by the textile industry. Pascual Madoz identified 13 121 looms for weaving throughout 3117 municipalities (of a total of 9000) having some textile production in the mid-nineteenth century (see Figure 13.4). Often, these textile activities tended to disappear as the factory system was adopted, as happened in the case of Galicia, where during the mid-nineteenth century some textile activity was recorded in 923 towns, the greater part of which disappeared during the first third of the twentieth century. In other cases, however, industrial activity focused on small-scale firms within rural centres (Morella, Segorbe, Alcoy or Elche, in Valencia; a third of the two hundred villages of Cataluña). This gave rise to industrialisation processes in these areas (Aracil and Garcia-Bonafé, 1978).

Among the factors that favoured the transformation of rural industry into a process of industrialisation in rural areas are the folowing: the existence of a local industry previous to the introduction of the factory system, the development of commerce (interregional and with the colonies) of local products during the nineteenth century, the transfer of resources (financial and human) from the agricultural and commercial sectors to rural industry, and the late formation of the highly protected industrial market.

The Formation of the Industrial Market

Apart from the consolidation of the national market, and the introduction of the capitalist mode of production within the agricultural

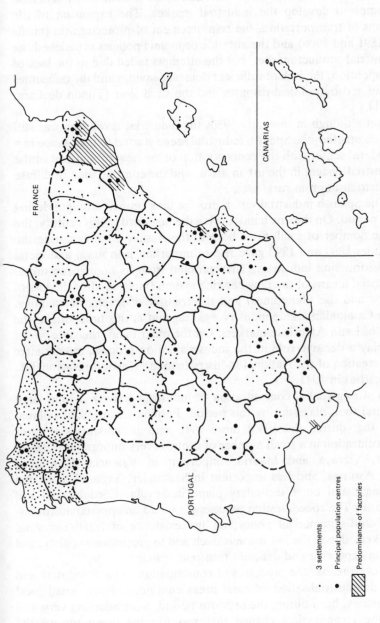

Figure 13.4 Dispersion of textile industry in the mid-century

Source: Aracil and García-Bonafé (1978) according to P. Madoz.

sector, what really defines the first half of the twentieth century is the attempt to develop the industrial market. The expansion of the means of transportation, the reinforcement of protectionism (tariffs of 1891 and 1906) and the autarkic economic policies broadened the industrial product market, but the attempts failed due to the lack of competition, the lack of sufficient domestic savings and the difficulties generated by political disputes and the Civil War (Tuñón de Lara, 1961).

But although in the early 1950s the industrial revolution was still not completed, the Spanish industrial scene started to take shape in a 'modern' sense, with the concentration of the new component of the industrial system in the urban areas, and the consolidation of diffuse industrialisation in rural areas.

The Spanish industrialisation process took on new strength during this period. On the one hand, during the first third of this century, the large number of small firms born in the Basque country during the decades 1880 and 1890 gave rise to important iron naval and metal transformation industries. They profited from its mining resources, financial means of the new banking system (built up after the loss of Cuba and the Philippines) and the transfer of foreign technology. The Catalonian textile industry was stagnant at this time, due to the loss of Latin American markets. On the other hand, the state began to play a decisive role in the industrialisation process, mainly after the creation of the National Industry Institute (Instituto Nacional de Industria) in 1941.

A strong spatial concentration of industrial activity (within large plants) took place during this period. Perpiña Grau (1936) pointed out that during the 1930s there were serious tendencies towards concentration in a small number of centres (very important in Barcelona, Vizcaya and Madrid; important in Valencia, Guipúzcoa and Asturias, and less important in Santander, Vigo Alicante and Málaga; and on a secondary plane in Sevilla, Córdoba and Zaragoza). The concentration process was based on an autarchic industrial and commercial policy, on the existence of small industrial markets, due to the low income levels and to protectionist policy, and on an expensive and deficient transport system.

Nevertheless, the processes of consolidation of rural industry and the deindustrialisation of rural areas continued. Some small local industries, born during the previous period, were adapting very well to the technological change that was filtering down toward the Spanish productive system. Local firms introduced modern machinery and produced new goods. Despite this, new industrialisation processes in rural areas appeared as well. As example of this we can mention the cases of the birth of the wood transformation industry in Lalín and Barra de Miño in Galicia and Yecla in Andalucia, or of marble transformation in Olula-Macael during the first third of the century, and the starting of the co-operatives in Mondragón and Guissona during the 1950s.

The local industrialisation process continues during this period, and the new system of urban firms overlaps the traditional system of local firms because of a set of factors. On the one hand, the new products of these urban firms do not exclude the products of the rural firms from the markets because the domestic demand grows slowly due to the low levels of income and to its bad distribution, and also because transport costs made the urban products significantly more expensive. Furthermore, an important part of the new urban products (naval industry, the iron and steel and metal transformation) make up a range of products different from traditional rural goods. Lastly, the radial character of the transport system favours mainly the exchange between the large cities of the network; but this fact and the deficiencies of the communications allow the local firms to control important regional markets.

Modern Economic Growth

During the last thirty years the Spanish economy has achieved what Kuznets has called 'modern economic growth'. It has passed through two well-differentiated periods. The first (up to 1973–75) was one of growth (annual GDP growth rate of 7 per cent during 1961–74) and structural change. The second (from 1974 onwards) is a period of crisis (unemployment rate increased progressively from 1.6 per cent in 1974 to 22 per cent in 1985).

The factors explaining the Spanish industrial development and the 1970s crisis of the industrial system, and the transformation of industry have been studied elsewhere (Vázquez-Barquero 1986). What should be stressed here is the contribution of small-scale industry in rural areas to the transformation of the industrial system in Spain.

Above all, it should be pointed out that rural areas began to be of interest as possible plant location from the early 1960s. The (large) urban industrial firms of the developed regions began increasingly to appreciate location in diffuse regions and in non-metropolitan areas as a result of the progressive cost increases, the appearance of agglomeration diseconomies and the 'liberalisation' of the economic policy. The process takes on special force in the early 1970s as a result of the changes in the demand of industrial products, the large increase in production costs and the increasing growth of modern services in the adjustment of the last decade (Vázquez-Barquero, 1984b).

The industrial diffusion process, however, is due not only to the functional or productive decentralisation or urban firms' activities which adopt a new location strategy. It is also due to the strengthening of the local industrialisation process in rural areas.

The 'liberalisation' of the Spanish economy, and the widening of the national market, allowed local firms to use the existing potential within rural areas and attend national and foreign markets. In the 1960s and 1970s the competitive advantage of rural firms was basically due to the lower production costs in rural areas. The favourable conditions of the Spanish and international markets and the dynamism of local entrepreneurs allowed the small local firms' systems to strengthen despite the fact that economic and sectoral policies favoured industrial concentration in only a few urban centres.

During the last decade the system of local firms took on a greater momentum, not so much because the industrial crisis and urban deterioration gave a differential value to this industrialisation pattern, but because of its better adaptation to the changing economic conditions. The leading local enterprises have changed their strategy. They no longer base their comparative advantage on lower production costs, but on the differentiation of production and in the production of new goods. The increase in local enterprise competition and labour productivity has been possible thanks to the introduction of new technologies into the production process, and the transformation of the plants' organisation system.

The leading local firms are more competitive when markets change quickly (such as clothing) and a territorial or functional segmentation of demand exists. Not all firms are successful in adapting to the new conditions. In those cases where firms have been incapable of achieving the necessary changes, we can observe processes of deindustrialisation. Frequently however, the basic factors that have favoured the start of the local industrialisation process have precipitated the surge of new industrialisation process, either linked to the previous process, or not.

5 TECHNOLOGICAL CHANGE AND LOCAL INDUSTRIALISATION

One wonders if the local industrialisation model continues to be useful today? Is local development a process that can make up one of the structural change strategies of the Spanish economy? Or is it a phenomenon that has changed character in the past decade only to disappear in the new phase of the economic cycle?

It is no doubt rash to put forth a judgement as to the future of a process so complex as that of local development. We can nevertheless explore its future from the perspective of today's technological change. Although local industry is often shaped by labour intensive activities, local development will undoubtedly be feasible if technological progress is introduced into the system of local industry. But, are local firms capable of adopting and adapting new technologies?

The analysis of case studies of local industries shows the penetration of modern technology within the local enterprise systems. Leaving aside the outstanding fact that the more dynamic local firms today have improved their communications systems (through the introduction of the telex or the connexion with national and international data banks), we should point to the adoption of new technologies in production processes too. It should be stressed that local industrialisation is largely based on the adaptation of technology, and recently, even on the 'creation' of modern technology.

In the Alto Deva, in Lalín, in Olot, in the villages of the province of Alicante or in Puente Genil, firms that are leaders in the machine tools, clothing, plastic extrusion, toys, shoes and mass-production pastry industries, have abandoned old-fashioned production processes and have introduced modern equipment, often electronic control machines. If the new communication technologies have improved the accessibility of local systems, the application of the new production processes have increased labour productivity and have improved the local firms' competition within the markets.

Beyond this, in clothing manufacturing, machine tools and extrusion of plastics the plants' production function is ever more closely adapted to a multi-product function system, that will allow firms to diversify their products and meet the requirements of different markets with several final products. Undoubtedly local firms are more efficient; but the introduction of new technologies in the production process also allows them to produce goods suited to customer demand. This has given the firms a greater flexibility which makes them more profitable and more competitive.

A major question in local development is certainly the choice of technologies that will permit an efficient use of the available local resources, and at the same time, be competitive within the products market. According to Morawetz (1974) there are three possibilities: to import the technology from abroad through transfer of technology, generate it locally, or adapt the technology available in another area to local needs. Traditionally, local entrepreneurs have sought to use production methods from abroad, but they have often been capable of adapting it to local production needs by introducing small changes in the more or less modern machinery.

While visiting toy firms in Alicante, plastic transformation firms in Olot, or mass-production pastry plants in Puente Genil, one realises that a large part of the machinery in the more modern plants has German, Italian or Japanese patents. Leading entrepreneurs are proud of their new equipment, and painstakingly describe how they have had to transform the organisation of the production process, and even the distribution of the machinery within the plant in order to make production more efficient. The majority of local entrepreneurs, however, use foreign (as well as Spanish) machinery and production methods, often somewhat outdated, and at times even second-hand.

With this same enthusiasm, however, local entrepreneurs show the machines in use, old or modern, which they or their technicians and/or skilled workers have designed or adapted. Occasionally, local firms need to fill orders for a new product, or must improve productivity in order to continue being competitive within the market and cannot change their equipment quickly enough. The lack of financial resources, the lack of information about the new equipment markets, or the need for an efficient use of local resources press them to look to themselves and their own capacity, to their own engineering know-how and so transform a piece of available machinery or equipment in the plant, or design a new one, in order to overcome the situation.

Some neo-Schumpeterian economists, on finding out that local entrepreneurs are more adaptable than innovative with respect to technology, react negatively and scorn the results obtained. My intention here is not to criticise this neo-Schumpeterian point of view, or to discuss Schumpeter's concept of the role of innovation within the economic growth process. I wish only to recall Rosenberg's (1976) emphasis on adaptation of technology in economic development processes.

We are witnessing an important change during this last decade in the behaviour of local firms in Spain, that has given rise to the creation of Research and Development Centres in local development areas, dedicated to innovation, design and quality control. Some have already achieved important results, as happened in the case of IKERLAN in Mondragón, ITEP in Mahón or INESCOP in Elda.

The best-known case is that of IKERLAN (Thomas and Logan, 1982), a co-operative of the enterprise system of Mondragón that undertakes research and development. Among their activities stands out the identification and adaptation of technologies, innovations, the diffusion of technology to the production co-operatives of the Mondragón group, and personnel training for firms within the group using new technologies.

Partly financed by the Basque government, the state administration, the Mondragón group, and the clients themselves, its most important feature is that it develops specific projects in the fields of electronics, mechanics, data information and production systems, directly related to the specific needs of the local firms. What also stands out is the development of innovations in the field of robotics and numerical control machines.

If the need to solve technical problems and increase competition and productivity on the part of Mondragón's co-operative firms gave rise to the creation of IKERLAN, the urgency for overcoming problems related to glues and leather for the shoes exported and returned from the USA induced local entrepreneurs in Elda to create INESCOP. Thus began, in the late 1970s the Research and Development Centre of Elda, initially financed by local entrepreneurs, and later by clients and the Ministry of Industry. Its activities are evolving from quality control of products and raw materials to the development of modern design and the creation of machinery for shoes.

In short, the evaluation of local industrialisation processes with respect to the introduction of technological change within the local enterprise system speaks for itself. The major factors of the local industrialisation process (local entrepreneurship, the local communities, capacity for solving their own problems, industrial culture) are ever present in local economies, and push them forward to adjust their productive structure to the new conditions of the international economic system. The local enterprise systems show a capacity for developing old/new products with new technologies, and begin new activities as well. In other words, the industrial centres in rural areas may assume new functions within the international (or national) division of labour.

6　CONCLUDING REMARKS

This paper has shown that within a national economy several paths of growth can be identified. Local industrialisation can become a development strategy but it will take different forms, according to the conditions of the particular local economy. The reason is that any local area is a product of its own history and the new rounds of investment have different implications for different productive structures.

The Spanish experience shows that the industrial revolution was completed not only through the (large firms) polarised urban/industrial growth model, but also through the (small firms) diffuse rural/industrial growth model. At the present time, industrial growth continues in rural areas because local firms are able to introduce new technologies within the production processes.

The problem is to design a long-term strategy for local development. Spain cannot serve as an example, given that local industrialisation took place despite the fact that the state's policies favoured the traditional concentration/diffusion model. In any case, we can say that the overlapping of at least two development models demands a complex system of objectives and of policy instruments (Vázquez-Barquero, 1986).

If both these models are to shape development, the economy's system of growth objectives must change. The maximum growth objective of the functional paradigm should be submitted to the limitation of satisfying the local communities, needs. Polarised development's objective should be changed for that of diffuse development. Faced with the fact of centralised, hierarchical growth, the local and regional communities potential should be fostered as well as its participation in the control of productive processes.

If the development objectives change, so too should the instruments and the agents of local development strategy change. On the one hand, only those actions focused towards the mobilisation of their own resources would be valid, and therefore, to the development of the economic, sociocultural and politico-administrative dimensions of local development. This, however, would mean accepting the fact that when the market mechanisms function, as happens in the case of local industrialisation in Spain, it is not advisable to interfere and that the enterprises' services would be promoted and managed by the entrepreneurs themselves.

This does not erase, however, the responsibility of public institutions. As Coffey and Polesi (1985) point out, public involvement is necessary for the preparation of the institutional and economic environment that allows endogenous development to begin in the areas, stimulating local entrepreneurship through social animation, information and financing.

References

Aracil, R. and Garcia-Bonafé, M. (1978) 'Industria Domestica e Industrialización en España', *Hacienda Pública Española*, no. 55, pp. 113–29 (Madrid).

Carande, R. (1977) *Carlos V y sus Banqueros* (Barcelona: Grijalbo).

Coffey, J. W. and Polese, M. (1985) 'Local Development: Conceptual Basis and Policy Implications', *Regional Studies*, vol. 19(2), pp. 85–93 (Madrid).

Crouzet, F. (1975) 'Quelques Problèmes de l'histoire de l'industrialisation en XIXe Siecle', *Revue d'Histoire Economique et Social*, vol. 53, pp. 526–40 (Paris).

Friedmann, J. and Douglass, M. (1978) 'Agropolitan Development: towards a New Strategy for Regional Planning in Asia', in Lo, Fu-chen and Salih, K. (eds) *Growth Pole Strategy and Regional Development Policy* (Oxford: Pergamon).

Friedmann, J. and Weaver, C. (1979) *Territory and Function* (London: Edward Arnold).

Fuà, G. (1980) 'Problems of Lagged Development in OECD Countries. A Study of Six Countries', *OECD*, mimeo. (Paris).

Fuà, G. (1983) 'L'industrializzazione nel Nord- Est e nel Centro' in Fuà, G. and Zacchia, C. (eds) *Industrializzazione senza fratture* (Bologna: Il Mulino).

Gore, C. (1984) *Regions in Question* (London: Methuen).

Guindani, S. and Bassand, M. (1982) *Maldéveloppement Regional et Indentité* (Lausanne: Presses Polytechniques Romandes).

Instituto del Territorio y Urbanismo, (ITUR) (1986) 'Areas Rurales Españolas con Capacidad de Industrialización Endogena', mimeo. *MOPU* (Madrid). Research carried out by CEAM.

Mendels, F. (1984) 'Des Industries Rurales à la Protoindustrialisation: Historique d'un Changement de Perspective', *Annalles*, E. S. C. 39e année, no. 5, pp. 977–1008.

Morawetz, D. (1974) 'Employment Implications of Industrialization in Developing Contries: A Survey', *Economic Journal*, vol. 84, (September), pp. 491–542.

Nadal, J. (1973) 'The Failure of the Industrial Revolution in Spain 1830–1914', in Cipolla, C. M. (ed.) *The Fontana Economic History of Europe. vol. 2, The Emergence of Industrial Societies* vol. 2 (Fontana/Collins, 1975.)

Perpiña Grau, R. (1936) 'De Economia Hispana', in Perpiña Grau, R. (1982) *Economia Critica* (Valencia: Institución Alfonso el Magnanimo).

Robert, J. (1982) 'Mobilising the Indigenous Potential of Disadvantaged Regions: A New Dimension of Regional Planning', European Regional Planning Study, no. 40. (Strasbourg: The Council of Europe).

Rosenberg, N. (1976) *Perspectives on Technology* (Cambridge: Cambridge University Press).

Sachs, I. (1980) 'Strategies de l'Ecodéveloppement', in *Economie et Humanisme* (Paris: Les Editions Ouvrières).

Stöhr, W. (1981) 'Development from Below: The Bottom-Up and Periphery-Inward Development Paradigm', in Stöhr and Taylor (1981).

Stöhr, W. (1985), 'A Selective Self-reliance and Endogenous Regional Development', in Nohlen and Schultze (eds), *Ungleiche Entwicklung und Regional Politik in Südeuropa* (Bochum: Studienverlag Dr N. Brockmeyer).

Stöhr, W. and Taylor, D. R. F. (eds) (1981) *Development from Above or Below? The Dialectics of Regional Planning in Developing Countries* (Chichester: J. Wiley & Sons Ltd).

Thomas, H. and Logan, C. (1982) *Mondragón: An Economic Analysis* (London: Allen & Unwin).

Tortellá Casares, G. (1975) *Los Origenes del Capitalismo en España* (Madrid: Technos.).

Tuñón de Lara, M. (1961) *La España del Siglo XIX* (Barcelona: Laia).

Vázquez-Barquero A. (1983) 'Industrialization in Rural Areas', *OECD*, Inter-governmental meeting, Senigallia (June).

Vázquez-Barquero, A. (1984b) 'Politica Regional en Tiempos de Crisis', *Estudios Territoriales* nos 15–16, pp. 21–32.

Vázquez-Barquero, A. (1986) 'Transformation of the Industrial System in Spain', in Hamilton, I. F. E. (ed.) *Industrialization in Developing and Peripheral Regions* (London: Croom Helm) pp. 114–35.

14 Small-scale Industry in Rural Areas: the Italian Experience

Giorgio Fuà
UNIVERSITY OF ANCONA

1 A HISTORICAL RETROSPECT

In Italy, as in other countries, the beginning of modern industry was largely based on small firms operating in rural areas or 'putting out' work to rural dwellers. A comprehensive account of Italian experiences with 'small-scale industrialisation in rural areas' would have therefore to start from a remote past, and would be too large a subject for the present paper.

So I will focus only on a singular feature of recent Italian history. But let me introduce it with a few historical statistics (detailed in the Appendix Table A 14.1).

On the eve of the twentieth century Italy was still a predominantly agricultural country. If we take as a rough indicator of industrialisation the percentage of the active population in industry[1] to total active population, we find this index to be scarcely 20 (see Figure 14.1, which provides a geographical partition of the country). Nineteen of the twenty present administrative regions have been grouped in three partitions, North–West, North–East and Centre (hereafter labelled NEC), and South, each of which is sufficiently homogeneous as concerns recent economic history. The remaining region, Latium, is shown apart, because its evolution is strongly marked by the presence of Rome, the Italian capital, which accounts for about three-quarters of Latium's total population.

It appears from Figure 14.1 that at the turn of the century the industrialisation index was near the national average in all geographical partitions.[2]

Since the turn of the century, however, the industrialisation index shows a strong increasing trend in the North–West, while there was

259

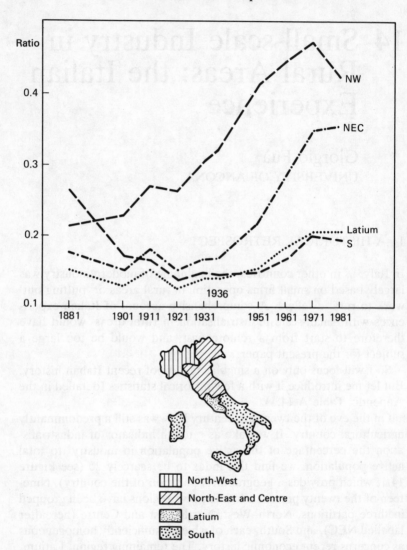

Figure14.1 Ratio of active population in industry to total active
population

not such a trend in other parts of the country. Consequently, at the
last Census preceding the Second World War the index for the
North–West was twice as high as the index for other partitions: the
North–West had become a moderately industrialised economy, while
all the rest of Italy was still mainly pre-industrial.

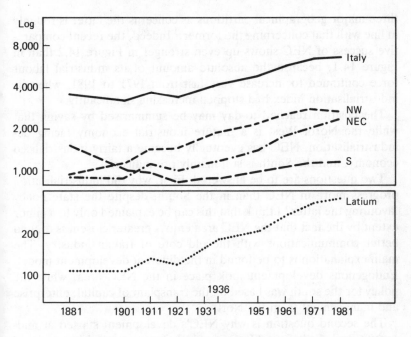

Figure 14.2 Active population in industry (000)

Around the middle of the century major changes took place in the still pre-industrial part of Italy. In the NEC partition, an endogenous industrialisation process gained speed, without any explicit state support, and resulted in a development pattern based on small firms and diffuse location.

In the South there was massive state action for promoting industrialisation, largely through an inflow of capital and of managerial and entrepreneurial capacity from the North.

As shown in Figure 14.1, the industrialisation index for NEC rose appreciably between 1936 and 1951, and very rapidly from 1951 to 1971. The index for the South also moved, but later and slower. Thus NEC regained much of the ground previously lost, while the South went on losing.

After 1971 the index kept approximately stable in NEC and the South, and declined in the North–West, reflecting a marked evolution towards a service economy.

We may be interested in considering – besides the industrialisation index – the absolute number of population active in industry (see Figure 14.2). It is found that the comparative performance of the three major geographical partitions as concerns the latter is roughly in line with that concerning the former.[3] Indeed, the recent comparative success of NEC shows up even stronger in Figure 14.2 than in Figure 14.1, because the absolute amount of its industrial labour force continued to increase very fast from 1971 to 1981, when its industrialisation index had stopped increasing significantly.

The position reached to-day may be summarised by saying that while the North–West is a mature industrial economy facing de-industrialisation, NEC has eventually become a fairly industrialised economy, and the South is still mainly pre-industrial.

Two questions are to be answered. First, why did industrialisation progress more in NEC than in the South, despite the state policy favouring the latter? I think that this can be explained only to a minor extent by the fact that the NEC area enjoys greater closeness to, and better communications with the old core of Italian industry. The main explanation is to be found in the different development model. Endogenous development took place in the NEC area, while the policy for the south was based on the transplant of capital, enterprise and management from the North.

The second question is why NEC's development started at mid-century and not before. My answer is that two prerequisites matured just at that time, namely excess supply of labour in agriculture (due to technological progress there), and improved transport and communication, that created new opportunities for contacts with distant markets.

In the following I will expound the NEC industrialisation model,[4] because I think it provides a lesson about the potential for development latent in local resources, and how not to waste it; a lesson that might be found interesting in other countries confronted with the need to industrialise rural regions.

2 THE NEC MODEL

2.1 The Starting Point

A key factor in the model is the environment. The original environment is typical of the Italy of the independent Communes, e.g., Tuscany (as opposed to the territories of the former kingdom of Naples).

Thus the territory is rich in small and medium-sized towns – urban centres with long traditions of efficient and democratic local government and vigorously engaged in commerce, the professions and handicrafts.

The countryside is covered by a good road network, is fairly well endowed with infrastructures, and has reasonable access to services. The family-run, small-scale enterprise (owner, share-cropper or tenant) is common in agriculture. The rural population is large and has close links with the population of the towns.

In the whole population (rural and urban) there is a high proportion of self-employed workers. The economic role of the family is often not confined to consumption, but covers production too. A large part of the population has a house, a small-holding or a family shop to fall back on. Relationships within the extended family and with the neighbourhood are supportive and there is marked community participation and social integration. This sort of environment has a high potential for development.

Let us see, now, how the industrialisation process is set in motion.

2.2 The Industrialisation Process at Work

On the one hand, we have a mass of workers who are no longer able to find satisfactory jobs in agriculture, but are unwilling to leave their homes where they feel integrated and protected, and are therefore looking for work as near home as possible. On the other hand, in this world of family businesses and self-employed workers, there is some management experience, some spirit of initiative, some sense of responsibility, and all these gifts, even in small doses, are widespread among the population. This potential is then mobilised to harness the surplus agricultural labour, and the result is the setting up of small, or even tiny, industrial initiatives.

The new enterprises and their growth and propagation are mainly financed directly from family savings. Given the limited savings available, the investment strategy adopted proceeds by small steps. The enterprises are set up in places where local labour is available and where existing private and public infrastructures can be used; the enterprises are therefore scattered widely over the territory as befits a logic of development which exploits existing structures as far as possible, while minimising the break with tradition.

This type of industrialisation also allows enterprises to avoid excessive wage claims and labour conflict. There are two points to consider here. First, as they can continue to live at home, the new industrial workers find themselves in a favourable position (compared to those workers who operate at some distance from their home) as concerns the opportunity of supplementing their wages with other income sources, and also as concerns the cost of living, the quality of life, and social security. This leads to moderation in wage claims. Secondly, there are few social distinctions between the new entrepreneurs and their workers; there are indeed often family ties, and, moreover, there is considerable social mobility, which favours a climate of co-operation.

The goods produced and the technologies used are in line with the other characteristics of the NEC model which I have outlined above. The new industry concentrates on those branches, technologies and types of product which do not present insuperable disadvantages for small-sized firms. It specialises, wherever possible, in a type of production which allows it to make use of local craft tradition. Production such as that described above rarely finds an adequate outlet in the neighbourhood. Therefore a large proportion of the industries which develop within the NEC area work chiefly for markets outside the region or abroad, which is possible because of recent progress in transport and communications.

One can now answer the question posed by those students of the economics of industrial location who ask whether the development of industry in certain districts rather than others depends on the presence of market outlets, the presence of raw materials or on other factors. Undoubtedly in the NEC model 'other factors' play the largest role. In this model, industrialisation finds fertile soil in the local (if still latent) supply of entrepreneurial energies, labour and savings, and in the existence of a well-run society with its institutions, its culture and material infrastructures. The success of the model relies on its capacity to combine all the strong points and resources of the existing organisation and harness them to modern development. This assumes that transplants and changes are not so drastic as to shatter the existing social pattern, thereby squandering valuable resources.

Two development phases – in the first phase, due to underemployment and depressed local conditions, the new enterprises are faced with an abundant and undemanding labour supply. Moreover, both the local authorities and public opinion are favourably disposed to enterprises creating new opportunities for employment, and the regulations are not too strictly applied to these enterprises. On the other hand, in this first phase new enterprises are unlikely to be able to compete on equal terms, technically and organisationally, with well-established firms. These two characteristics of an industrial world still in its infancy – modest productive capacities and modest social demands – offset each other. Enterprises which are still technically and organisationally inferior to established firms can be profitable and competitive if they pay lower wages, lower taxes and do not have to conform strictly to regulations on working conditions and environmental pollution.

At a later stage, when the industry has grown, labour becomes more demanding and social controls more rigorous. The wages, charges and regulations which are borne by the enterprises tend to equal those of established industries, and the firms can maintain their profitability and competitivity only by raising their productivity.

In this second phase, the NEC industries make rapid technical and organisational progress by perfecting the organisation of the integrated system of small firms and increasing specialisation in quality production, that of small batches or even customised production (for example, robots).

After this brief outline of the model as a whole, I shall examine some details.

2.3 The Entrepreneurs and the Workers

The labour force comes mainly from the families of agricultural workers, at least in the beginning. The majority of the workers have some sort of family property (small-holding, shop or house), and so have a safety net to catch them in hard times. They are not 'proletarians'.

While the leaders of the first wave of industrial development in North–Western Italy came mainly from the upper classes, those of the NEC development come from all classes. Indeed, the great majority come from the lower-middle and lower classes. After the pioneers, the entrepreneurial ranks are swollen by people who started as wage earners and who have then set up their own business in the same industry.

Thus, class differences are not marked. Workers and employers come from the same or similar social backgrounds, and are connected by family ties and social mobility. They have a common work ethic handed down to them from the pre-existing society of family-run farms and craft activities. It is an ethic based on the traditional conviction that there is a necessary relationship between effort and reward, between commitment to one's work and social success. This leads to emulative behaviour and to labour relationships based on co-operation rather than strife. Even the problem of the loss of a job can be faced with less anxiety, when, as is most often the case, the worker has an economic base in the family which can temporarily give him refuge, and when a large number of ways are open to provide his return to the labour market. For this reason, enterprises face little resistance to plans for reconversion or retrenchment.

It may also be noted that, in this situation, a whole series of factors serve to keep wage claims within bounds. They are briefly examined below.

Wage levels and standard of living – in the first place, certain factors permit the achievement of a given volume of real purchasing power with a money pay lower than that which would be necessary under conditions of concentrated industrialisation. Thus, the average cost of housing is lower because old houses remain in use and the price of new dwellings is not so high as in large cities. Family ties with agriculture mean that certain foodstuffs can be provided on favourable terms. Commuting between home and work is generally less expensive, both in time and money, than it is for workers who live in the cities.

There are many other advantages, which are not so easy to quantify in terms of money, but are none the less appreciated, and which accrue from the workers remaining in their own surroundings. I will pass over these and take up one final point.

This is the high degree of utilisation of the labour potential. The widespread existence of productive activities within the family and the close network of family and neighbourhood relationships creates the conditions for the employment – although without formal work contracts – of those marginal elements of the work force (housewives, retired people, students) who, in other circumstances, have difficulty in finding work. As well as giving employment to these 'second rank' workers, the socioeconomic structure favours a super-utilisation of the 'first rank' workers. Men who own small businesses always tend to work long hours, and they are numerous here. Wage-earners here often have a second job to which they devote part of the time left over from their primary jobs. These second jobs often consist simply in giving a helping hand in a family small-holding or shop. This is also the temporary solution to unemployment found by many workers when they are on the dole. And, moreover, it serves for some as a means of taking advantage of their holidays.

2.4 The Small Enterprise System

The small size of the enterprises is a key element. In these particular environmental conditions, it is undoubtedly the formula which gives the greatest possibility of success and also that which best preserves the environment.

It is the formula most suited to local entrepreneurs who would not be able to raise large amounts of capital or manage complex organisations even should they wish to do so. It is also what makes it easier to find manpower in an essentially rural area, studded with small and medium-sized towns. Such a territory does not offer a pool of labour suitable for large industrial agglomerations, but it does provide labour for smaller and more numerous industrial units.

Furthermore, industrialisation based on small enterprises does not cause so much of an unpheaval as that based on large concentrations, as regards not only urbanistic and landscape values, but also the existing social structure. For example, the system of small enterprises maintains the continuity of the productive role of the family and of the old work tradition, and does not upset the balance of democratic local government as much as would the creation of large-scale industry.

Type of production preferred in the NEC model – choices of types of product and technology are influenced by three considerations, whose relative weight is modified as development proceeds.

First, production lines are chosen which are within the cultural horizon and the technical and financial capacities of the local entrepreneurs. In the early stages of industrialisation, this implies the adoption of technologies which are not too alien for a world of small farmers and artisans. Moreover, those industries are preferred which have a link with the earlier craft specialisations of the individual areas. A large number of important industrial districts have an ancestry of this sort. The fact that these industries evolve, without a break in continuity, from a pre-existing craft tradition makes their first steps easier and does not stop them, as they develop and diversify, from gradually adopting advanced technology.

Secondly, the conditions of under-employment existing at the outset encourage the firms specialising in those production lines which allow them to take advantage of the relatively low cost of labour and the lack of rigidity in the regulations concerning the protection of the environment and the health of the workers. Both cause and effect will disappear with industrial progress.

Thirdly, those industries are preferred in which it is possible to break down production into stages or products without having to use inferior techniques. Thus, even a very small enterprise can, by concentrating exclusively on one stage of the process – and/or on a few component parts of the product – avoid the risk of being below the optimal size from a technical point of view. I have left this point to the last, because, as we shall see in a moment, it has the most important consequences for the NEC industrial structure. Of the three points mentioned above, it is the one which remains valid for the longest time. It combines with the other two points to condition the entrepreneurs' choices in the early stages of industrialisation. Then, as development proceeds, its influence increases, while that of the other two declines.

Division of labour and methods of integration – the division of labour among a number of different manufacturing firms can solve the problem of making small size compatible with the technological optimum only as concerns production in the strict sense; but there are other important functions, such as finance and control, marketing, management of human resources, in which the small manufacturing firm would still find itself at a disadvantage. It is, therefore, expedient for the small enterprise to entrust these functions to specialised agencies, which can work on a reasonably large scale by serving a number of manufacturers. We thus have a combination of two closely-knit networks: the division of labour among a number of manufacturers and the division of labour between manufacturers and tertiary firms offering the necessary services.

To say that enterprises make use of the division of labour is the same as saying that they form an integrated system, and, in fact, the development of a system of integrated small enterprises is one of the most commonly recognised characteristics of the NEC model. Writers have spoken of 'industrial districts' (borrowing the name from Marshall), 'area systems', 'clusters of enterprises', or 'constellations of enterprises'. Each of these writers was obviously thinking of a different variety of the integrated system, which had indeed many different forms. Some systems are clearly circumscribed (the majority of transactions are carried out within the system), while others have vaguer boundaries; some systems are restricted to a limited territory, while others are not, and, finally, in some systems the association of enterprises is formally regulated while in others it is not.

Methods of co-operation vary from financial participation to supply contracts, from simple family relationships to informal temporary agreements. In order to give a few instances, I can start by mentioning the co-ordination of small Tuscan industries by private export firms with offices in Florence, which not only co-ordinate foreign demand with Tuscan production, but at the same time carry out important complementary functions, giving mercantile and financial assistance and controlling quality.

In other cases, there are forms of association. For instance, the associations of artisans and small entrepreneurs in Emilia have created centres which prepare wage packets, keep the books, pay VAT contributions, and fill in tax forms for their members. There are also co-operatives for the sale of products and, still more important, co-operatives which act as guarantors to the banks for the solvency of the single entrepreneur and negotiate the most favourable interest rates possible.

I may conclude these examples by considering the highly individual model of integration offered by the Prato wool industry. In this system there are many leading firms which have no employees whatever, consisting only of the entrepreneur himself. It is he who designs the good to be produced and commissions the spinning, weaving, finishing and mending from different firms.

Industrial districts specialising in one product – a phenomenon found fairly frequently is the geographical agglomeration of small enterprises either producing similar goods or vertically integrated; in other words, the formation of areas specialising in one single production line.

It is a well-known fact that the contiguity of many enterprises producing similar goods creates a complex of economic factors and stimuli influencing each single firm, and for this reason, the process of agglomeration, once under way, has an avalanche effect, caused by the reciprocal strengthening of the firms inside the area, by the arrival of other firms from outside, and by the involvement of the surrounding territory through overspill or annexation.

The luxuriant growth of which these agglomerations are capable is, in the short term, an important component of the overall growth of the NEC industry, but, if it is not properly channelled, it runs the risk of causing long-term difficulties. Two dangers must be considered. First, it is better to avoid the total, or almost total, dependence of a highly-populated area on one very limited specialised product; the first crisis in the sector would cause a social disaster. Secondly, one must fear a situation in which the 'area-systems' act as magnets attracting a concentration of population and activities, thereby causing congestion within the area and abandonment outside it; should this happen, the territorial balance from which the NEC model draws its strength would no longer exist.

Problems of services – as noted above, industrialisation based on small enterprises following the NEC model demands and stimulates considerable growth in the supply of services for these enterprises.

The range of services offered by existing private agents is rich and varied, but it could be improved. Not only are there certain services where either quality or selling price is exposed to criticism, but there is also a whole series of services that is excluded or seriously neglected. I refer to scientific services, to basic educational facilities, and to all those services which a small firm (without the wider operational horizons of a large enterprise) is unwilling to pay for by itself, as in any case the greater part of the benefits produced from these services will not accrue to its own production alone but be spread through the system.

Given the fundamental importance of services to production in the NEC model, and the gaps in the structures created by private enterprise, we must consider the possibility of supplementing them from public sources. Experiments on these lines have been carried out especially at local and regional level, but results so far have been modest. This is hardly surprising given the difficulty of finding forms of public aid compatible with the NEC model's way of working, i.e., which invigorate it without spoiling it (by, e.g., bureaucracy, 'welfarism', and favouritism).

The service activities stimulated by NEC industrialisation show a marked tendency to concentrate in the towns. This gives rise to a paradoxical situation in which a deconcentrated, rural model of industrial development leads to a concentrated, urban model of tertiary development. This spontaneous tendency is reinforced by certain local administrations who are planning to develop major regional towns as capitals of the 'tertiary sector'.

If things continue in this way, and if, as is generally considered likely, the tertiary sector is destined to absorb an increasing proportion of the work force, there will be a progressive weakening of those decentralised structures which today form the strength of the NEC model. This is not all, however. If this territorial dualism persists, whereby the services go to the towns, while industry remains in the country, the differentiation between services and industry will widen, and, in the final analysis, reach a complete antithesis. Should the service industries continue to offer higher wages and better working conditions, the feeling that the towns are prospering at the country's expense could be aggravated and thus could recreate a potential rivalry and distrust between town and countryside of the kind familiar to us in other situations in history, when 'countryside' conveyed the idea of an exploited peasantry.

For all these reasons, we cannot but be preoccupied by present tendencies. It is, however, obvious that the development of service industries is to be encouraged, and that, as things are at present, firms in this sector secure considerable economies from a marked urban concentration. But the existing situation is also the result of the policies adopted, and we can attempt to change that by giving our policies a different slant in the future. In particular, we may envisage a policy aimed at taking advantage of the considerable possibilities for deconcentration offered by new technological developments in telecommunications and telematics.

The strengths of the system – the analysis we have carried out shows the logic underlying the formation of the system of small enterprises. Small dimensions are adopted because this is the highway to a development based on local resources, and the enterprises must be linked together to form a system, in order to avoid the diseconomies which would otherwise stem from their smallness. It must now be asked whether the results obtained – the system of small enterprises – is simply a poor man's second best, something which poor countries have to accept because they are not (yet) able to construct a system based on large enterprises, or whether the decentralised model may not in some ways be actually superior. The answer is that the system of small enterprises has certain strengths (just as it has obvious weakness). I will now review the most important of these.

I should first stress the favourable environmental conditions produced by the overall working of the NEC model, such as low cost of living, intensive utilisation of the labour potential, and survival of the old attitude to the work. On the one hand, the small enterprises, as essential elements in the model, help to produce those conditions, and on the other hand, they benefit from them in terms of lower costs and more efficient business management.

Moreover, 'smallness' allows faster adaptation to continually changing markets and technologies. In the first place, the small firm, which is less bound than the large one by the dead hand of bureaucracy and trade union rules, is quicker to modify the allocation and size of the labour force and other resources. In the second place, a system of small enterprises makes it possible, by the simple transfer of subcontracts, to solve problems which would require closures and relocation of personnel in a large firm system. In the third place, the NEC system gives an outlet to the inventiveness and spirit of initiative of a large number of people, and encourages these qualities through competition and emulation. So, even though, as we have seen, basic research may be neglected, there is a profusion of the type of research which is the closest to industrial application and which leads to a continual flow of small innovations (almost of the 'learning by doing' kind).

Greater flexibility, and a more open attitude to innovations, make the small enterprise the most suitable one for production on a small scale or for single items. It is therefore at an advantage in those markets where demand is either fragmented for geographical or social reasons (down to the exceptional case of 'customised' demand), or variable in time (rapid fashion changes or frequent innovations.)

This position in the international division of labour gives the NEC model a lead, because the relative importance of these markets is increasing. The NEC-type industry can, therefore, seize on this opportunity. Indeed, it has already begun to do so. It can rely on its greater flexibility to beat the competition of more advanced economies as it can rely on qualitative and technological superiority to beat the competition of emerging economies with low wages.

2.5 Capital Formation

The following are the main characteristics of capital formation in the NEC model. Families have a high propensity to save, and these savings tend to be invested directly within the family. The investments are made with an eye to producing immediate results in terms of production (i.e., the incremental capital/output rate is kept low). The result is that local industry achieves a good growth ratio relying on local savings and depending little or not at all on a net capital inflow from outside.

As to the characteristics of savings, in the NEC model family savings are used mainly to build and improve the family's premises and equipment: the house, the small-holding, the workshop and the shop. This gives them two important qualities. In the first place, while serving as a reserve for the future and as an income-yielding asset, this type of savings, more than any other, satifies the saver's desire for self-fulfilment. Secondly, it offers the saver a certain security as to maintaining the value of his money in times of inflation. These two considerations, self-fulfilment and security, help to explain why the family's propensity to save is generally higher in the NEC model than in other communities where concentration of settlements and productive structures offers less opportunity for direct investment.

It should be noted that differences in savings as shown in statistics reveal only part of the truth. Some of the time off from 'official' work is spent in accumulating resources, eg., family house-building during weekends. Activities of this kind create income, savings and investment which the national accounts ignore. Of course, this use of free time is found everywhere, but there are signs that it is particularly common in the NEC districts. This is not surprising, considering that the whole NEC rationale encourages and facilitates it.

The above description portrays a world of largely self-financing investors, and this is a strong point in the system in the sense that the enterprises are not deep in debt and are therefore less vulnerable.

I shall now examine the characteristics of real investment, and first comment on its volume. As the location of new productive initiatives tends to be chosen on the basis of pre-existing structures, past investments can be recouped, and there is a reduction in the new investments needed to launch these projects. This observation holds good for every type of infrastructure – from workers' houses to power lines and roads, and includes the whole network of services needed to create civilised surroundings. It is also valid to some extent for the factory buildings and plant. Small firms frequently start out in buildings not designed for the purpose, and adapted, for example, from warehouses, storerooms or stables, with makeshift equipment. This allows them to begin production with a minimum of new investment. If production is successful, and as both the funds available and the cultural horizon expand, they will gradually adopt more sophisticated technological and logistic solutions. And so on, step by step, without great leaps forward. When one firm leaves its buildings and equipment for better ones, the old assets are frequently taken over by another firm which is trying to move one step up the ladder, too. So the progress made by one firm makes things easier for another, and, by a chain reaction, the whole group gradually moves upwards, making the maximum use of the capital available.

We must not expect the results of this investment model to be impressive from all points of view. They may not be so for technicians and town planners, as the model produces an industrial landscape dotted with provisional solutions consisting of makeshift buildings and outdated technologies. This may be cause for regret, but, given the limited quantity of investment, the model has the great advantage of allowing the largest number of people possible to find work and to improve their qualifications by experience. It should also be noticed that this gradual progress reduces the risk of serious errors.

3 REPERCUSSIONS ON AGRICULTURE

While agriculture makes a positive contribution to NEC industrialisation, it is also important to examine the influence of this industrialisation on agriculture.

Some problems arise from the fact that industry competes with agriculture in the use of land and water resources, but only in a few particular zones has the damage suffered by agriculture been very serious.

Repercussions on the labour market are much more important. NEC type industrialisation brings wide-ranging opportunities for extra-agricultural work in rural zones, and triggers the phenomenon of the 'multi-activity family' (whose members are employed both in agriculture and in other types of work) which gives a breathing space to agriculture. The possibility of income from extra-agricultural sources helps the family to remain in its place of origin and thus averts the danger of the countryside being abandoned – so common in models of concentrated industrialisation. From a plurality of activities the family both derives a higher income and gains wider experience advantageous for agriculture. Those members of the family employed in extra-agricultural activities bring new technological and administrative skills to the management of the family farm, and employ their savings in agricultural investment, with possibly profound changes in agriculture.

We must also remember the ability of multi-activity families to weather the seasonal variations in agricultural work.

Agrarian policy will, however, have to face dramatic choices in the future, following the effect of industrialisation on young people's professional ambitions. Among today's multi-activity families, the leading role in the small family farm remains, on the whole, in the hands of the older generation. The younger generation is not interested in taking over, because youth find extra-agricultural employment more satisfying and less demanding. Of course, a great many young people appreciate the fact of belonging to a family owning a small-holding, but very few are anxious to run it themselves. If this trend continues, the small family farm, which is one of the pillars of the NEC model, will gradually cease to exist for lack of new generations willing to take it over. A policy must be devised to cope with this possibility. On the one hand, we should ask ourselves whether it is possible to concentrate on a really substantial package (in education, finance, public services, prices, etc.) that would make small farm management attractive to young people again. Following the same line of reasoning, we should also consider a plan to change the small farm into a diversified business, e.g., agro-tourism, which would make its management both financially and personally more rewarding. Looking at things from the opposite point of view, one might suggest a policy which would accept the decline of the small farm and favour the setting up of farms large enough to permit the exploitation of brillant managerial capacities and thus attract the best qualified type of youth. We need not even dismiss the possibility of separating the two functions present up to now in small family farms; indeed a system could be envisaged in which large farms take over market production, while family small-holdings produce for domestic consumption.

4 THE OUTLOOK

There is a widespread agreement that, up to now, the NEC model of rural industrialisation has been a relatively successful experience. Without an explicit plan, it has succeeded, area by area, in rallying local potential for entrepreneurship, work and savings, and in using to advantage the material and social structures, probably with better results than would have been possible using imported models and resources. The material well-being and the cultural level of the

population have improved substantially; social integration and mobility have been strengthened, and there has been no serious disrup-
tion.

This, on the whole, bright picture, however, is not without some
shadows. Industrialisation has brought with it certain evils which a
more sagacious public policy could have avoided. But the positive
results greatly outweigh the negative ones.

While an assessment of the results obtained can easily be made,
future developments are controversial. We have to consider whether,
precisely as a result of the progress made, the deconcentrated model
which has been the basis of the NEC economy (small enterprises, low
territorial concentration, fundamental importance of the family and
the agricultural environment) is destined to lose its pride of place to a
completely different model of development, characterised by large
enterprises and complex organisation, by metropolitan concentration
and a sharp break between town and countryside. Should the NEC
economy develop in this way, it would be a repetition of events in
earlier developed regions and countries. There, too, industrialisation
began in a deconcentrated form, and only became concentrated in a
second phase of development.

The history of earlier developed countries, however, presents a
third phase which has been manifest for some time, and which gives
cause for reflection. Urban congestion and huge industrial centres
have begun to make their negative effects felt (ungovernability,
sclerosis, lack of individual responsibility), and this has led, both in
theory and in practice, to a new movement towards deconcentration.
This should serve as a warning to the later developed countries and
regions, such as NEC. We must ask ourselves why the latter should
slavishly copy the policy of concentration, only to discover one fine
day – too late, as usual – that they, too, will have to make a U-turn
and begin to deconcentrate again.

The solution suggested here has little chance of being automati-
cally adopted. In an earlier phase of NEC development, both cultural
survivals and automatic economic mechanisms were leading society
towards deconcentrated development, without any explicit plan having been adopted; but today the situation is different, and the
automatic bias in favour of concentration is now growing stronger,
and threatening the deconcentrated model. Thus the increase in
income and international contacts through business, tourism, and
education abroad are all leading to the adoption of 'consumeristic'
models. Young people who now have easy access to higher education

want safe careers such as are afforded by large bureaucracies. Commercial attempts to 'sell' consumerism as a life-style are highly organised on a world scale, whereas there are no similar organisations to sell competing life-styles.

The progress of the NEC development in a way which will guarantee the advantages of the deconcentrated model cannot therefore be left to chance, but calls for a clear realisation of the situations and an explicit policy.

Appendix Table A14.1 Basic statistics

	1881	1901	1911	1921	1931	1936	1951	1961	1971	1981
Active population in industry ('000)										
North-West	946	1 122	1 409	1 459	1 757	1 867	2 211	2 537	2 766	2 653
NEC	921	883	1 112	1 008	1 119	1 181	1 425	1 758	2 054	2 336
South	1 564	1 024	969	824	884	899	976	1 061	1 153	1 151
Latium	106	105	128	116	155	176	205	262	321	353
Total Italy	3 537	3 133	3 618	3 407	3 914	4 123	4 817	5 618	6 294	6 493
Ratio of active population in industry to total active population										
North-West	.215	.230	.271	.264	.309	.322	.417	.451	.479	.428
NEC	.175	.153	.182	.151	.167	.168	.223	.288	.353	.359
South	.266	.175	.165	.139	.149	.147	.149	.164	.202	.197
Latium	.151	.128	.154	.127	.140	.140	.156	.186	.208	.208
Total Italy	.217	.181	.201	.179	.202	.204	.246	.287	.334	.321

Notes

1. In the present paper I refer to Population Census figures, corrected for changes of boundaries and of industrial classifications, and I include in 'industry' items 2, 3, 4 of the International Standard Industrial Classification (United Nations).
2. Actually, in 1881 the South was above the rest, but this was due to female labour precariously employed in traditional textile activities, a phenomenon which dwindled away in subsequent decades.
3. Things are different for Latium. Due to the attraction exerted by Rome, population increased in this region at a much faster rate than in average Italy. The same applies to total active population, and to active population in industry. But the ratio of the latter to the former increased less in Latium than elsewhere.
4. I shall largely draw from a previous study (Fuà, 1983).

Reference

Fuà, G. (1983) 'L'industrializzazione nel Nord-Est e nel Centro', in Fuà, G. and Zacchia, C. (eds) *Industrializzazione senza fratture* (Bologna: Il Mulino).

Discussion on Part II

The first part of the discussion focused on specific historical experiences. The main points that emerged were:

(1) The absence of a sharp dichotomy between agriculture and industry in the work of earlier writers such as Petty, suggests the need for placing theories in their particular historical context and the need for methodological caution in transferring concepts to other economic subject areas.

(2) The importance given to wage goods and to subsistence as necessary parts of production in classical political economy, finds an analogue in more recent development literature.

(3) The work of early economists such as Quesnay suggests that there may be serious difficulties – in terms of accumulation and resource raising – of relying on a protectionist industrialising strategy. But such analyses should only provide questions to ponder on the best means of industrialisation, rather than specific policy prescriptions.

(4) As regards the process of economic development – the classical economists were emphasising the importance of institutional freeplay, better property relations, factors, types of contracts in agriculture and so on; their lesson is still valid.

(5) The basic question remains one of working out ways of industrialisation and labour absorption, given prevailing farm conditions and activities, in specific contexts such as that of India.

The second part of the discussion moved from a consideration of the classical economists' perceptions to possible policy conclusions for developing countries. The issues which emerged were:

(1) The problem of labour absorption in agriculture needs to be tackled, given the failure of the heavy industrialisation strategy to generate sufficient employment and the limits to increased labour absorption in agriculture.

(2) New technology is creating a trend towards economies of

specialisation rather than economies of scale. This furthers the growth of small-scale, locally-based industries.

(3) Direct intervention by the state may create distorted structures. State support to small-scale enterprises and rural industrialisation schemes should be less and less in the form of financial subsidies and more and more in the form of real services; it should be mainly indirect, in the form of training and marketing support, provision of specific infrastructures, technical assistance, etc.

(4) The question is how to make the best use of available local resources, organisations, communities and entrepreneurial abilities, rather than relying on the instalment of factories decided from outside.

(5) Hand in hand with fostering the growth of small-scale units of production, the concern should be with improving the quality of life and furthering equity considerations.

More specifically, during the course of the discussion:

A. M. Khusro (New Delhi) explained how in India both the city-centred and decentralised rural-based strategies had been inter-twined in the process of development since the 1950s. He also pointed out how the urban manufactured goods found markets in rural areas and not vice versa. To raise the quality of life in rural areas, he advocated the shifting of large infrastructure facilities to the people and the diversion of more plan resources to rural areas.

S. C. Patnaik (Utkal University, Cuttack, India) cautioned against ignoring the problem arising out of certain patterns of development and the functional aspects of the economic system at different points of time in different countries. He urged disaggregative planning strategy and active peoples' participation to change the development perspectives.

Stantacana (Spain), while acknowledging the influence and impact of high technology in the productive process, put more stress on how to commercialise the resources of a region.

K. K. Khakkar (Saurashtra University, Rajkot, India) was interested to know from Professor Fuà whether the rural-oriented industries were diffused in the Italian experience as found in West European countries and India.

Kamal Kabra (Indian Institute of Public Administration) argued how subsidies given to small-scale industrial units would be counter-productive. State help in the form of improved marketing methods and accessibility to infrastructure facilities were advocated for the development of small units.

Uma Devi (University of Kerala) raised the point as to whether the growth of small units was compatible with ensuring social justice.

Ajmer Singh Sidhu (Punjabi University) asked two questions – is the problem we are facing today a consequence of our process of change, having taken a wrong direction, or is it concerned with a process which has yet to work itself out? He also pointed out how state regulation had inhibited investment in housing, transportation and small scale industry in the Punjab.

Kamal Mitra Chenoy (Indian Institute of Public Administration), quoting the Italian experience, emphasised the need for an analysis of both the forward and backward linkages in the developmental process of small units.

Tirpath Gupta (Indian Institute of Management) stressed the necessity of human resources and localisation of small industrial units, not only in rural areas but also in other parts of the economy as well. He laid particular emphasis on the development of the forestry system.

H. K. Sahay (Patna University) drew attention to the significance of increasing institutional mobilisation and allocation of surpluses for rapid development of the agricultural sector. He added that the determinants of the successful performance of the entrepreneurial function, particularly in the context of backward areas, deserved special care.

R. M. Tungave (Sahu Institute of Business Management) deprecated the subsidy system and favoured E.A.G. Robinson's technical optimum norms for the development of small-scale units.

C. B. Padmanabhan (National Institute of Educational Planning and Administration) placed more emphasis on growth, productivity and quality of life, i.e., better human resources, and was interested to know what type of industrialisation strategy could be introduced for remote rural areas.

K. M. Parchure (Poona University) said that an open economy would be fraught with so many challenges in terms of modernisation, consumerism and increase of defence expenditure.

Vedagiri Shanmugasundaram (University of Madras) decried the exaggerated importance given to the development of industry and the underrated significance attached to agriculture, and pinpointed the statistical lacuna in giving the demand for agricultural production.

To C. S. Barla (University of Rajasthan), the historical experience of development outlined in the papers of, for example, Professors Fuà and Sachs, obviated the structure of markets prevalent in developing countries particularly in rural India. Referring to Mr Eltis's paper, Arun Majumder (Visva-Bharati Calcutta) felt convinced that what was a more relevant aspect in Quesnay's contribution to the Third World countries was the concept of 'productive labour'.

In his response, Professor Fuà clarified that the growth of small-scale industrial units in rural areas of Italy was in no way an anti-urban development. Instead, each small unit was operating as a tiny part in the local development path. Due to the availability of local resources, the adoption of technology, the economy's helpful role in the market and the state, there were no problems in the development of small units in Italy and Spain.

Deepak Nayyar (Jawaharlal Nehru University) asked how to reconcile the diminishing returns proposition of Ricardo with that of Adam Smith's conception, and P. Patnaik (New Delhi) wondered whether he had to follow a complete free trade policy.

In response, Mr Eltis contended that Adam Smith and Quesnay assumed constant cost and constant returns in their expositions and the texture of free trade policies prevalent in Smith's times would be different from that of present day.

Professor Sylos-Labini, in his summing up, underlined that the issues like unemployment, scale economies, emphasis on self-employed small industrial units and state participation have found concurrence both in the contents of the papers presented and in the points of the discussion. To him, understanding of historical ideas, that is, past experiences, are prerequisites to theorising about the real situation.

Name Index

Scitovsky, T.   27, 176
Scott, M.   176
Sekiguchi, S.   103
Selowsky, M.   128, 136
Sen, A.K.   viii, xiv, xxii, 105–37, 228
Senguptal, N.K.   xiii, 94, 97, 101
Sengupta, S.   119, 120
Shanmugasundaram, V.   xiii, 283
Shiraishi, T.   ix
Sidhu, A.S.   282
Simon, H.A.   223, 229
Singer, H.W.   139
Singh, K.S.   129
Singh, M.   xi, xiii, xiv, xviii, 3, 23, 138–50
Sinha, R.K.   xiii
Skinner, A.S.   197
Smith, A.   xix, 28–9, 34–5, 42, 166, 169, 175–97, 198–9, 201, 203–9, 210, 215, 220, 283
Snowdon, B.   128
Sobhan, R.   130
Soderlund, E.F.   173
Solow, R.M.   29, 128
Sraffa, P.   166, 207, 214, 216
Stein, P.G.   197
Stephens, I.   129–30
Stigler, G.J.   169
Stiglitz, J.   31
Stöhr, W.   234, 235, 237
Subramanian, V.   129
Svedberg, P.   128
Swaminathan, M.S.   128, 228
Sylos-Labini, P.   vii, xii, xv, 153–5, 173, 283

Tawney, R.H.   174
Taylor, C.E.   119, 120
Taylor, D.C.   101
Taylor, D.R.F.   235
Taylor, L.   128

Thirsk, J.   162
Thomas, H.   255
Thomas, J.W.   137
Thorner, D.   228
Tilly, L.A.   128, 130, 131
Todd, W.B.   197
Tonveronachi, M.   173
Tortellá Casares, G.   257
Tsuru, S.   ix
Tungave, R.M.   282
Tuñón de Lara, M.   250
Turgot, A.R.J.   177, 203, 206, 215
Tyagi, R.P.   17, 59

Urquidi, V.L.   ix, 231
Usher, D.   40

Vahlquist, B.   132
Vaughan, M.   128
Vázquez-Barquero, A.   xv, xxi, 232–58
Visaria, P.   130

Walras, L.   25
Watkins, M.H.   101
Watson, E.   135
Weaver, C.   234
West, E.   188
Wheeler, E.F.   120
Wickham, T.H.   101
Williamson, J.G.   vii
Wilson, T.   163–4
Wittfogel, K.A.   100

Yellen, J.   31
Young, A.A.   xxi, 26, 29, 139
Yuanzheng, L.   ix

Zacchia, C.   279

Subject Index

290